A CENTURY OF JEWISH LIFE IN SHANGHAI

Touro University Press Books

Series Editors
Michael A. Shmidman, PhD (Touro College, New York)
Simcha Fishbane, PhD (Touro College, New York)

A CENTURY OF JEWISH LIFE IN SHANGHAI

Edited by STEVE HOCHSTADT

Library of Congress Cataloging-in-Publication Data

Names: Hochstadt, Steve, 1948- editor.
Title: A century of Jewish life in Shanghai / edited by Steve Hochstadt.
Description: New York : Touro University Press ; Boston Academic Studies Press, 2019. | Proceedings of a conference which took place in Shanghai in June 2015. | Includes bibliographical references and index. | Summary: "For a century, Jews were an unmistakable and prominent feature of Shanghai life. They built hotels and stood in bread lines, hobnobbed with the British and Chinese elites and were confined to a wartime ghetto. Jews taught at the Shanghai Conservatory of Music, sold Viennese pastries, and shared the worst slum with native Shanghainese. Three waves of Jews, representing three religious and ethnic communities, landed in Shanghai, remained separate for decades, but faced the calamity of World War II and ultimate dissolution together. In this book, we hear their own words and the words of modern scholars explaining how Baghdadi, Russian and Central European Jews found their way to Shanghai, created lives in the world's most cosmopolitan city, and were forced to find new homes in the late 1940s"-- Provided by publisher.
Identifiers: LCCN 2019025634 | ISBN 9781644691311 (hardcover) | ISBN 9781644691328 (adobe pdf)
Subjects: LCSH: Jewish refugees--China--Shanghai--Congresses. | Jews--China--Shanghai--Congresses. | World War, 1939-1945--China--Shanghai--Congresses. | Shanghai (China)--Ethnic relations--Congresses.
Classification: LCC DS135.C5 C355 2019 | DDC 951/.132004924009041--dc23
LC record available at https://lccn.loc.gov/2019025634

Copyright © Touro University Press, 2019
Published by Touro University Press and Academic Studies Press.
Typeset, printed and distributed by Academic Studies Press.

ISBN 9781644691311 (hardcover); ISBN 9781644693315 (paperback)
ISBN 9781644691328 (electronic)

Touro University Press
Michael A. Shmidman and Simcha Fishbane, Editors
320 West 31st Street, Fourth Floor,
New York, NY 10001, USA
tcpress@touro.edu

Academic Studies Press
1577 Beacon Street
Brookline, MA 02446, USA
press@academicstudiespress.com
www.academicstudiespress.com

Book design by Lapiz Digital Services.
On the cover: Leo Meyer leading exercises at the Kadoorie School. Courtesy of Ilana Diamond.

Contents

List of Illustrations	vii
Preface *Rodger Citron*	ix
Introduction	**1**
How Many Shanghai Jews Were There? *Steve Hochstadt*	3
Shanghai before the War	**27**
Shanghai Remembered: Recollections of Shanghai's Baghdadi Jews *Maisie Meyer*	29
The Burak Family: The Migration of a Russian Jewish Family through the First Half of the Twentieth Century *Anne Atkinson*	73
Russian Jews in Shanghai 1920–1950: New Life as Shanghailanders *Liliane Willens*	85
Shanghai and the Holocaust	**97**
Desperate Hopes, Shattered Dreams: The 1937 Shanghai–Manila Voyage of the "Gneisenau" and the Fate of European Jewry *Jonathan Goldstein*	99
Diplomatic Rescue: Shanghai as a Means of Escape and Refuge *Manli Ho*	116
305/13 Kungping Road *Lotte Marcus*	127
Survival in Shanghai 1939–1947 *Evelyn Pike Rubin*	137

What I Learned from Shanghai Refugees 143
Steve Hochstadt

Chinese Responses to the Holocaust: Chinese Attitudes toward
Jewish Refugees in the Late 1930s and Early 1940s 158
Xu Xin

Looking Back at Shanghai 177

Imagined Geographies, Imagined Identities, Imagined Glocal Histories 179
Dan Ben-Canaan

Ephemeral Memories, Eternal Traumas and Evolving Classifications:
Shanghai Jewish Refugees and Debates about Defining a Holocaust Survivor 203
Gabrielle Abram

Bibliography 232

Index 236

List of Illustrations

Family of Edward Ezra	32
Outdoor party at D.E.J. Abraham's home	36
Lawrence and Horace Kadoorie	47
The Buraks in Shanghai in 1920	79
Thomas Vickers, head officer of the Ichang Fire Station, inspecting bomb damage in 1937	82
Bella Burak's grave	83
Map of Manchuria and Chinese Eastern Railway	86
Map of Shanghai in 1939	88
US Immigration Visa of Liliane Willens	96
Letter of Martin Foerder to Manuel L. Quezon, President of the Philippines, April 3, 1939	114
Feng Shan Ho, Chinese Consul General to Vienna, c. 1938	118
Jewish visa applicants in line at a consulate in Vienna	120
Shanghai Visa #3639 issued by Feng Shan Ho (courtesy of Manli Ho)	121
Oskar and Grete Lustig, parents of Lotte Marcus, before emigration	128
Chinese visa issued by Feng Shan Ho to Oskar Lustig	134
Laura Margolis, representative of the Joint in Shanghai	135
Japanese ship "Hakozaki Maru"	138
1943 class at the Shanghai Jewish School	139
1944 pass for Evelyn Popielarz to leave Designated Area	141
Big belly laughing Buddah	184

Jason Joseph Isaac and Vera Dobrolovskii-Diniz with
    friends at a Shanghai night club, c. 1944.   187
Isak Grigori on a pile of coal at his lumberyard in
    Harbin in the 1930s   191
Workers construct the cemetery for fallen Russian soldiers at
    Huangshan Public Cemetery in Harbin   200

Rodger Citron*

Preface

When Patricia Salkin became the Dean of Touro College Jacob D. Fuchsberg Law Center ("Touro Law") in 2012, one of her many ideas for the law school was to hold a conference on the history of the Jews of Shanghai. While teaching Chinese Law at Albany Law School, she developed a relationship with the Law School of the Shanghai University of International Business and Economics (SUIBE). It was during her visits to Shanghai that then-Dean Salkin learned about the Jewish refugees from Germany and other European countries who sought refuge from Nazi Germany in the late 1930s and early 1940s.

Touro Law is part of the Touro College and University System, which was founded under Jewish auspices. As such, Touro Law has an abiding interest in the history of the Holocaust, especially how the law and the legal system in Germany enabled the rise of Adolf Hitler and the Nazis. Prior to Dean Salkin's arrival in 2012, the law school held international conferences on the infamous Wannsee Conference in Berlin, in 2002, and the Nuremberg trials, in 2006. However, never had Touro Law explored the history of the European Jews who found refuge in Shanghai.

---

* Rodger Citron graduated Phi Beta Kappa from Yale College in 1988 and earned his JD from Yale Law School in 1992, where he was a senior editor of the Yale Law Journal and a recipient of the C. LaRue Munson Prize. He clerked for the Hon. Thomas N. O'Neill, Jr., of the US District Court for the Eastern District of Pennsylvania, and then, among other things, worked as trial attorney at the United States Department of Justice. His articles have been published in a number of law reviews, including the Stanford Journal of Complex Litigation, the South Carolina Law Review, and the Administrative Law Review, and he is a coauthor of *A Documentary Companion to Storming the Court* (New York: Aspen Publishers, 2009). In 2004, he began teaching at Touro Law Center, becoming Professor of Law in 2012 and serving as Associate Dean of Academic Affairs from 2014 through 2018. Before this conference, he organized an international conference in Paris on the Alfred Dreyfus affair and the Leo Frank case.

Dean Salkin approached her colleagues at SUIBE. It quickly became apparent that a conference about the Jewish refugees in Shanghai would be of great interest. As Dean Salkin and her team moved forward, they learned about the diverse history—really, histories—of the Jews in Shanghai. Baghdadi Jews came to Shanghai in the nineteenth century and prospered, Russian Jews emigrated in the early twentieth century, and as many as 18,000 Jewish refugees escaped Nazi persecution in the 1930s and 1940s.

After more than a year of work that included extensive collaboration with SUIBE, the conference took place in Shanghai over three days in June 2015. It never is easy to organize a conference. Here the organizational and logistical challenges were all the more difficult because the two schools were more than 7,000 miles apart and in completely opposite time zones! When it was morning in New York, it was evening in Shanghai, and vice versa. Through all of the planning—the extensive correspondence, the international phone calls, the various demands of protocol—SUIBE always was a gracious and generous partner and host.

The conference featured a presentation by Manli Ho, the daughter of Dr. Feng Shan Ho, who had received the title of Righteous Among the Nations, Israel's highest award, for courage in issuing Chinese visas to save Jews from the Shoah while he was the Chinese Consul General in Vienna from 1938 through 1940. Other distinguished scholars gave talks, including Maisie Meyer, Pan Guang, Dan Ben-Canaan, Jonathan Goldstein, Xu Xin, and Steve Hochstadt. Former refugees and others who lived in Shanghai before World War II—Evelyn Pike Rubin, Lotte Marcus, and Liliane Willens—and emigrants' family members—Anne Atkinson—told family histories.

The conference was delightful. It kicked off with an elegant evening reception at the Shanghai Jewish Refugees Museum that drew media reception from television and print journalists in Shanghai. This event combined the feelings of a joyous reunion with respect, even admiration, for the tolerance shown by Shanghai's residents to these various Jewish populations from the nineteenth century through the mid-twentieth century. Over the next two days, there were a number of panel sessions at SUIBE. Many of the panelists agreed to publish their papers and graciously worked with Professor Hochstadt, who edited the papers and brought this book to life. Thank you to the authors and the editor, who have assembled a volume that contributes to the scholarly literature in this area and commemorates a fascinating history.

And thank you to Dr. Alan Kadish, President of the Touro College and University System, for his generous support of the publication of this volume.

It takes a village to put on an international conference. Along with Touro Law, the cosponsors were SUIBE, the Center for Jewish Studies Shanghai, the Shanghai Society for People's Friendship Studies, and the Shanghai Jewish Refugees Museum. Conference underwriters and supporters included the Capobianco family, the Jacob D. Fuchsberg law firm, the Herman Goldman Foundation, the Sino-Judaic Institute, and the Florence and Laurence Spungen Family Foundation. Your generous support made this conference possible.

Thank you also to the Conference Planning Committee. It included Vice President Xu Yong-lin, SUIBE; Dean Shoubin Ni and Professor Joan Tang, Law School of SUIBE; Professors Jonathan Goldstein, Pan Guang, Ben Kahn, and Steve Hochstadt; and now-Provost Salkin, Dr. Susan Thompson, Assistant Dean Linda Howard Weissman, and myself, of Touro Law. Although he was not officially a member of the committee, Danny Spungen must be mentioned here for his tireless support of the conference. Finally, thank you to the Israeli Consul General and the US Consulate for advice and support along the way, and to Rabbi Shalom Greenberg at the Chabad in Shanghai, who provided sound advice about working in Shanghai and capably handled all aspects of the conference food needs. Thank you, all of you. Your dedication and hard work enabled the conference to go as planned and to make it look easy.

Introduction

Steve Hochstadt*

How Many Shanghai Jews Were There?

For a brief historical moment, there were more Jews in Shanghai than in any other Asian city. Outside of Europe, the Middle East, and North America, the only cities with more Jews in 1940 were Buenos Aires and Johannesburg.[1] Shanghai was the most exotic and cosmopolitan of them all. This book takes the reader inside three distinct Jewish communities in twentieth-century Shanghai. Baghdadi, Russian, and Central European Jews describe their social and political worlds, all of which vanished after World War II.

Touro Law Center organized an ambitious conference in Shanghai in 2015 about the Jews of Shanghai. Cosponsors were the major local

---

* Steve Hochstadt taught history at Illinois College in Jacksonville 2006–2016, after teaching at Bates College in Maine for twenty-seven years. He was educated at Brown University: BA 1971, PhD 1983. His research has focused on migration in Germany and on the Holocaust. *Mobility and Modernity: Migration in Germany 1820–1989* (Ann Arbor: University of Michigan Press, 1999) won the Allan Sharlin Prize of the SSHA. *Sources of the Holocaust* (New York: Palgrave Macmillan, 2004) is an annotated documents collection widely used in Holocaust courses. His grandparents escaped from Vienna to Shanghai in 1939. He has published two books about the flight of Jews from Central Europe to China: *Shanghai-Geschichten: Die jüdische Flucht nach China* (Berlin: Hentrich und Hentrich, 2007) and *Exodus to Shanghai: Stories of Escape from the Third Reich* (New York: Palgrave Macmillan, 2012). He has consulted with the Shanghai Jewish Refugees Museum on their exhibits, and is treasurer of the Sino-Judaic Institute, supporting scholarship and teaching about Jews in China. He wrote a weekly column for the Jacksonville (IL) Journal-Courier from 2009 to 2018.

1 "Statistics of Jews," *American Jewish Year Book* (1941–1942): 672–73.

institutions which focus on Jewish history, the Shanghai Jewish Refugees Museum and the Center of Jewish Studies Shanghai, as well as the Shanghai University of International Business and Economics. Bringing together eyewitnesses and scholars for the three Jewish communities demonstrated the conference's broad vision. The experiences of each community connected at least two continents, so their personal histories are also world histories. Every year, there are fewer survivors: this conference may be the last of its kind.

Let's begin by putting the Jewish minorities into their Chinese context. Shanghai was and is one of the world's largest cities, counting over twenty-three million in the last census in 2010. Exactly where Shanghai ranks among large cities depends on varying definitions of city boundaries, urban agglomerations, and metropolitan areas, but Shanghai is certainly near the top of any list. In 1930, Shanghai had three million inhabitants.[2] That included about 49,000 foreigners. The largest group were Japanese (18,800), followed by British (8450), Russians (7400), and Americans (3150). There were only 1400 Germans at that time, few of them Jews.[3] The census did not count people by religion, so it is only possible to estimate the number of Jews.

The first Jews to live in Shanghai came from the Middle East, mostly from the Ottoman Empire, via Bombay, Calcutta, and other South Asian cities. There were probably nearly 1000 Baghdadi Sephardic Jews in the years before World War II.[4] Maisie Meyer, whose work puts her at the center of the study of the Baghdadi Jews, uses the biographical memories of many members of this community to sketch their hundred-year history. Through her we hear them talk to us directly. A few Baghdadis achieved fantastic wealth, enabling them to help many who came later to Shanghai.

---

2 *Cambridge Sentinel* 26, no. 35, August 30, 1930, 2.
3 "Census and Population," *Tales of Old China*, 2018, accessed April 9, 2018, http://www.talesofoldchina.com/shanghai/business/census-and-population.
4 Maisie Meyer says they "never numbered more than 1,000": "Baghdadi Jews in Early Shanghai," Iraqi Jewish Association of Ontario, 2009, accessed April 9, 2018, https://ijao.ca/baghdadi-jews-in-early-shanghai/. David Kranzler says about 700 and notes other sources saying between 500 and 700: Kranzler, *Japanese, Nazis and Jews: The Jewish Refugee Community of Shanghai 1938–1945* (New York: Yeshiva University Press, 1976), 47, 71, note 29. Gao Bei and Irene Eber estimate the number at 1000: Gao Bei, *Shanghai Sanctuary: Chinese and Japanese Policy toward European Jewish Refugees during World War II* (New York: Oxford University Press, 2013), 63; Irene Eber, *Wartime Shanghai and the Jewish Refugees from Central Europe: Survival, Co-Existence, and Identity in a Multi-Ethnic City* (Berlin: De Gruyter, 2012), 1.

In the late nineteenth century, millions of Jews fled antisemitic violence in the Russian Empire to the West. Anne Atkinson and Liliane Willens tell their family stories of travel in the opposite direction. Their ancestors took the Trans-Siberian Railroad eastward out of Russia to Harbin, which at that time housed the largest Jewish community in Asia. Although there was no native antisemitism in China, Russian Jews were not able to escape their tormenters. Non-Jewish Russians who opposed the Communists, the so-called White Russians, also fled to China in large numbers after 1917. Atkinson and Willens describe how their families escaped the hostile attitude of the White Russians and the invading Japanese to the relative safety of Shanghai.

Atkinson focuses on the many long migrations of the Burak family, which originated in eastern Europe, crossed the vast Russian Empire at the beginning of the twentieth century, and settled in Harbin. They soon left to join the Russian Jewish community in Shanghai, where they stayed through World War II. Like too many Jewish families in the mid-twentieth century, they ended up dispersed across the globe, with some branches ending up in Australia, where Atkinson was born. Willens was born in Shanghai and writes about her Ukrainian-Russian family, which also made its way across Russia to Shanghai via Harbin. She and her family came to the United States after World War II.

The Russian Ashkenazic Jews remained quite distinct from the earlier Sephardic Baghdadis. The size of their community can only be roughly estimated. Rena Krasno, born in Shanghai in a Russian family, estimates that there were 500 Russian Jews in Shanghai in 1921, 800 by 1924, and more than 4000 by 1940.[5] Other scholars offer varying figures for this last date: Kranzler says 4000 to 6000, Gao Bei says 6000 to 8000, Irene Eber "nearly 7000" in one place and 6000 in another.[6] Among a total of 16,000 Russian emigrants in 1933, Jews were greatly outnumbered by non-Jews.[7] It is clear that there were many more Russian Jews than Baghdadis, but the Russians were much less likely to be wealthy or to be well integrated into Shanghai high society, dominated by Western businessmen. The overlapping

---

5   Rena Krasno, *Strangers Always: A Jewish Family in Wartime Shanghai* (Berkeley, CA: Pacific View Press, 1992), 8–10.

6   Kranzler, *Japanese, Nazis and Jews*, 57–65; Gao Bei, *Shanghai Sanctuary*, 63; Eber, *Wartime Shanghai and the Jewish Refugees*, 1; Avraham Altman and Irene Eber, "Flight to Shanghai, 1938–1940: The Larger Setting," *Yad Vashem Studies* 28 (2000): 61.

7   [7] Marcia Reynders Ristaino, *Port of Last Resort: The Diaspora Communities of Shanghai* (Stanford, CA: Stanford University Press, 2001), 72.

patterns and unique particulars of the Burak and Willens families offer us first-person insights into the origins, lives, and ultimate fate of the Russian Jewish community in Shanghai.

Shanghai's largest Jewish community lived there for only about ten years, but the connection to the Holocaust has made the Central and Eastern European Jewish refugees the best known among Shanghai's Jews. The refugees brought little more than a few suitcases. Their stories are both more tragic and more moving. Their survival depended on the aid of the Baghdadi and Russian Jews, supplemented by financial assistance from American Jews.

Jonathan Goldstein and Manli Ho write here about the desperate efforts of German-speaking Jews to find safe haven from deadly Nazi persecution. Goldstein shows how the Philippines appeared to offer sanctuary in 1937, but eventually closed its borders to Jewish refugees. Manli Ho describes how her father, Feng Shan Ho, used his diplomatic position in Vienna to save thousands of Jews, many of whom ended up in Shanghai.

The meaning of living a refugee life comes out of personal stories, told in personal styles. Lotte Marcus and her parents were one of the many Viennese families who survived with one of Ho's visas. She sketches the living conditions that most refugees endured in Shanghai. Evelyn Pike Rubin's father was arrested during *Kristallnacht*. Only her mother's purchase of ship tickets to Shanghai enabled his release, and the family traveled from Breslau (now Wrocław in Poland) to Shanghai on a Japanese ship. Both families lost their fathers in Shanghai and both eventually were able to come to the United States.

My own grandparents were able to escape from Vienna to Shanghai and eventually to come to the United States after the war. I have interviewed about one hundred former refugees, from whom I learned much about their lives and much about life itself. My essay later in this book discusses how hard it was to become a refugee, what it means to write about refugees, and how much solidarity Jews displayed toward fellow Jews in distress.

Professor Xu Xin is the foremost Chinese scholar of Jewish life in China. He provides us with a clear description of the surprising effort of the Chinese government, forced to flee before the Japanese army, trying to find a way to provide a new home for thousands of Jewish refugees. This effort eventually fell through. Yet paired with Manli Ho's description of her father's rescue work, official Chinese attitudes are clearly displayed. Although the Chinese had little power in Shanghai before 1945, their humanitarian regard for their new Jewish neighbors provided an important context for Jewish survival in Shanghai.

The first refugees came from Germany and Austria, followed by a smaller number from Czechoslovakia, mostly in 1938 and 1939, traveling mainly by ship. After the Nazis invaded Poland in 1939 and then moved further east into the Soviet Union in 1941, Jews from Poland and Lithuania took the Trans-Siberian Railroad across Asia. Many of them spent up to a year in Kobe, Japan, before being shipped by the Japanese to Shanghai in 1941. Because so much attention is currently being paid to the refugees in Shanghai, it is worth outlining the contours of this community as well as numbers can manage. How many Jews escaped the Nazis and made their way to Shanghai? There is no precise answer to that simple question, and published approximations differ widely.[8] Counting them is made difficult by several circumstances.

A small number were successful in continuing their journey to safer, more desirable places before the Pacific War exploded at the end of 1941. Goldstein notes that 28 of the earliest German refugees to Shanghai managed to get to Manila in September 1937. Adolf Storfer, publisher of the biweekly *Gelbe Post*, an intellectual magazine in Shanghai, from 1939 to 1940, was able to go to Australia in 1941.[9] Leon Szalet arrived in Shanghai on the "Conte Verde" in 1940, but was able to get a visa and left for the US in October 1941.[10] Jacob Rosenfeld, who arrived in Shanghai after he was released from Buchenwald, joined the Red Army as a field doctor in 1941. Kranzler says that before Pearl Harbor "several hundred" refugees managed to leave Shanghai.[11]

---

8   This is not the case only for Shanghai. Leo Spitzer, in *Hotel Bolivia: The Culture of Memory in a Refuge from Nazism* (New York: Hill and Wang, 1998), 203, note 2, points out the wide spectrum of estimates for German Jewish refugees to Bolivia, ranging from 7,000 to 60,000. Spitzer's estimate is 20,000.

9   Storfer was evidently one of twelve actors, writers, directors, and journalists who traveled to Australia on an American troop transport "SS Cape Fairweather," which left Shanghai just before the Japanese took over the city in the wake of Pearl Harbor: "Who Were The Shanghai Twelve?," *For the Life of Me*, accessed April 9, 2018, https://forthelifeofme-film.com/2016/06/01/shanghai-12/. On Storfer, see Christian Pape, "Verdrängt, Verkannt, Vergessen? Ein Beitrag zu Leben und Werken von Adolf Josef Storfer," in *Chilufim. Zeitschrift für jüdische Kulturgeschichte* 12 (2012): 5–26.

10 Szalet's papers are housed at the Leo Baeck Institute in New York: Johanna Schlicht, *Guide to the Papers of Leon Szalet (1892-1958), 1914-1996*, accessed April 15, 2018, http://findingaids.cjh.org/?pID=121455.

11 Kranzler, *Japanese, Nazis and Jews*, 128.

Should these brief sojourners be counted the same as those who spent the war in Shanghai? And how does one count Sonja Mühlberger, born in Shanghai on October 26, 1939, seven months after her parents had fled from Frankfurt am Main?[12] Technically she was not a refugee, but a native of Shanghai. What about other children born in Shanghai who died there, some after only a few days?[13] Some refugees were defined by the Nazis as Jews, but had converted to Christianity or were not religious at all. Some families who had to leave Germany came from mixed marriages, but their members were not counted separately in Shanghai. When the Japanese government decided to put restrictions on entry of refugees to the part of Shanghai that it controlled, and the other foreign powers represented in the Shanghai Municipal Council immediately followed suit, the definition of "refugee" suddenly became significant. The shipping companies needed to know whom to allow on their ships to Shanghai.[14]

Thus assessing precisely how many Jewish refugees came to Shanghai requires arbitrary decisions about the definition of "Jewish refugee." The number of questionable cases, however, is small compared to the total flood of refugees. Much larger errors in published approximations of the number of Shanghai refugees are caused by careless estimation and deliberate political exaggeration. This can be seen by comparing the numbers given in different types of sources.

Scholars have been fairly consistent in their estimates. David Kranzler was the first serious scholar of the Jewish refugee experience in Shanghai in his 1971 Yeshiva University dissertation, which was published in 1976 as *Japanese, Nazis & Jews: The Jewish Refugee Community of Shanghai, 1938–1945*. His thorough exploitation of available sources led him to estimate that a maximum of 17,000 refugees in Shanghai was reached when 1000

---

12 Sonja Mühlberger, *Geboren in Shanghai als Kind von Emigranten, Leben und Überleben im Ghetto von Hongkew (1939–1947)*, vol. 58 of *Jüdische Miniaturen* (Berlin: Hentrich und Hentrich, 2006).
13 The list of refugees who died in Shanghai includes three newborns who died in the refugee hospital on December 7, 1944. This tragedy is discussed in my interview with Doris Grey, the head nurse: Hochstadt, *Exodus to Shanghai*, 152.
14 There was considerable correspondence in August to October 1939 among representatives of the Shanghai Jewish community, the Japanese Consulate General, the Shanghai Municipal Council, and shipping companies like Lloyd Triestino about the new restrictive rules for entering Shanghai, especially about the definition of "refugee": file 73, Prof. Irene Eber Collection about the Fate of Jews in China, Yad Vashem Archives O.78, Jerusalem, Israel.

Eastern European Jews were sent from Kobe to Shanghai in late 1941.[15] Most scholars, including myself, have concurred approximately with this conclusion.[16] That number can also be found in some newspaper articles and websites which discuss the Shanghai refugees.[17]

Sometimes the number 20,000 is used as the total of the German-speaking arrivals in Shanghai.[18] Wolfgang Benz, one of the foremost Holocaust historians in Germany, says 25,000.[19] The Wikipedia article about Shanghai's Jewish refugees says 23,000 were forced into the Designated Area in 1941, doubly wrong.[20] Such large numbers are frequently encountered in the popular press.

In recent years, the number 30,000 has become common. I believe it was first used by Chinese writers in an effort to draw more attention to the role played by China in providing a safe haven to Jewish refugees when the rest of the world was not welcoming. Perhaps the earliest reference to

---

15   Kranzler, *Japanese, Nazis and Jews*, 146–147, note 34.
16   Hochstadt, *Exodus to Shanghai*, 60; Françoise Kreissler, "Exil in Shanghai: Problematik und Schwerpunktthemen," in *Deutsch-chinesische Beziehungen vom 19. Jahrhundert bis zur Gegenwart*, ed. Heng-yü Kuo and Mechthild Leutner, vol. 19 of *Berliner-China Studien* (Munich: K.G. Saur Verlag, 1991), 294; Elisabeth Buxbaum, *Transit Shanghai: Ein Leben im Exil* (Vienna: Edition Steinbauer, 2008), 8; Gao Bei, *Shanghai Sanctuary*, 3. See also the website of the US Holocaust Memorial Museum, which says "17,000 German and Austrian Jews": "German and Austrian Jewish Refugees in Shanghai," accessed April 9, 2018, https://www.ushmm.org/wlc/en/article.php?ModuleId=10007091. Eber says 18,000 to 20,000: *Voices from Shanghai: Jewish Exiles in Wartime China* (Chicago: University of Chicago Press, 2008), 7.
17   Tom Tugend, "'Jewish Refugees in Shanghai' tells story of survival," *Jewish Journal*, October 16, 2013, discussing an exhibit at UCLA, says "some 20,000 Jews".
18   Frank Stern, "Wartezimmer Shanghai," in *Das Exil der kleinen Leute: Alltagserfahrung deutscher Juden in der Emigration*, ed. Wolfgang Benz (Munich: C.H. Beck, 1991), 109–120; Altman and Eber, "Flight to Shanghai, 1938–1940," 51, 84. An article by Alvin Mars, which appears to have been an undergraduate seminar paper, gives various incompatible numbers: the number who arrived in 1939 was 17,000; 4000 to 6000 arrived after the restrictions were put in place in August 1939; the total exceeded 20,000: "A Note on the Jewish Refugees in Shanghai," *Jewish Social Studies* 31 (1969): 286–291. See also the website of Shanghai Jewish Center, "Shanghai Jewish History," accessed April 15, 2018, http://www.chinajewish.org/SJC/Jhistory.htm.
19   Wolfgang Benz, ""Das Exil der kleinen Leute," in *Das Exil der kleinen Leute*, 7–37. An early use of that number was by Juliane Wetzel, "Auswanderung aus Deutschland," in *Die Juden in Deutschland 1933 bis 1945*, ed. Wolfgang Benz (Munich: 1988), 496. Kranzler notes that the number 25,000 was already being "thrown about" in the 1980s "with no basis in fact": *Japanese Nazis and Jews*, 294, note 24.
20   "Shanghai Ghetto," *Wikipedia*, accessed April 9, 2018, https://en.wikipedia.org/wiki/Shanghai_Ghetto.

that number was in 1992 by Pan Guang, the Dean of the Center of Jewish Studies Shanghai at the Shanghai Academy of Social Sciences, and one of the best known Chinese experts on Jews in Shanghai.[21] He has lectured worldwide and written for many Western publications, consistently using that number.[22] Soon 30,000 became the official Chinese estimate.[23] That number was picked up by Western media and repeated countless times, by National Public Radio, TIME, Reuters, the Jewish Journal, and Haaretz.[24] As part of the heavy promotion of China's role in the victory over Japan for the 70th anniversary of the end of the war in 2015, this official Chinese number was proclaimed all over the world.

As late as 2015, the Shanghai Jewish Refugees Museum, opened in 2007, employed the number 30,000 on its website.[25] At the dedication of a new exhibit in 2014, a wall listing all the names of Jewish refugees listed in the 1944 Japanese census, the Museum referred to "over 18,000." More

---

21 Pan Guang, "A New Quest for Jewish Refugees in Shanghai during World War II," *SASS Papers* (1992): 363.

22 He repeated that number in "The Central European Jewish Community in Shanghai," in *Reading Asia: New Research in Asian Studies*, ed. Frans Husken Huskin and Dick van der Meij (London: Curzon Press, 2001), 178, and in "Shanghai: a Haven for Holocaust Victims," *Discussion Papers Journal*, vol. 2 of *The Holocaust and the United Nations Outreach Programme* (New York: United Nations, 2012), 65.

23 "Former Jewish refugees revisit Shanghai," *China Daily*, March 27, 2014, accessed April 9, 2018, http://www.chinadaily.com.cn/photo/2014-03/27/content_17384167.htm; on CCTV by Li Kun, "Shanghai serving as haven for Jewish refugees during wartime, " August 21, 2015, accessed April 9, 2018, http://english.cntv.cn/2015/08/21/ARTI1440143683868404.shtml; repeated by Iris Pan Lu of the University of Hong Kong, "Remembering the Pain of 'Others': Reflections on Shanghai Jewish Refugees Museum and Beyond," *Writing the War in Asia—a documentary history*, October 14, 2015, accessed April 9, 2018, https://www.polyu.edu.hk/cc/images/Article/Doc/paper/dissertation/panlu/06_dissertation_PanLu.pdf.

24 Louisa Lim, "Center Revives Shanghai's Jewish History," National Public Radio, June 16, 2006, accessed April 9, 2018, https://www.npr.org/templates/story/story.php?storyId=5488614; Ling Woo Liu, "Shanghai Sanctuary," *TIME*, July 31, 2008, accessed April 9, 2018, http://content.time.com/time/magazine/article/0,9171,1828102,00.html; Royston Chan, "Play tells tale of Jewish refugees in WW2 Shanghai," Reuters, March 28, 2012, accessed April 9, 2018, https://www.reuters.com/article/china-jewish-shanghai/play-tells-tale-of-jewish-refugees-in-ww2-shanghai-idUSL3E8EN1FK20120323; Lia Mandelbaum, "The Jewish Refugees of Shanghai, " *Jewish Journal*, December 30, 2013, accessed April 9, 2018, http://jewishjournal.com/latest_blogs/125658/the-jewish-refugees-of-shanghai; "New Database Gathers Tales of Shanghai's Holocaust Refugees," *Haaretz*, June 6, 2008, accessed April 9, 2018, https://www.haaretz.com/whdcMobileSite/1.4989120.

25 Accessed August 11, 2015, http://www.shanghaijews.org.cn/English.

recently, the Museum has abandoned the 30,000 figure in favor of 20,000, which is now therefore sometimes used by Chinese media.[26] But other Chinese institutions cling to the 30,000 number.[27] Some official sources employ other sloppy formulations about the total number of refugees or the number who were forced into the "Designated Area" in 1943.[28]

Numbers are important. Can we use all available evidence to reach a definitive, if still imprecise, total number of refugees in Shanghai? Many authorities tried to count the refugees for their own purposes. The German Consulate General, the steamship companies, the Shanghai Municipal Police (SMP), the Japanese occupation authorities, the American Jewish Joint Distribution Committee, and the Shanghai Jewish committees helping the refugees all tried to keep track of refugees arriving, in place, or leaving. They each used different language and definitions to categorize people. Refugees often didn't want to be counted, and some refugee families escaped all official notice and survived to eventually create a new life in some other Jewish community.

So all we have are partial estimates. Each of these official efforts to count and list the European refugees provides a window into the size and demographic composition of the refugee stream. If we consider all of these estimates, we will come closest to an accurate understanding.

At first nearly all European Jewish refugees from the Nazis arrived in Shanghai on ships out of European ports. The first German Jews came already in 1933 and attracted little notice, so there are conflicting reports

---

26 Kou Jie, "Shanghai Jewish Refugees Museum aims to add archives of Jewish refugees to heritage lists," *People's Daily Online*, September 07, 2016, accessed April 9, 2018, http://en.people.cn/n3/2016/0907/c90000-9112086.html.

27 An article by Pan Zhen, "JEWS IN SHANGHAI | Shanghai Jewish Refugees Museum Committed to the Mission of Collecting Evidence of History," on the website of the Shanghai International Studies University, September 15, 2016, accessed April 9, 2018, http://en.shisu.edu.cn/resources/features/jews-in-shanghai-17; "Shanghai wants to register its Jewish refugee history with UNESCO," *China Daily*, December 12, 2017, accessed April 9, 2018, http://www.chinadaily.com.cn/a/201712/12/WS5a2fcca8a3108bc8c672a0d8.html; "JEWS IN SHANGHAI | Peter Finkelgruen: Memories of a Shanghai Baby," Shanghai International Studies University, September 25, 2016, accessed April 9, 2018, http://en.shisu.edu.cn/resources/features/jews-in-shanghai-8.

28 The website of the US Embassy and Consulates in China refers to "25,000 Jewish refugees from Europe and the Soviet Union from the 1920s through the 1940s" living in Hongkou: accessed April 9, 2018, https://china.usembassy-china.org.cn/ambshanghai092117.

on their number.[29] Even as late as 1938, authorities paid little attention to the small contingents of Central European Jews landing in Shanghai. Then suddenly their numbers grew. In the wake of the *Anschluss* of Austria into the Nazi Third Reich in March 1938, and the subsequent violent attacks on Jews and their property in Vienna, Austrian Jews began desperately to seek a way out. As the Nazi government increased the pressure to emigrate, Jewish organizations and periodicals began to bring up Shanghai as a possible destination, undesirable but with no restrictions on entry.[30]

About two-thirds of Central European refugees were brought on Italian ships of the Lloyd Triestino line that traveled through the Suez Canal and around India to Shanghai. German ships left Baltic or North Sea ports and sometimes took the longer route around the southern tip of Africa. Japanese liners also left from Mediterranean ports. Someone tried to count the number of Jewish refugees on each ship. Although it is not clear who made these counts, it was probably the shipping companies themselves counting the passengers to Shanghai who had a "J" marked in their passports.[31] The Shanghai Municipal Police reported on each ship's arrival and the number of refugees, and local newspapers also reported on refugee arrivals. Here, too, conflicting figures are provided by different sources. For example, the "Conte Biancamano" out of Genoa, a giant Italian luxury liner, docked on February 22, 1939. The SMP reported that there were 780 refugees on board; the *North China Herald* reported 820; the *China Press* reported 841.[32]

---

29 The SMP reported 26 families had arrived on November 6, 1933: "Arrival of German-Jewish Emigrants in Shanghai," November 7, 1933, file D5422 (c), Shanghai Municipal Police Files, 1894–1945, accessible on microfilm. Irene Eber says about 30 Jewish families had arrived by the end of 1933: *Wartime Shanghai and the Jewish Refugees*, 40, note 4. In October 1934, 32 Jewish doctors from Germany were reported to be practicing in Shanghai: "Refugee Doctors Settle in Orient," Jewish Telegraphic Agency, October 5, 1934, JTA Jewish News Archive. James R. Ross describes some of these early refugees in *Escape to Shanghai: A Jewish Community in China* (New York: Free Press, 1994), 24–25.

30 Astrid Freyeisen, *Shanghai und die Politik des Dritten Reiches* (Würzburg, Germany: Königshausen und Neumann, 2000), 390–395; Antonia Finnane, *Far from Where? Jewish Journeys from Shanghai to Australia* (Melbourne: Melbourne University Press, 1999), 21–23.

31 The Nazi government decreed on October 5, 1938, that Jews' passports were invalid until they had a "J" stamped in them. Thus it would have been easy to identify Jews leaving the Third Reich for Shanghai after that date.

32 *North China Herald*, March 1, 1939, 376; *China Post*, February 23, 1939, 3. The inaccuracy of many reports about refugee arrivals was not just due to questions about

Nevertheless, the various efforts to keep track of refugees arriving by ship provide us with useful approximations of how many came and when they arrived. From various sources, I have collected records of the number of refugees who arrived in Shanghai on 90 ships between October 1933 and August 1941.[33] Some ships carried only a handful, while others such as the "Conte Biancamano" brought over 500.[34] The total from the 90 ships is about 13,300. This is only a partial accounting: the German Consul General reported that the "Conte Verde," which arrived June 7, 1940, was the "150th ship since the beginning of the big wave of immigration" of Jews.[35] Data for some of the arrivals of the largest liners are missing, but most of the missing ships are probably smaller carriers.[36]

There are varied estimates of how many refugees reached Shanghai in 1938. Perhaps the first large group, about 180, arrived on November 24 on the Italian ship "Conte Verde." The *North China Daily News* reported that the total of recently arrived refugees was now 400.[37] The regular landings of two other large passenger ships of the Lloyd Triestino line, the giant "Conte Biancamano" and the "Conte Rosso," and the Norddeutscher Lloyd's

---

whom to count. The Gestapo chartered the "Usaramo" of the Deutsch-Afrika line to carry exclusively Jewish passengers to Shanghai, especially those released from concentration camps along with their families. Nearly all sources report their number as 459, but the *China Press*, June 28, 1939, 2, the day before arrival in Shanghai, reported 339 passengers.

33 The most useful sources were the individual reports by the SMP as each ship landed, contained in file D5422(c), supplemented by other sources about ships for which I could find no SMP report: Ross, *Escape to Shanghai*; Deutsches Generalkonsulat Shanghai; Eber, *Wartime Shanghai and the Jewish Refugees*; *Shanghai Jewish Chronicle*. Where sources provided conflicting numbers, I have relied on the SMP report.

34 For example, the freighter "Protesilaus" of the British Blue Funnel Line landed 3 refugees in Shanghai on April 6, 1939.

35 "Judentum in Shanghai," Deutsches Generalkonsulat Shanghai, June 30, 1940, 1, in file 73, Irene Eber Collection.

36 For example, an online list of Norddeutscher Lloyd ships leaving Bremen for Shanghai in 1938 and 1939 shows 8 voyages for which I have no passenger data, including 4 large passenger liners. This list, too, is incomplete, as I have data for 7 Norddeutscher Lloyd ships which arrived in Shanghai which are not on the online list, mostly freighters with less than 20 passengers. Accessed April 19, 2018, http://www.public-juling.de/passagierlisten/passagen.php?ankunftshafen=Shanghai,%20China&lang=de.

37 *North China Daily News*, November 25, 1938.

"Potsdam" in December added another 860.[38] A variety of sources place the total for 1938 between 1100 and 1500.[39]

The numbers increased rapidly during 1939, as Jewish men who had been arrested during *Kristallnacht*, November 9–10, 1938, were released from concentration camps if they could show proof of immediate emigration. Over 1000 landed in Shanghai in February, including 780 on the "Conte Biancamano," bringing the total to over 2650.[40] The flow increased to at least 1500 in March, 1750 in April, and over 2000 in June. The German Consulate General reported a total of about 10,000 by the end of May, and the *North China Herald* said 10,500 after the "Conte Verde" had carried 526 in early June.[41] The flood of refugees abated somewhat in July and then was severely restricted in August. The Japanese authorities were already in May discussing plans to restrict entry to the districts of Shanghai they controlled. In early August the Japanese military announced that no further refugees would be admitted to the area they controlled in Hongkou after August 21, and the Western-controlled Shanghai Municipal Council followed suit by closing entry to the International Settlement.[42] These restrictions were relaxed somewhat to allow those who had already embarked before August 21 to land, and to permit immigration to immediate family of those already in Shanghai and to those who could show US $400 in so-called "guarantee money."

Various sources tried to estimate how many refugees had arrived in 1939. The German Consulate General reported 12,667 and a report from official Shanghai Jewish sources said 12,089.[43] The ships for which I have

---

38 Other large liners from these two companies, plus passenger ships of other lines, arrived in these months, but there is no documentation of how many refugees traveled on them.

39 Dr. Kurt Marx, "Bericht über die Organisation des Committee for the Assistance of European Refugees in Shanghai," July 18, 1939, 14, file 46, Irene Eber Collection; Heinz Ganther, ed., *Drei Jahre Immigration in Shanghai, ihr Beginn, 1939, ihre Leistung, 1940, ihr Erfolg, 1941* (Shanghai: Modern Times Publishing House, 1942), 15, file 58A, Yad Vashem Archives, O.78, says 1374. The *Shanghai Times* reported on December 24 that 1000 had arrived, which would make 1340 by the end of the year.

40 The *North China Herald* reported 2500 before two more ships landed at the end of February with another 150: February 22, 1939, 327.

41 *North China Herald*, June 7, 1939, 415.

42 The development of these restrictions is more fully discussed in Steve Hochstadt, "Shanghai: a Last Resort for Desperate Jews," in *Refugees from Nazi Germany and the Liberal European States*, ed. Frank Caestecker and Bob Moore (New York, Oxford: Berghahn Books, 2009), 109–121.

43 Report on "Judentum in Shanghai," Deutsches Generalkonsulat Shanghai, February 2, 1941, file 73, Irene Eber Collection; Ganther, *Drei Jahre Immigration in Shanghai*.

reports carried about 11,200 through the end of September. Given the spectrum of estimates for 1938, the total by the end of 1939 should range between 13,200 and 14,200. The Jewish relief committee estimated that total to be 13,527, right in the middle of that range.[44]

For 1940, when the stream of refugees was much smaller, estimates vary less: the German Consulate General said 1900 and Jewish sources put the number at 1988.[45] That puts the total somewhere between 15,100 and 16,200 at the end of 1940. 1941 was the final year that European Jews might flee to the East. In October, Heinrich Himmler forbade further emigration of Jews, as the Nazis moved fully toward mass murder.[46] The records of Jewish arrival in Shanghai in 1941 are very sparse, not permitting an estimate of how many landed that year.

One more large group of Jews arrived in 1941, having followed a different path from those who originated in Central Europe. After the German and Soviet armies divided up Poland in 1939 and the Soviets began to move into the small Baltic countries, Jews in Lithuania discovered that the Japanese Consul, Chiune Sugihara, and the Dutch Consul, Jan Zwartendyk, were willing to issue visas for Japan and Curacao. Brandishing these papers, at least 2000 Jews were able to cross the Soviet Union in 1940 and 1941, and land in Kobe, Japan.[47] The German invasion of the Soviet Union in June 1941 then cut off the final means of escape. The Japanese government helped these refugees to survive in Kobe until the summer of 1941. Many, perhaps about 1000, were able to move further to destinations in North and

---

44 Report on "Judentum in Shanghai," Deutsches Generalkonsulat Shanghai, June 30, 1940, 8, file 73, Irene Eber Collection.

45 Report on "Judentum in Shanghai," Deutsches Generalkonsulat Shanghai, February 2, 1941, file 73, Irene Eber Collection; Ganther, *Drei Jahre Immigration in Shanghai*. The records of the SMP are less helpful about ships arriving in 1940: I found reports of only 770 arrivals for that year. The Jewish relief committee registered only 284 arrivals for the first four months of 1940. Not all arriving refugees registered with the Committee if they did not need financial help: Report on "Judentum in Shanghai," Deutsches Generalkonsulat Shanghai, June 30, 1940, 8, file 73, Irene Eber Collection.

46 A translation of the order from the Reich Security Main Office can be seen at "Order Banning the Emigration of Jews from the Reich," *Jewish Virtual Library*, accessed April 15, 2018, http://www.jewishvirtuallibrary.org/order-banning-the-emigration-of-jews-from-the-reich.

47 The story of Sugihara has been told a number of times in print, often with exaggerated figures of the numbers of Jews saved. An example is Hillel Levine, *In Search of Sugihara: The Elusive Japanese Diplomat Who Risked his Life to Rescue 10,000 Jews from the Holocaust* (New York: Free Press, 1996). Nothing extensive has yet been written about Zwartendyk.

South America, Australia and New Zealand. In July and August 1941, the Japanese put about 900 on ships and sent them to Shanghai.

The best work on these refugees has been accomplished by the Australian scholar Andrew Jakubowicz. Using the same kind of partial estimates by varied authorities, he judges the total of Polish Jewish refugees in Shanghai to be somewhat more than 1000.[48] There were no representatives of this smaller group at the Shanghai conference.[49]

The International Committee for the Organization of European Immigrants in China, often called the IC, or the Komor Committee, after its chair Paul Komor, had counted 15,469 refugee registrations by January 14, 1941. The three main authorities who had been trying to keep track of all Jewish arrivals in Shanghai, Jewish relief workers, the SMP, and the German Consulate General, offered their final assessments in 1943. The newly established Shanghai Ashkenazic Collaborating Relief Association reported that 15,342 refugees had registered with Jewish authorities.[50] The SMP reported a total of 15,250, which may have been based on the SACRA figures.[51] The Germans put the total at about 16,000.[52]

Given an unknown number of refugees who did not register with the relief committees and escaped everyone's notice in the extreme confusion of 1939, the number 16,000 should be considered a minimum approximation. I would place the upper limit at 17,000 who were present in 1943. Kranzler estimated that several hundred had been able to leave Shanghai soon after arriving. The list of deaths to refugees compiled by the Jewish authorities shows about 770 who died by the middle of 1943, when the above estimates

---

48 Andrew Jakubowicz and Aleksandra Hądzelek, "The Polish Jews of Shanghai and the Political Sociology of Historical Memory," *Holocaust Studies: A Journal of Culture and History* 19 (2013): 27–64; Andrew Jakubowicz, "Transnationalism in the Analysis of Global Refugee Movements: The Case of the Second World War Polish Jews in Shanghai," *Australian Humanities Review* 62 (2017): 111–134; Andrew Jakubowicz, "Stopped in flight: Shanghai and the Polish Jewish refugees of 1941," *Holocaust Studies: A Journal of Culture and History* 23 (2017): 1–18.

49 The most recent book about this community is by Vera Schwarcz, *In the Crook of the Rock: Jewish Refuge in a World Gone Mad—The Chaya Leah Walkin Story* (Brighton, MA: Academic Studies Press, 2018).

50 *Bulletin of the Shanghai Ashkenazic Collaborating Relief Association* (SACRA) 3 (April 30, 1943) as described at "Guide to the Shanghai Collection, 1924–1950 (bulk 1939–1948) RG 243," YIVO Institute for Jewish Research, accessed April 10, 2018, http://findingaids.cjh.org/?pID=109124.

51 "Stateless Refugees—Removal to the Designated Area," SMP, May 22, 1943.

52 Telegram from Martin Fischer, Deutsches Generalkonsulat Shanghai, February 20, 1943, file 73, Irene Eber Collection.

were made.⁵³ This list will be discussed in more detail below. Those two corrections would add at least 1000 other refugees who had arrived in Shanghai, placing the total arrivals between 17,000 and 18,000.

A postwar report by the American Jewish Joint Distribution Committee, the outside relief organization most responsible for helping the refugees survive, provides a final attempt at a complete count. In 1946, the Joint estimated a total of 14,600 refugees in Shanghai.⁵⁴ Again, adding in all those who had managed to leave soon after arrival, those who had died, and those who were able to get out of Shanghai right after the war, which came to at least 1400 by 1946, the total would be close to 17,000, not far from the estimate above.

In 1944, the Japanese initiated the most extensive effort to count all European refugees, a house-to-house census of all foreigners in Hongkou. The result of the census is a list of 14,794 people considered as "Foreigners residing in Dee Lay Jao police district" of Shanghai, as written on the first of 473 pages of the census results.⁵⁵ This census remains a mysterious undertaking. The results were typed in English, apparently by three young Jewish refugee women. The people listed were put into detailed categories according to national origin and bureaucratic status, such as "census forms with old numbers," "mail from other districts," and "pending cases," whose meaning is not clear. Within each category, names were put in alphabetical order. For each person, first and last name, gender, age, address, occupation, and origin category are listed. There is no known documentation about exactly when and how the information was gathered. Along with residents from all over the world, a total of 12,364 refugees are listed, well short of the sum of refugees discussed above. Many refugee families are not listed at all,

---

53   A list of deaths to Jewish refugees was compiled by the Communal Association of Central European Jews between 1940 and 1946. This list does not include Polish refugees: all the places of origin cited are in German-speaking Central Europe.

54   Cited in Ellen Pressler, "Überlebt in Fernen Osten," *Aufbau*, New York, September 16, 1994, 24.

55   A copy of the original document is available on a CD accompanying the book *Exil Shanghai 1938–1947: Jüdisches Leben in der Emigration* (Teetz, Germany: Hentrich und Hentrich, 2000), ed. George Armbrüster, Michael Kohlstruck, and Sonja Mühlberger. The list is described in an appendix, 256–259. Because the typed sheets have been scanned and made into an Excel file, it is possible to use these data to analyze the demographic composition of the refugees, keeping in mind their incomplete coverage.

as the list covers perhaps only about 70%, but overall the records contain invaluable information about most Jewish refugees.[56]

One issue that the 1944 census can elucidate is the nature of the gender disproportion among Shanghai refugees, the much larger number of males. Other major refugee streams from Central Europe were nearly evenly divided: males were 52% of refugees to Palestine in 1933-37 and 51% of those to the United States in 1938–41.[57] Data covering nearly all refugees who landed in Shanghai between January and September 1939, more than half of the total, show 61% male, with nearly twice as many adult men as women in the early months of 1939.[58] If we assume that the 1944 census, although incomplete, accurately reflects the gender ratio, we can use the age data to pinpoint the location of the extra men. At the time of arrival in Shanghai, children until age 15 were equally divided. A strong preponderance of men shows up after age 25 and persists past 60 years old, including at least 2000 adult men.

While the data from Shanghai offer no other clues about these men, it is reasonable to assume that this preponderance of men is related to the arrest of 30,000 men in the wake of *Kristallnacht*, after which the heaviest movement toward Shanghai commenced. Both single and married men could be released from the concentration camps if they showed tickets out of the country, which were very hard to obtain. Presumably many families decided simply to get their men out of the camps and out of the country. The rest of the family often followed, as in the case of Lisbeth Loewenberg

---

56 Armbrüster, Kohlstruck, and Mühlberger, "Exil Shanghai: Facetten eines Themas," in *Exil Shanghai 1938–1945*, 15. My own grandparents are not listed, because they, along with several dozen other refugees, mainly doctors, were given permission to remain outside of the Designated Area. Other refugees who were known to have been living in Hongkou are not listed.

57 The data for the United States for 1938–1939 come from "Statistics of Jews," *American Jewish Year Book* 42 (1940-1941): 613; for the United States for 1939-1941 and for Palestine from Arieh Tartakower, "The Jewish Refugees: A Sociological Survey," *Jewish Social Studies* 4 (1942): 328, 330.

58 The Shanghai data for 1939 cover 9035 refugees who arrived between January 15 and September 12, 1939, as reported in two sources: Marx, "Bericht über die Organisation," 14, and the reports of the SMP on individual landings. They were originally divided into three categories of men, women and children, with no explanation of the precise boundaries of the category "children." The children have been equally apportioned to male and female.

and her mother from Vienna.⁵⁹ But for thousands of families this was not possible.

The Polish refugees who arrived mostly in 1941 were even more heavily dominated by males, 75% according to the 1944 census. About one quarter of those counted were male rabbinical students between ages 15 and 35. But even without them, males still outnumbered females nearly exactly two to one, concentrated in ages 15 to past 55. This predominance of males has yet to be explained.

Where did the refugees come from? Again, various authorities tried to keep track of the origins of the refugees.⁶⁰ Each offers useful data, but none covers all the refugees with precision.

The geographic origin of the refugees shifted during 1938 and 1939 because of the nature of Nazi persecution. Because systematic violence struck Austrian Jews first, immediately after the *Anschluss* in March 1938, they were the first to take the desperate step of fleeing to Shanghai. Of those who landed in Shanghai before March 1939, nearly two-thirds were from Austria. By that time the proportions were already shifting, because thousands of Jews were arrested in Germany in June and then tens of thousands during *Kristallnacht* in November. In the months after March 1939, about 70% came from the so-called *Altreich*.⁶¹ The German Consul General reported on the Jewish committee's data for the end of 1939, which covers about 13,500 refugees. Among those, 7900 (59%) came from Germany, 4500 (33%) from Austria, and about 1000 from other places or of unknown origin.⁶² At that moment, few Polish refugees had arrived, so the remaining 1000 were mainly other German speakers.

After the war was over and Jews began to leave Shanghai with help from American relief organizations, an attempt was made by the Joint to record the origins of refugees. In their 1946 report referred to earlier, the Joint provided the following groupings: 7000 from Germany, 4000 from Austria, 1200 from Poland, 600 from Italy, 300 from Czechoslovakia, and

---

59 See interview with Lisbeth Loewenberg, reproduced in an edited version in *Exodus to Shanghai*, 47–49.
60 Most of the data on origin does not specify whether birthplace or place of previous residence is meant.
61 Christiane Hoss, "Abenteurer: Wer waren die Shanghai-Flüchtlinge aus Mitteleuropa?," in *Exil Shanghai 1938–1947*, 107.
62 From report "Judentum in Shanghai," Deutsches Generalkonsulat Shanghai, June 30, 1940, 9, file 73, Irene Eber Collection.

1500 other or stateless.⁶³ In a later report on those who had already left Shanghai by August 31, 1948, the *American Jewish Yearbook* cited these figures: Germans 5658, Austrians 2325, Poles 960, Czechs 113, and others 513.⁶⁴

When we consider all of these sources together, they agree that among the German-speaking Jews from Central Europe, about two-thirds came from Germany, just less than one-third came from Austria, and about 1% from Czechoslovakia, not more than 250. It appears that we can be relatively certain that the number of Polish refugees was somewhere around 1000.

The Nazi government had tried to extract every possible item of value from Jewish families before they left the country. Once in Shanghai, finding work was difficult. Wealthy Baghdadis were able to offer some financial help and occasionally jobs to the first few hundred arrivals, but once the number of refugees reached several thousand, that kind of assistance was no longer possible. Nevertheless, most refugees were able to establish an independent existence, however precarious, during their long years in Shanghai. They were helped by infusions of funds from the US, funneled through the Joint Distribution Committee, which were distributed in the form of daily meals to thousands of refugees. Possessions were sold on the street to pay for food and rent.

The most destitute families and those who could not find work ended up living in the so-called *Heime*, supported by funds from Baghdadi Jews and from the Joint. The number of refugees in the *Heime* rose rapidly during 1939: about 1300 in May, 1800 in June, 2350 in July, and 2500 in August.⁶⁵ According to SACRA statistics in early 1943, 2819 lived in five *Heime*.⁶⁶ Thus one out of every six refugees spent years living in crowded barracks in Shanghai, supported by relief agencies. There is little information about

---

63   Pressler, "Überlebt in Fernen Osten," 24.
64   Cited by Zhava Litvac Glaser, "Refugees and Relief: The American Jewish Joint Distribution Committee and European Jews in Cuba and Shanghai," PhD dissertation (City University of New York, 2015), 311.
65   SMP reports, "Jewish Refugee Camps," D5422(c), dated May 19, June 24, and August 5, 1939. The July figure comes from Dr. Kurt Marx, "Bericht über die Organisation des Committee for the Assistance of European Refugees in Shanghai," July 18, 1939, 14, file 46, Irene Eber Collection. Sometimes the *Heime* are referred to as camps; this is a misleading label, since they did not resemble either concentration camps or internment camps. Residents could come and go as they pleased.
66   "SACRA Statistik," on disk accompanying *Exil Shanghai 1938–1947*. This report was originally published in SACRA's *Bulletin* in May 1943.

whether many refugees moved in and out of the *Heime*, but that was possible given changing financial circumstances.⁶⁷

Who lived in the *Heime*? Although there have been many interviews recorded with former Shanghai refugees, very few of those were in the *Heime*. Few former *Heim* residents got involved with the reunion activities of former refugees or wrote memoirs. The memories of extreme deprivation may well have been too painful to relive. The only source which offers some information about *Heim* residents is the 1944 census, which recorded 2605 people living at the addresses of five *Heime* in Hongkou.⁶⁸ Although the 1944 census was incomplete, it is reasonable to assume that the coverage of people living in the *Heime* was more easily accomplished and thus might be more complete. The characteristics of these recorded *Heim* residents helps us to understand something of the selection process among refugees.

Men were more likely to live in the *Heime* than women: they made up two-thirds of the *Heim* population. Two-thirds of the residents gave no occupation to the census-takers, while this was true for only 40% of those who were recorded living independently. The *Heime* each had unique character, based on who lived there. Families were placed at the Wayside Road Heim, men and women were equally represented, and children made up nearly 20% of the residents. There were also many families at the Chaoufoong Road Heim. At Alcock and East Seward Road, four out of five residents were men, and there were virtually no children.

Another important number in our understanding of the life of Shanghai refugees represents how many had been living outside of the Designated Area when it was declared in early 1943, and thus had to give up their residence, and usually their jobs, to move to Hongkou. The SACRA reported in May 1943 that 7990 refugees already lived in the Designated Area and 7352 had to move.⁶⁹ That same month, the SMP reported slightly different numbers: 7000 already lived in the Designated Area, 6600 had moved in recently, and 1650 who lived outside had received permission to delay their

---

67 See interview with Gerard Slaxon Kohbieter, reproduced in an edited version in *Exodus to Shanghai*, 142–143. He describes living in the Alcock Heim.
68 The Ward Road Heim was located at 138 Chang Yang Lu; Chaoufoong Road Heim at 680 Kao Yang Lu; Wayside Road Heim at 150 Hok San Lu; Alcock Road Heim at 66 Ankuo Lu, and East Seward Road Heim at 961 Tung Zangdze Lu. These addresses were spelled in a variety of ways in the census report.
69 "SACRA Statistik," on disk accompanying *Exil Shanghai 1938–1947*.

move.⁷⁰ Thus about half of the refugees had to move because of the Japanese creation of the Designated Area.

While both scholarly and popular works about Jewish refugees in Shanghai emphasize survival, not all of the refugees who made it to Shanghai survived to see the end of the war. The semitropical climate in Shanghai and primitive hygienic conditions made life difficult for Central Europeans, whose memoirs are filled with stories of illness.

Any accounting of Jewish deaths during the Holocaust must attempt to distinguish deaths by government action from deaths as part of normal life, which can include sickness, accidents, even crimes. It is notable that only a handful of refugees died because of their treatment by the Japanese authorities in Shanghai, who shared a military alliance with Nazi Germany, but not the Nazis' desire to kill Jews. Fred Schranz, a Jewish man who served in the Pao Chia, a force of Jewish guards organized by the Japanese to patrol the borders of the Designated Area, got into a dispute with some Japanese soldiers who had damaged his bicycle, and was later found dead. He may have been the only refugee murdered by the Japanese.⁷¹ Hermann Natowic, a popular soccer referee in his thirties, was accused by the Japanese of spying and operating a radio transmitter. He was subjected to months of torture in 1943 and released only when it appeared he would die. A refugee doctor, Samuel Didner, saved his life.⁷² Six Polish Jews who refused to move into the Designated Area contracted typhus in a Japanese prison and died.⁷³

The government action which killed the most refugees was the American bombing of the Designated Area on July 17, 1945. Much has been written about this incident, which may have been the result of unfortunate aim or mistaken targeting.⁷⁴ On no other occasion did the American bombing program kill Jewish civilians. The bombs struck a Chinese market and a building used by the SACRA to house refugees. All reports agree that thirty-one Jews died that day.

The Communal Association of Central European Jews compiled a list of refugees who died in Shanghai between January 1940 and February

---

70   "Stateless Refugees—Removal to the Designated Area," May 22, 1943, SMP file D5422(c).
71   Ross, *Escape to Shanghai*, 208.
72   Ernest G. Heppner, *Shanghai Refuge: A Memoir of the World War II Jewish Ghetto* (Lincoln, NE: University of Nebraska Press, 1993), 108. A more detailed discussion of Natowic and Didner can be found in Ross, *Escape to Shanghai*, 181–93.
73   Kranzler, *Japanese, Nazis and Jews*, 529.
74   Kranzler, *Japanese, Nazis and Jews*, 553–554.

1946, with 1433 names, cities of origin, and birth and death dates.[75] This list appears not to include any Polish Jews, as all the places of origin are in Germany, Austria, and Czechoslovakia. Like every list of Shanghai Jews, this list of deaths is incomplete, but how incomplete is difficult to measure. For example, the death list contains only twenty-two names who died in the July 17 bombing. But Jews who were not refugees, for example, Russian Jews, might have been among those killed. None of the Jews listed as dying on that day were children; most were in their forties and fifties. The bombs landed during the day, when children living in the building were at school. Although a kindergarten class met in the SACRA building, it had been dismissed early that day.[76]

The increasingly difficult economic plight of the refugees in Shanghai is clear from the sharply climbing numbers of deaths recorded by the Jewish authorities.[77]

Table 1: Deaths among Central European Refugees

Year	Deaths
1940	126
1941	185
1942	312
1943	305
1944	231
1945	248
1946	14

The sharp rise in deaths during in 1942 is evidence that living conditions deteriorated after the Japanese took over Shanghai at the end of 1941. The worst years were 1942 and 1943. Although about half of the refugees had to leave their residences early in 1943 to move into the much more crowded Designated Area in Hongkou, this does not appear to have made their

---

75 We should not assume that this list is complete or completely accurate. Like all the sets of data about the refugees, it offers us general clues about their lives and deaths. The number of deaths per year in this list corresponds very closely, although not exactly, with the number reported by the Joint for 1940–1942: Glaser, "Refugees and Relief," 251. The list was published in *Aufbau*, the New York journal for German-speaking Jews. Digitization was organized by Ralph Hirsch of the Council on the Jewish Experience in Shanghai.

76 Ross, *Escape to Shanghai*, 220.

77 Kranzler, *Japanese, Nazis and Jews*, 605–606, offers slightly variant numbers, differing by less than 10%.

collective health worse. Fewer died in 1944 and 1945. The data cover only January in 1946, but that month appears to have been much better than in previous years, indicating that the death rate had fallen after the American liberating forces brought a much improved food supply.

If we assume that about 17,000 to 18,000 Central European refugees arrived in Shanghai, then the 1433 deaths in the list would mean an average annual mortality rate of about 140 per 10,000 people. Mortality rates in Germany during the 1930s ranged between 110 and 120 per 10,000, and in Europe from 85 and 125 per 10,000.[78] Jewish mortality rates in Germany were somewhat lower than the rest of the German population, which is usually explained as due to lower infant and child mortality.[79] Thus, only after 1941 did Jewish refugees in Shanghai experience significantly higher mortality than would have been expected in Europe.[80]

As with most collective issues concerning the Shanghai Jews, it is not possible to precisely enumerate the postwar destinations of members of the three Jewish communities, because the authorities who controlled the exodus from China did not distinguish refugees from earlier Shanghai residents. It was difficult to find passage out of Shanghai and entry into a desirable destination in 1945 and 1946. The Joint tabulated 16,025 Jewish emigrants from Shanghai 1946–1952, when probably over 20,000 Jews were living there at the end of the war. The great majority left in 1947–1949, and the remaining 2000 or so in 1950–1952.

A tabulation of 9569 Jews from Central Europe, thus probably refugees, who left Shanghai in 1946–1948, shows at least where the majority went, which was heavily influenced by origin. Nearly 80% of former Germans came to the United States, 9% returned to Germany, 6% to Latin America,

---

78   Jörg Baten and Andrea Wagner, "Autarchy, Market Disintegration, and Health: the Mortality and Nutritional Crisis in Nazi Germany, 1933-1937," Cesifo Working Paper No. 800, Category 7: Trade Policy, October 2002, 2, accessed April 10, 2018, https://www.cesifo-group.de/DocDL/cesifo_wp800.pdf.

79   Maristella Botticini, Zvi Eckstein, and Anat Vaturi, "The Chosen Many: Population Growth and Jewish Childcare in Central-Eastern Europe, 1500–1930," Pinhas Sapir Center for Development, Tel Aviv University, Discussion Paper No. 4–16, March 2016, 92-101; Steven M. Lowenstein, "The Beginning of Integration, 1780–1870," in *Jewish Daily Life in Germany, 1618–1945*, ed. Marion A. Kaplan (New York: Oxford University Press, 2005), 115.

80   Of course, this comparison is based on expected mortality in the absence of organized persecution. After 1933, Jewish mortality was raised by deadly Nazi government policies. It is worth noting that even with somewhat higher mortality in Shanghai, thousands of Jews survived who would have been killed in Europe.

and 4% to Australia. Former Austrians were much more likely to return home: 42% were repatriated to Austria, 24% came to the United States, 20% to Australia, 7% to Latin America. Among Polish refugees, 64% came to the United States, 14% to Australia, 9% to Canada; virtually none returned to Europe. Most Czechs also came to the United States. Only 1% of these refugees went to Palestine, which had only become an independent Israel in May 1948.[81]

Leaving Shanghai was not the end of the Shanghai experience. Although arrival in another country in the late 1940s made Shanghai appear far away, memories of refugee life remained to be processed for the rest of their lives. Some memories were attached to objects brought back from Shanghai, placed in new homes as reminders of personal histories. I remember Chinese figurines and pictures on my grandparents' walls, mixed in with Viennese artifacts, representing the stations of their peripatetic lives. The final two essays in this book close the narrative of Jewish life in China by considering what a past refugee life means today.

Dan Ben-Canaan investigates the psychological transformation in the minds of former refugees from Harbin and Shanghai, as they reimagined their histories, combining local experiences with global travels. Understanding how former refugees perceive their histories is crucial for historians who rely heavily on those memories, in the forms of interviews and memoirs, to recreate the past.

Gabrielle Abram describes how former refugees have been perceived by others, particularly regarding their connection to the Holocaust. She shows how scholars have moved gradually towards including former refugees into the category of Holocaust survivors, and how this has changed self-perceptions among refugees.

For about a hundred years, Jews were important to Shanghai and Shanghai was important to Jews. The essays in this volume demonstrate how Jews from Europe and the Middle East created communities in China, communities of achievement and of survival. Those communities have dispersed, leaving traces both in the consciousness of their descendants and in emerging institutions in Shanghai, like the Shanghai Jewish Refugees Museum.

---

81   Glaser, "Refugees and Relief," Appendices, 9–10, 310–11.

Shanghai before the War

Maisie Meyer*

Shanghai Remembered: Recollections of Shanghai's Baghdadi Jews

This essay aims to provide a deeper insight into Shanghai's Baghdadi Jewish community through the study of individual people who were significant participants during a crucial period within Chinese history. While animating the dry facts of history, it enriches our understanding of the unique way of life of a Jewish community that acquired influence and status and successfully became the center of Shanghai economic life, though elsewhere Jews were often a despised minority. Amidst a host of other nationalities, they maintained their own customs and traditions, and created a way of life adapted to their environment.

Baghdadi Jews were originally Ottoman subjects.[1] For convenience, the term "Baghdadi" in this context encompasses Arabic-speaking Jews from Baghdad, Basrah (Basra) and other parts of the Ottoman Empire,

---

*   Maisie Joy Meyer was born in Calcutta in 1939 in a Baghdadi Jewish family and was brought up in India. She married Benjamin Meyer, a structural engineer, in 1961, and has three children. She earned the BA in English at Loreto College in 1961, and the BA in humanities in 1986 at Middlesex University. She earned an MA at London School of Economics and Political Science in 1988 and a PhD in International History in 1994. She is the leading expert on the Baghdadi community in Shanghai. Her books are *From the Rivers of Babylon to the Whangpoo: A Century of Sephardi Jewish Life in Shanghai* (Lanham, MD: University Press of America, 2003); and *Shanghai's Baghdadi Jews: A Collection of Biographical Reflections* (Hong Kong: Blackman Books, 2015).

1   Incidentally, it is not appropriate to refer to them as Iraqi Jews before October 1932, when Mesopotamia achieved official independence, in accordance with an agreement signed by the United Kingdom in 1930.

from Cairo and Egypt, as well as non-Arabic-speaking Jews from Persia and Afghanistan. From the 1830s onwards, these Jews migrated to escape persecution, conscription, and frequent epidemics of plague. They were attracted to Bombay, where David Sassoon was recruiting Judaeo-Arabic-speaking Jews to launch a vast commercial empire. His son Elias pioneered the settlement of Baghdadi Jews in Shanghai after the Treaty of Nanking in 1845 ended the infamous Opium Wars and Shanghai became a so-called Treaty Port, open to foreign trade and settlement.

Initially, Jews left their families in Baghdad for lengthy periods, to take advantage of China's lucrative trading opportunities. They were undeterred by the arduous seventy-day journey from Bombay to Shanghai, including occasionally being grounded for days, the cargo being thrown overboard, and passengers sitting through the night with guns at the ready in case of pirates. It was also necessary to break the journey often and disembark into small sampans.[2]

Biographical accounts collated in my recent book, *Shanghai's Baghdadi Jews: A Collection of Biographical Reflections*, illustrate the remarkable global outreach of these peripatetic migrants. They wandered with their families from one Baghdadi Jewish settlement to another, notably Bombay, Calcutta, Rangoon (Yangon), Singapore, Hong Kong, and Batavia (Djakarta in the Dutch East Indies), in search of a livelihood, before finally settling in the foreign concessions of Shanghai. Shaul Ghazal, to avoid conscription into the Turkish Army, migrated with his wife and three sons to Burma, then Malaysia. When seven-year-old Silas Isaiah Jacob was stoned in an anti-Jewish riot in Baghdad, his mother traveled with her three sons to Shanghai via Bombay, where Silas worked as a clerk for the Sassoon firm. Catherine Levy Hardoon's family migrated to Basrah, Turkey, Calcutta, and settled in Bombay for about two years. Nineteen-year-old Maurice Dangoor's trade in diamonds took him to France, England, and Holland. He returned to Baghdad during World War I and then went to Germany, where a Baghdadi friend encouraged him to go to Shanghai, which was experiencing an economic boom. Sassoon Reuben's quest to expand his import-export business led him from Egypt, Syria, and Lebanon to Bombay and Kobe, Japan, where there were three Jewish families. His daughter Helen recalls that she attended synagogue services for the first time in a hotel room, when the outbreak of Sino-Japanese hostilities in 1937 compelled

---

2   *Israel's Messenger* (hereafter *IM*), Shanghai, March 20, 1908, 13.

the Hillaly, Toeg, and Isaac families from Shanghai to extend their holiday during the festivals. Isaac Toeg taught them religious traditions. When her family later settled in Shanghai, the feeling of belonging to its Baghdadi community meant a great deal to them.[3]

Economic Success

Shanghai's Baghdadi Jews had a high profile in financial circles. Benjamin David Benjamin (1844–1889), a former Sassoon employee, became a stockbroker in 1875 and was content at first with commissions on small transactions. Four years later he was referred to as the "Lion of the Shanghai Stock Exchange." The cry in the stock market was, "What is Benjamin doing?"[4] For five years he was the largest shareholder of the Hong Kong and Shanghai Banking Corporation. He boasted that a quarter of the bank belonged to him. Benjamin was the preeminent speculator and land proprietor in the burgeoning Treaty Port, and allegedly owned more than a quarter of the International Settlement in the late nineteenth century. He had interests in virtually all the local companies and could manipulate the markets in property and commodities at will. Overspeculation sparked the collapse of his business. He was responsible for the boom and subsequent crash in real estate values leading to years of depression. Benjamin was reduced to penury. The self-confidence and pride of the Jewish merchants regarding their good reputation within the wider community is palpable. They complacently believed that they were building for the future and that their community would live on through their offspring. Marcella Rubel wrote: "Elaborate private estates are owned by the Baghdadi Jews, who made their fortunes in the Orient. Almost half the shopping, business and residential district is owned by these wealthy Jews."[5] Rose Jacob Horowitz recalls that Baghdadi Jews felt they had built Shanghai. The children even chanted along with the Chinese laborers.[6]

---

3   Meyer, *Baghdadi Jews*, 25, 151, 195, 272, 274.
4   John George Thirkel, *Some Queer Stories of Benjamin David Benjamin and Messrs. E. D. Sassoon & Co.: Wealth Fraud and Poverty: Les Juifs Entre Eux* (Shanghai: Celestial Empire, 1888), 2.
5   M. C. Rubel, *IM*, October 9, 1925, 7.
6   Rose Horowitz to author, Los Angeles, February 12, 1992.

Family of Edward Ezra

The community possessed considerable property in the foreign concessions, including two synagogues and cemeteries. N. E. B. Ezra boasted that Jewish financiers kept architects busy with their large investments in apartment buildings, theatres, hotels, offices, storage facilities, residences, factories, and cinemas. He hoped that when historians recorded the history of Shanghai, they would give credit to the Jewish merchants who developed the city into reputedly the fifth largest in the world.[7] The grandeur and scale of the Sassoon, Ezra, Hardoon, Benjamin, and Somekh edifices located in the heart of the city and, not least, their palatial homes were spectacles of power and entrepreneurial energy. Today, they are monuments to a once-vibrant community, particularly as their tombstones and cemeteries have long since vanished. Baghdadi Jewish merchants expanded trade and family networks and there was constant interaction among Judaeo-Arabic speaking Jews who had settled in a string of trading posts in Southeast Asia. Flower Elias explains: "In this way, their horizons stretched far beyond the confines of their homes, for 'home' to them was not a house, but anywhere

---

7   Meyer, *Baghdadi Jews*, 245.

the family dwelt."[8] In an era when communication was difficult, the mutual interdependence of the Baghdadi Jews, not unlike that of an extended family, was astonishing. Sasson Jacoby's father regularly sailed to Kobe to perform circumcisions for the cluster of Baghdadi families who lacked this facility, earning him the nickname "China Clipper."

Community Life

A keen sense of community, awareness of their common background, tradition, shared values and attitudes were vital threads in the fabric of the community. As Matook Nissim put it, "One filled in where one was needed. We were a good strong group of youngsters with the same value system." He learned to play the trumpet because the Calef Band needed a trumpeter. Joe Jacob, Ezekiel Abraham, Isaiah Jacob, and others studied *sheita* (the ritual slaughter of livestock), realizing that the youngsters would have to take over this role from the older generation. A salient theme strongly reflected in these biographical accounts was a robust Baghdadi Jewish identity, reinforced by tradition, close commercial ties, distinctive cuisine, kinship, and endogamy. Ethnic tensions arose when Daniel Moalem's father (whose family were Yemenites) married a Baghdadi, Girgee Ghazal. Her family were not invited to the wedding. All three Moalem brothers were ostracized when Simeon Moalem married Emma, a Baghdadi, and Joe married Anna, a Russian. Marriage between Baghdadis and Ashkenazim was actively discouraged. None of Isaiah Jacob's relatives attended his wedding to Rebecca Soloduhin, a Russian, and they had no further contact with him until his wife was pregnant. The community was astounded when brothers Theodore and Arthur Sopher married Ludmilla Menshikoff and Lydia Bistroff, both White Russians, a group renowned for their antisemitism. Biographies by their sons reveal that their parents divorced. Julie Abraham, from a strictly Orthodox family, married an Ashkenazi US Army soldier, Melvin Freedman. Moselle Cohen is unique in marrying a student of the Lithuanian Mir Yeshiva, Lazare Hendeles. Such marriages were more acceptable from the 1930s, but marriage to a non-Jew remained an anathema.[9]

Members of this community lived in close proximity and were generally either related by marriage or linked commercially. It was clannish and

---

8 Flower Elias and Judith Elias Cooper, *The Jews of Calcutta: The Autobiography of a Community 1798–1972* (Calcutta: Jewish Association of Calcutta, 1974), 52.
9 Meyer, *Baghdadi Jews*, 80, 113, 199, 217, 309, 340.

parochial, retaining its culture and its own social functions. The community did not ostracize those who had almost completely abandoned their traditions, but welcomed them on the rare occasions when they attended religious services. One did not have to be a member to attend the synagogues. A high degree of tolerance is evident. Leah Jacob Garrick notes that on Friday nights some guests excused themselves and disappeared outside to smoke a cigarette, which was prohibited on the Sabbath. Even so, they continued to be the family's Sabbath guests.[10]

Even secular Baghdadis did not sever family and communal ties. Maple Hardoon, one of the eleven adopted children of Silas Aaron Hardoon and his devout Buddhist wife Liza Roos, recalls the Buddhist monastery in their forty-acre garden and the huge sums her father spent on preserving China's rich cultural heritage. By contrast, he donated the magnificent Beth Aharon Synagogue to the community and stipulated that his adopted sons should be brought up as Jews. Maple reveals: "My brothers were circumcised when they were quite old—Rubin at the age of nine. Mother might well have left it so late because she was delaying and father insisting. The *mohel* who performed the circumcision came to the house with all the equipment." The girls were excluded when the boys were taught Hebrew and given instruction for their bar mitzvah. Kosher food was cooked for Silas Hardoon separately. When he died, he wished to be buried according to Jewish tradition.[11]

Among a portion of the community, a drift away from strict observance began during World War II and became quite manifest in the final stages of the community's existence in Shanghai. They turned their backs on their religion, but not on their cultural affiliations. Thus, Baghdadi Jewry's links to their Babylonian heritage endured, even when they were alienated from Baghdad, which aligned with Nazi Germany, adopting its brutal persecution of Jews.

Socioeconomic Differences

The community was by no means homogeneous: even their nationalities were different—Iraqi, British, French and Spanish—and there were varying degrees of orthodoxy and religious observance among them. The reality

---

10   Meyer, *Baghdadi Jews*, 113.
11   Meyer, *Baghdadi Jews*, 58.

was that there was social stratification generally based on family background and wealth. There was a conspicuous social divide between those Baghdadis who lived in the salubrious International Settlement and French Concession and the less well-to-do residing in the Chinese and Japanese neighborhood of Hongkou. However, there was a great deal of social mobility, as many poor immigrants went on to become wealthy.

The social life of the middle and lower classes of Baghdadis revolved around their homes, as was customary in Baghdad. Dan Moalem, who had over fifty cousins, recalls that they studied and played together. Relatives continually dropped in and cousins often stayed the night. Almost every week, someone in the extended family had a birthday party.[12]

Warm hospitality was characteristic of most families and there was always room for unexpected guests. Leah Jacob recalls: "Guests from all over the world graced our table. No formal schooling could possibly give us the education that so extended our horizons."[13] The courtyard of the Ohel Rachel Synagogue functioned as the Shanghai Jewish School playground from 1931 on. It was a convenient meeting place for youngsters whose social and sporting activities centered on the school and the synagogue. There was little need for a Jewish club.

The social lives of the elite were poles apart. Homes of well-to-do businessmen provided the setting for many social gatherings, earning them a reputation for lavish hospitality. Their large private gardens were the venues for picnics, fun fairs, and other communal events. The names Hardoon, Ezra, Kadoorie, and Sassoon were emblazoned over the business and social life of East Asia for a century. Their biographies reveal that their unparalleled level of commercial achievement, wealth, and privilege gave them status within the colonial establishment. Edward Isaac Ezra's palatial residence, Adeodata Hall, was situated amidst over twenty-five acres of land with monumental gardens and a picturesque park. The house was furnished with Louis XV furniture, the ballroom accommodated one hundred fifty dancers, a music room comfortably seated an audience of eighty, and a banqueting hall was the scene of many social functions.[14] Sir Victor Sassoon had a flair for hosting extravagant parties in the penthouse of his Cathay Hotel (now the Fairmont). His sensational "Shipwreck," "Circus," and "Toy Shop" fancy-dress parties dominated the social columns of the

---

12 Meyer, *Baghdadi Jews*, 309.
13 Meyer, *Baghdadi Jews*, 114.
14 Meyer, *Baghdadi Jews*, 253.

local press, which even published a detailed list of the several hundred guests at his "Toy Shop" party.¹⁵ Children enjoyed the school's annual visit to Marble Hall, the palatial residence of Sir Elly Kadoorie, which was well known to a wide spectrum of visitors from all parts of the world, among them high-ranking British officers, Zionist emissaries, politicians, and men of letters, including the famous Bengali poet Rabindranath Tagore. At a ball in his honor, the Panchen Lama, second only to the Dalai Lama, brought along his Tibetan orchestra, replete with mountain trumpets. Sports Days were held on a large tract of land behind the Abrahams' house. By all accounts, on Sabbath afternoons, adults and teenagers would socialize in the Abrahams' home and play croquet, tennis and volleyball in their garden. Boys played soccer on the adjacent land. The Jacob brothers and cousins were such a large group that they fielded a soccer team against another group from the Sephardic community. The game was known as "The Jacobs against the rest." The Jacobs usually fared well, except when it rained, when they generally lost, because most of them wore spectacles and had to keep stopping to wipe them.¹⁶

Outdoor party at D. E. J. Abraham's home

---

15   *IM*, February 10, 1937, 8.
16   Meyer, *Baghdadi Jews*, 88, 125.

The Abraham family were undoubtedly the nucleus of the community, who looked to them for leadership, particularly in times of trouble, as in January 1927, when Chinese crowds, incited by the Chinese Communist Party, burst through the barricades of the International Settlement, causing extensive destruction to property. Widespread relief greeted the British troop ships carrying the Shanghai Defense Force. Aziza Abraham Mowlem recounts that her brother Reuben arranged for Jewish servicemen to have meals in their home and in other Jewish homes. Sebag Montefiore, a member of the distinguished English Sephardi family, was one of the guests for the Passover Seder and several soldiers stayed at their home during the festivals. The family arranged the table according to military protocol and had a separate table in a different room for the soldiers.[17] Major General John Duncan acknowledged, "The way in which the Jewish community has come forward to help us is greatly appreciated and will never be forgotten."[18]

Affinity to the British

Some 340 Shanghai Baghdadis were British subjects, since they were born in British India, or settled over an extended period in a British possession, or worked in British firms in Shanghai. This accorded them valuable economic, political, legal, and social privileges; a British passport was a much sought-after means to privilege. Joe Jacob explains that this was not a question of simply opting for some foreign nationality; it was the one with which they were familiar, because of the British domination of Baghdad after World War I. The British, with their global empire, had power and organizing ability. It made sense to identify with this empire and to have its backing in Shanghai, where each community had its own protection and consuls, and the Municipal Council provided security and stability. In addition, the British controlled India and Hong Kong, through which some Shanghai Baghdadis had passed. A British national had the legal status of a foreign resident or a foreign investor. They were convinced that their prosperity correlated to British rule. In sharp contrast, those who were not British subjects were severely handicapped without the benefits of extraterritoriality. They were subject to Chinese law, and their commercial enterprises and travel were seriously inhibited.

---

17   Meyer, *Baghdadi Jews*, 78.
18   *IM*, March 4, 1927, 4.

Baghdadi Jews had an extraordinarily cosmopolitan outlook. Being able to communicate in English identified them with the British oligarchy that held power in the foreign enclave. Common commercial interests made them valued partners of the British elite and they were able to join them in the administration of the International Settlement. Over the course of time, Shanghai's Baghdadi Jews sacrificed, in part, their traditions and culture, creating a synthesis on the altar of pragmatic, or perhaps opportunistic, alignment with all-powerful Imperial Britain. Their slavish Anglicization and conviction that everything British was worthy of emulation molded the very structure of their lives. A thoroughly English education, involving the whole gamut of ballet, piano, deportment and elocution classes, generated strong British affinities, which continued over four generations. Rebecca Toeg explains that they considered themselves to be both thoroughly Baghdadi and thoroughly British, and were accepted in British society and British clubs. When her uncle Ezekiel invited them to swim at his rowing club, she noticed that he invariably put on a very British accent when talking to his English friends.[19] A European teacher, Miss Patterson, reported in 1904 that the Shanghai Jewish School inculcated more important lessons of patriotism, in addition to a secular education as good as that provided in many European schools.[20] Marcella Rubel, an American visitor to Shanghai in 1925, noted that the Baghdadi Jews spoke with a distinctly British accent and were as Westernized as she was. The Baghdadi Jews even had a high profile at the racecourse, the hallmark of the British colonial system and an integral part of the Treaty Port culture.

However, the Baghdadi Jews were born and bred into a culture to which they did not really belong. George Hayim reveals that his English governess threatened to make him and his brother into "little English boys"—after all, his father wanted his children to be *plus Anglais que les Anglais*. Even before they arrived in England for their education, they developed an inferiority complex regarding England. Most people could tell that they were not English, though they suffered no discrimination. He gained entry to Trinity College Cambridge. Rebecca Toeg acknowledges that she has yet to come to terms with her identity and considers Baghdadi Jews in Shanghai as birds that emerge from the eggs laid by the cuckoo in the British nest.[21]

---

19   Meyer, *Baghdadi Jews*, 240.
20   M. S. Perry, "Shanghai Jewish School First Annual Report: Report by a European Lady Teacher," *IM*, January 25, 1904, 20.
21   Meyer, *Baghdadi Jews*, 244, 365.

N. E. B. Ezra, editor of their journal *Israel's Messenger*, noted: "Here in Shanghai, where the community is wholly cosmopolitan, we Jews look upon the British flag with love and adoration. We venerate the King, the Queen and the Royal Family."[22] The community celebrated all royal anniversaries, vying with others to pay homage to the British monarch. Their tangible expressions of staunch British patriotism are exceptional. At the time of the Battle of Britain in 1940, when Spitfires and Hurricanes were Britain's saviors, Ellis Hayim and his wife organized seven nights of revelry in aid of the Spitfire Fund in their garden during May and June, which they called the "Follies." The Japanese accused him of spying. He replied, "I am English. I'm at war with Germany. I do all I can for my country just like you are doing at this moment." He insisted that his life and his work were open to any investigation, and that the "Follies" had taken place before Japan even entered the war. It did not save him from prison and daily questioning, but he stood his ground. Ironically, there were times when the Japanese camp commanders asked his advice on how to run things. He consistently emphasized he was Jewish, knowing that the Japanese respected religion. For his services to Britain, Hayim was honored with an OBE (Order of the British Empire), receiving the rank of Commander.[23]

Sir Victor Sassoon donated huge sums to the British War Fund and urged others to contribute. Hermann Goering, head of the German air force and Hitler's deputy, condemned him on the radio as a "mischievous Hollywood playboy." In New York, the FBI insisted on giving him two bodyguards, believing he might be a target of the Nazi Bund or Japanese gunmen. The Kadoorie family's home, Marble Hall, became the center of Allied activities immediately after the war. The British Consul General and his staff resided there rent-free for a lengthy period. The family also made good the shortfall when the Consulate had difficulties paying off their Chinese staff.[24]

At the outbreak of World War II, Theodore Sopher was among the three hundred French citizens mobilized in Shanghai. After three months, the French government decided that their services were not required. Theodore and his brother Arthur spoke little French but were fluent in English. They

---

22 *IM*, May 3, 1934, 7.
23 Meyer, *Baghdadi Jews*, 288.
24 Meyer, *Baghdadi Jews*, 103, 107, 215.

possessed a library of twelve thousand books. Except for Hebrew prayer books, most of these books were in English.[25]

Wealthy Baghdadis emulated the lifestyle of the British gentry. But British nationality and Anglicization did not guarantee full acceptance by the class-conscious British society, which recognized only fair-skinned Britons from the British Isles as bona fide British nationals. There was discrimination, an inflexible caste division and a practically unbridgeable social barrier between British people from the colonies and those born in England. Eze Nathan observed that in Singapore, the higher Jews moved up the social ladder, the more aware they became of the barriers that existed between them and their European peers.[26] Ida Bension, a Zionist envoy to Shanghai in 1929, observed that parents who were able to give their children a good education tried to turn them into "English gentlemen," but it rarely went beyond outward appearance.[27] Norman Stillman noted, "Jews might become Westernized in dress, education and even in tastes and habits, but most of them were first and foremost Jews, both in their own eyes and in the eyes of others."[28] They were aware that they were different and were not English. As in India, their status was ambiguous. They were sometimes treated as non-European or, at least, comparable to other "anomalous" people, like the Eurasians and Anglo-Indians, and were considered "marginal Westerners" within the foreign community.[29] There is little doubt that Shanghai's Baghdadi Jews suffered social discrimination.

In Shanghai, the long lists of British elites who were pleased to enjoy the lavish hospitality of affluent Baghdadis leaves the impression that wealth dissolved social taboos. They were members of British clubs, which generally enforced a network of sanctions and placed great emphasis on maintaining British standards of behavior. Evidently, in Shanghai's class-ridden society, wealth and social prominence were the major criteria for acceptance into the elite British Shanghai Club, considering that the billionaire Silas Hardoon was a member, notwithstanding his marriage

---

25 Meyer, *Baghdadi Jews*, 294.
26 Eze Nathan, *The History of Jews in Singapore, 1830–1945* (Singapore: Herbilu Editorial & Marketing Service, 1986), 67.
27 Ida Bension, *IM*, June 7, 1929, 14.
28 Norman A. Stillman, *The Jews of Arab Lands: A History and Source Book* (Philadelphia: Jewish Publication Society, 1979), 41, 52.
29 Walter Q. Zenner, "The Comparison of Jews of China and Jews of India" (paper presented at conference "Jewish Diasporas in China: Comparative and Historical Perspectives," Harvard University, August 1992), 4.

to a Eurasian Buddhist, a flagrant disregard of British social values. The Shanghai Club's membership list reveals only a handful of Baghdadi names, suggesting that some might not have applied for membership as they felt more comfortable in other European clubs. As one Englishman put it: "The Kadoories, after all, were almost one of us," and "Sir Victor was Jewish, but one could not very well snub a man who played golf with the Prince of Wales."[30]

Relationship with the Chinese

Prominent Chinese politicians were among the guests entertained in the homes of wealthy Sephardim. But the Baghdadi Jews generally had little social contact with the Chinese populace. Except for the Chinese elite, the only natives they met were servants, staff, compradores, rickshaw pullers, and interpreters. The Baghdadis were friendly, sometimes grateful, toward the Chinese they employed. In most ways, they adopted the Western sense of social and moral superiority. Leah Jacob Garrick family addressed their servants, who they employed for many years, by their positions: Cook, *Amah*, Boy, and Chauffeur.

The wealthy often had a retinue of servants. Silas Hardoon reputedly had nine hundred. Sir Elly Kadoorie's staff in Marble Hall after 1945 included two boys, three cooks, nine coolies, two *amahs*, and four gardeners, a significant reduction from his prewar splendor. Some sixty of their dependents, including children and grandchildren, were housed in the staff quarters. Edward Ezra employed over twenty servants, including cooks, *amahs*, gardeners, chauffeurs, pool attendants, and maintenance technicians from the 1920s until the early 1940s. After the Japanese occupation, the number was whittled down to ten.[31] By all accounts, most Shanghai Baghdadis had good relationships with their servants, who were well cared for.

Most families even of modest means had at least an *amah* to look after their children. She was generally considered a family member, a second mother. Often each child was pampered by their own *amah*. Several *amahs* hobbled about with bound feet. Generally, the families of the *amahs*, boys, cook, and laundryman lived behind the house. Childhood relationships

---

30 Quoted in Harriet Sergeant, *Shanghai: Collision Point of Cultures, 1918–1939* (New York, Crown Publishers, 1991), 127–129, 131.
31 Meyer, *Baghdadi Jews*, 107, 258.

sometimes broke through the social walls. Matook Nissim sneaked into his *amah*'s room to sleep in her bed and join the servants, seated around a large round table, at their meal of hot rice and a couple of vegetable side dishes. Ellis Jacob's mother could not understand why he was so reluctant to eat his dinner until she discovered that he would share his *amah*'s meals. She was horrified to see her pick up a morsel of food with her chopsticks and put it into her mouth, then pick up another titbit with the same chopsticks and pop it into Joe's. Sasson Jacoby's family could only afford servants who did not have a word of English, because those who spoke Pidgin English cost two or three times as much. His *amah* would take the children to the Quinsan Garden, like a mother duck with a string of ducklings, and loudly admonish them in Chinese. Rose Jacob Horowitz's early playmates were the children of servants, who encouraged her to feel, think, and speak Chinese just like them.[32]

Leah Jacob Garrick recalls that her grandfather Sasson Ezekiel Abraham raised a young Chinese boy named Huncha. Since only Arabic was spoken in the house, Huncha learned to speak it fluently. When ships with Baghdadi visitors were expected, he was often sent to the docks to bring them to the house. Imagine their surprise when they were greeted in fluent Arabic! After his wife's death, her grandfather went to Palestine in 1935, taking Huncha with him. When he died a year later in Jerusalem, Huncha returned to Shanghai.

The Chinese festivals remain a happy childhood memory, notably the Chinese New Year. Baghdadi families looked forward to their scrumptious feast and to sharing the Chinese custom of giving children coins wrapped in red paper to symbolize paying off their debts. Sasson Jacoby's father prepared bags of rice as gifts to their servants and readied money to hand out to the postman, street cleaner, and garbage men. The cook prepared kosher *jiaozi* and *yuanxiao* (traditional dumplings). Clive Levy's *amah* and her friends funded a lavish Chinese banquet for the family and a dining room jam-packed with guests. In appreciation, they gave her money in an envelope. By all accounts, it was heartbreaking for the Baghdadis to part from their *amahs*, their tears mingled. All their servants were given generous severance payments.[33]

---

32   Meyer, *Baghdadi Jews*, 81, 156, 247.
33   Meyer, *Baghdadi Jews*, 86, 118, 250.

Few foreigners bothered to learn the Chinese language. It was mainly youngsters who made the effort. Reginald Marcus Elias spent every possible moment with his Chinese boy, Mo Di Chow, and his family. In their company, he became fluent in Mandarin and in the Wu dialect (foreigners called it Shanghainese) spoken only in Shanghai and developed a deep love for the Chinese people. Mo Di Chow accompanied him to England and stayed with the family throughout World War II, returning to China in the early 1950s. Their relationship was generally good-humored and affectionate, but sometimes very stormy. His brother, Freddie Elias, spoke the Wu dialect perfectly and could pick up good racing tips from the locals. Rather than Latin, Matook Nissim chose Chinese for his second language at the Western District Public School and spoke the Wu dialect quite fluently.[34] Clive Levy spoke Cantonese so fluently that no one could detect he was not Chinese when he was out of sight.

Not all youngsters became so immersed in Chinese culture. Ellis Jacob's father, one of the few elders who spoke fluently in the Wu dialect, regretted that his son did not learn more about Chinese customs and culture in school. Leah Jacob Garrick is embarrassed to admit that she never learnt any Chinese, except to bargain and "cuss." Interestingly, when Maurice Dangoor, who was fluent in Arabic, French, Hebrew, Turkish, Dutch, English, and German, tried to learn Chinese, it angered his Chinese business associates, who did not want foreigners to learn their language.[35]

Yet, Rose Jacob Horowitz reveals that they totally identified with the refugee Chinese from the surrounding countryside, who poured into the International Settlement when war broke out between China and Japan in 1937. They carried their pitiful belongings on their backs, their feet barely shod, often bleeding, with an occasional family piling an assortment of furnishings on a large single-wheeled barrow, all of them with expressions both dazed and terrified, wandering aimlessly. Rose Jacob once saw a Chinese man gnawing the bark of a tree in hunger.[36] During the epidemics that accompanied the fighting, corpses were strewn on the road, because relatives could not afford a funeral. Leah Jacob Garrick recalls walking to school sidestepping packages of straw in which dead Chinese babies were wrapped and collected daily. A charity organization, styled the Blue Swastika Society, sent trucks cruising through the streets to pick up the

---

34 Meyer, *Baghdadi Jews*, 86.
35 Meyer, *Baghdadi Jews*, 25, 119, 259.
36 Meyer, *Baghdadi Jews*, 154.

dead. This went on constantly, as there were endless plagues, wars, floods, typhoons, though it was mainly starvation that took lives. Poverty led to the increasing presence of beggars on the streets. Many of the homeless had serious infectious diseases, including leprosy, and threatened to touch passersby if money was not readily offered.

Another Wave of Refugees: Jews from Europe

The Treaty Port's attraction for around 18,000 refugees who fled from Nazi persecution beginning in 1938 was that passport control no longer existed after mid-1937, allowing anyone to land without a visa. The newcomers were generally penniless, with limited personal belongings, and often had no comprehension of English. When hundreds of refugees arrived on each ship from Europe in early 1939, trucks were provided by the locals to bring the newcomers to shelter. They were loaned free of charge from two Jewish-owned firms, Mollers and Benjamins, or could be rented from Millers, which owned the largest local fleet. It had a profound impact on Matook Nissim to see bedraggled refugees, once well-to-do but now destitute, in a very different environment, with only the suit on their backs, lining up to have a meal in soup kitchens.[37]

From the moment the refugees arrived, they were transported, housed, and fed through the generosity of Baghdadi Jews. Wealthy Baghdadis, most notably the Kadoories, the Abrahams, the Hayims, and Sir Victor Sassoon, were at the helm of the relief work. Sir Victor's donations to Jewish refugee relief were reputedly the largest in the East. He set up various accounts that supported the refugees, under the pseudonym Val Seymour. In 1938 he purchased 10,000 square miles of land in Brazil and investigated the possibility of establishing a colony of refugees from Nazi Europe, stating, "I am all for the Jews living in a colony together, where the Jews do everything from being sweeper to President."[38] He maintained that further immigration to Shanghai should be discouraged, as the city could not cope with any great influx of people: "If any more Jews arrived, it would only mean a great deal of hardship for them. Shanghai was not a prosperous place and did not possess a bottomless purse."[39]

---

37 Meyer, *Baghdadi Jews*, 83.
38 *The Jewish Tribune*, Bombay, July 1938, 10.
39 *North China Herald*, July 8, 1938.

In early 1939, Sir Victor donated the first floor of the Embankment Building, which accommodated approximately 400 refugees and for about a year served as a receiving station for new arrivals. In May 1939 the kitchens operated by a Chinese caterer fed about 1,000 persons daily. Sir Victor found it incredible that 33 cents could provide three square meals a day: "I eat there myself very often, paying 20 cents per meal and don't mind being 'stung' because it is for a good cause."[40] Sir Victor replaced the Embankment Building with a more suitable property, San Sing in Pingliang Road, Hongkou, which accommodated 2,500 people. He employed many immigrants in his own offices and as gardeners in his home and urged others to do the same.

Sir Victor's charitable contribution was specifically earmarked *not* for relief work and "maintenance," but for "constructive purposes," in order that the recipients would become self-sufficient. He intended everything he put into charity to double or treble itself by wise investment, or to serve as an example to encourage others to contribute.[41] His Rehabilitation Fund loaned money to artisans and tradesmen to start businesses. It was generously supported by many Baghdadi Jews.

Some 200 young men received vocational training as mechanics, joiners, and carpenters at a small training camp provided by Sir Victor. In his workshop on Kinchow Road, 150 refugee women produced hand-knitted quality goods and ladies' and children's dresses. One of his other projects, the Immigrants Thrift Shop housed in his building at 55 Nanjing Road, became an outlet for refugees to sell their belongings and their handmade articles.[42] He donated $23,000 and provided enormous quantities of cotton and silk to help immigrants get started in business. In startling contrast to their former focus on his spectacular parties, the local press now featured the debonair millionaire escorting the British ambassador Archibald Kerr and other influential members of the foreign community to shops set up by the refugees around refugee camps.[43] Given Shanghai's languishing economy, it was no mean feat that some 1400 refugees became self-sufficient. Sir Victor explained, "I am mostly interested in rehabilitation, besides giving a man a chance to do some business, he is able, at the same time, to employ two

---

40 *North China Herald*, May 17, 1939.
41 Meyer, *Baghdadi Jews*, 220.
42 *IM*, July 14, 1939, 15.
43 Meyer, *Baghdadi Jews*, 221.

or three other refugees."⁴⁴ As John Ahlers, editor of the *Shanghai Evening Post and Mercury*, observed, "In the sight of the 5,000 needy refugees, the achievement of providing a living for 1,000 may not look a great accomplishment, but hats have to be taken off to the refugee committees."⁴⁵

Horace Kadoorie was the driving force behind the Shanghai Jewish Youth Association (SJYA) School, also known as the Kadoorie School, which opened in East Yu Yuen Road on January 2, 1942. It was equipped to accommodate 600 pupils, supported by seventeen teachers and a headmistress. Pupils were taught English, the Bible, Hebrew, and other general subjects. Extension courses were available to pupils over fourteen: some received a thorough business education and were assisted in finding employment. Numerous former pupils, who today are successful businessmen and professionals, attest to its high academic standards. Horace organized the SJYA eighteen-day summer camp: "To give the children an opportunity to have a little happiness, plenty of nourishment and fresh air and thus build up their health."⁴⁶ Jewish children from the host communities were encouraged to mingle with the refugees. Many of the biographical accounts speak of this father figure to thousands of Jewish children with deep affection and gratitude. Rose Jacob Horowitz recalled that he encouraged youngsters from all three Jewish communities to mingle, sensing that friendships formed in their teens would help bond them into one community. Coincidently, she met Vienna-born George Horowitz and they were married in San Francisco three years later.⁴⁷ Abe Abraham continued to recite *kaddish* (the mourner's prayer) for Sir Horace on the anniversaries of his death.⁴⁸

---

44   *IM*, May 5, 1939.
45   *Shanghai Evening Post and Mercury*, April 15, 1939.
46   Horace Kadoorie to B. S. Barbash, manager of the Shanghai branch of Jewish immigrant aid society HICEM (HIAS), July 7, 1938, no. 60, B'nai B'rith Archives, New York.
47   Rose Horowitz, interview by Steve Hochstadt, Los Angeles, June 28, 1991, Shanghai Jewish Community Oral History Project, Muskie Archives, Bates College, Lewiston, ME.
48   Meyer, *Baghdadi Jews*, 27.

Lawrence and Horace Kadoorie

The surge of generosity also came on an intimate, individual basis, exceptional considering their strained circumstances. The Jewish Girl Guides ran an outdoor sale organized by Aziza Abraham and Mrs. Diestel. Regular invitations to family meals led to lasting friendships, notably that of Cecilia Abraham's family and the Austrian refugees, Bruno and Gertie Breitbart. Abe Abraham recited *kaddish* for each of them for a year when they passed away in America. Every day between three and six refugees came peddling or requesting help from Rose Jacob's father, who invited them to remain for whatever meal was next. Moselle Cohen's home was open to European refugees. She married their Sabbath guest Lazare Hendeles. Daniel Moalem made lifelong friends with the new students with strange accents in the Jewish school.[49]

The Beth Aharon Synagogue was converted into a reception center for the refugees. It was here that local Jews brought food (mainly sandwiches of either boiled eggs or canned fish), fruit, and drinks. When Rose Jacob complained that she was missing school and all the end-of-year festivities, her father insisted that helping their fellow Jews took precedence even over learning. His words, "Don't ever forget you're Jewish and some day you

---

49 Meyer, *Baghdadi Jews*, 27, 156, 306, 340.

could be a refugee too," returned to haunt her some eleven years later when their family left Shanghai.⁵⁰

However, the welcome extended to the Central European newcomers had its limits. The traditionally Orthodox Baghdadis were appalled by the estrangement from traditional Judaism on the part of most of those refugees. It was ironic that they had become refugees solely because of their "Jewishness"! Contact with the Ashkenazim made the Sephardim more mindful of their distinctive Baghdadi identity. Rose Jacob recalled that what first struck locals about these newcomers was that their clothes were of a more severe cut. They seemed downcast and sullen, but the children sported rosy cheeks unusual in Shanghai's climate. She found the superiority complex of the German refugees, because they came from Europe, overbearing.⁵¹ Ironically, some local Jews believed their own status in the foreign concessions was undermined by these impoverished refugees, Jews like themselves, coming to their now battered and crowded town.

Isaac Abraham, who was nine at the time, highlights the visceral antipathy, even loathing, harbored by the Russian plebeian Jews towards the haughty German "*Yekkish* snobs" and their insufferable superiority complex, which militated against any form of genuine fraternization or real social intercourse. "There was no common language between the German refugees and either of the other two communities. They did not know enough Hebrew, nor were they sufficiently conversant in Yiddish. Arabic or Russian were patently non-starters. Their 'English' was either abysmal or non-existent, and valiant efforts were made to remedy this deficiency." He clearly remembers trying to teach several refugee girls befriended by his older sisters to pronounce "th" as in "this," "that," "those," the "English way," rather than "zis," "zat," "zose." He had little success.⁵²

The arrival of some three hundred Polish students of the Mir Yeshiva in 1941 also made a lasting impact on several Baghdadi Jews. The community placed mattresses on the floor of the synagogue and helped to set up temporary living quarters for the Yeshiva students. Matook Nissim's father stayed with the refugees on the night they arrived. Rose Jacob and her brother Joe bought crates of oranges and apples for them. They did not ask the servants to do this extra work, but stayed up at night to make the sandwiches and accompanied their parents to the synagogue, where

---

50   Meyer, *Baghdadi Jews*, 25.
51   Meyer, *Baghdadi Jews*, 156.
52   Meyer, *Baghdadi Jews*, 147.

they waited on the newcomers. The spiritual fervor of the students of the Mir Yeshiva was etched in the memory of nine-year-old Isaac Abraham, inspiring him and his brothers to study in religious academies in America. Rebecca Toeg's father employed one of their rabbis, Leo Adler, to teach his children. Adler influenced Toeg to place his two sons and two daughters in religious schools in Brooklyn, New York. They were attracted by the more sophisticated and questioning approach to Torah learning.[53]

The War Years

About three hours after the attack on Pearl Harbor on December 8, 1941, Japanese soldiers swarmed out of the area of Hongkou that they controlled and crossed the bridge into the European-controlled section of the International Settlement. They captured the American "USS Wake" and sunk the British "HMS Peterel," moored in the Whangpoo River. Rose Jacob recalls Japanese army trucks rumbling up and down Yu Yuen Road, soldiers in them calling through megaphones in Chinese, "We are taking over this area on behalf of the Ta Tao Government. Everyone continue in your usual way."[54]

Matook Nissim was an employee of E. D. Sassoon Banking Company, established by Victor Sassoon in 1928 to handle the financial affairs of the family business, E. D. Sassoon and Company Limited. Nissim heard on the radio that America had declared war in retaliation to Japan's attack on Pearl Harbor. He received a phone call telling him to be at the office at 5:00 a.m. and assumed that it was to shred all the documents. The shredders were not working fast enough, so they burned everything. At 8:00 a.m., they heard thumps on the corridors and sailors from the "Idzumo," Japan's largest warship, entered carrying guns and bayonets. All fifteen staff were herded into the boardroom and warned through an interpreter that they risked arrest if they touched any of the papers. The Japanese were extremely angry that the staff had destroyed the documents and kept them standing there the entire day, while the seamen sat around the board table. They told the staff to return to work the next day, because they wanted to maintain continuity and to see how they serviced the hotel, the bus company, and the brewery.

---

53 Meyer, *Baghdadi Jews*, 158, 245.
54 The Ta Tao Government was a puppet municipal government for Shanghai set up by the Japanese in 1938. It was headed by Fu Hsiao-en until he was assassinated in 1940, and then by Ch'en Kung-po.

It was a vast empire, and the Japanese needed to know how to manage it. They instilled fear in the staff.[55]

The biographies poignantly depict the effects of the Japanese occupation of the International Settlement at the outbreak of the Pacific War. Japanese troops seemed to just march in and take over the international concessions. They fanned out throughout the city, occupying strategic buildings, depots, police stations, and barracks. The mere sight of them was frightening. The foreign radio stations warned residents to stay indoors and not to behave "suspiciously" and that civilian life would go on as usual if they abided by the regulations devised by their new masters.

Proclamations, obviously prepared in advance in Chinese and English, were posted at all major intersections. These were titled "Imperial Rescript," issued in Hirohito's name, and announced that Japan would liberate Asia for the Asians. On the 8th of each month, a new "proclamation" was pasted atop each, until late in the year when no new ones appeared. One proclaimed that business was to continue as normal, but "supervisors" were assigned to all British and American businesses and took control of their assets and functions. Tenants were evicted from apartments in "enemy owned" buildings. The Japanese evicted many residents from the first floors of tall apartment buildings to store ammunition. Tenants above were prohibited from moving out and lived in constant fear of explosions, used as human shields to deter the Americans from bombing these targets.

Japanese gendarmes entered houses belonging to enemy nationals, after posting both front and back gates with "Enemy Property" notices advising that this was now Hirohito's. Every single piece of furniture was plastered with a shorter version of the notice and listed on an inventory which the owners signed. This did not preclude the odd gendarme entering at will, taking whatever he fancied, announcing with a straight face, "I do this for my Emperor." Cars, buses, and trolleys were confiscated and sent to Japan. Seared in Dan Moalem's memory was the incident when he was walking along Seymour Road and a truck full of Japanese soldiers stopped suddenly and several hopped out. At the officer's command, they bent on one knee and aimed their rifles at passing pedestrians. Although they did not fire, there was general panic, people scattering in all directions. This was clearly one of numerous methods designed to keep the local population in a state of fear. He also witnessed a group of soldiers marching down

---

55 Meyer, *Baghdadi Jews*, 85.

Peking Road kicking over any street vendor's goods and stalls they deemed were in their way.[56]

Frequent roadblocks were set up to check identification papers and health documents. If residents had left these at home, the soldiers would administer an on-the-spot cholera injection, despite protests that it had already been done. Whenever soldiers appeared, civilians would scurry in the opposite direction. Pedestrians never knew what to expect and were constantly alert. Cissy Jacob Flegg's mother was walking to the hospital to give birth. The Japanese opened her suitcase of baby clothes and scattered them on the street. They pointed a bayonet at her stomach and would not allow her to pass through the barriers until the sirens announcing an all clear went off. A young foreigner approached them and said he was a doctor and would help. Fortunately, the sirens went off and they got to the hospital in time.[57]

Daniel Moalem describes how the invasion brought mercantile trade to a halt. No American or British ships could come to the port. His uncle Silas, who worked a large stevedore company, was devastated when he was made redundant, since he had six children and a wife to support. He lived temporarily on his savings, but things soon got desperate and despite all his efforts it was difficult to find another job. The family had to live frugally throughout the rest of the war, at times selling valuables to make ends meet.[58] Cut off from its foreign trade, this once-dynamic commercial center was in the grip of an economic crisis. The cost of living rose, inflation spiraled, and the stock market was out of control.

Ellis Jacob recalls that shortages became apparent immediately, but most imported goods, especially from the United States and England, were available on the black market for a price quoted in American dollars. The *fabi* (Nationalist currency) was recalled and replaced with CRB notes issued by the puppet government, which devalued even faster. Food became scarcer, the water supplies diminished, electricity was cut off at odd hours, always during air raids. They resorted to home-made oil lamps. Heat in winter was a luxury they could no longer afford. Without fuel for the household boiler, hot water was bought in two pails once a week. Rose Jacob Horowitz writes that the first pail served for a joint bath for her mother and her. Before

---

56   Meyer, *Baghdadi Jews*, 308.
57   Meyer, *Baghdadi Jews*, 267.
58   Meyer, *Baghdadi Jews*, 308.

letting out the water, it was reused to soak and soap their laundry. The next pail, after the men had bathed, was used to rinse the laundry.[59]

The lack of news, music, and, not least, the Hollywood movies, to which he always had access, made the greatest impact on Ellis Jacob. Instead there were endless reruns and Japanese propaganda newsreels, which began with the flourish of music of "The Entrance of the Guests" from Wagner's *Tannhäuser*. "The Japanese strictly controlled the local radio station and broadcast their preposterous version of the news. By listening to the Japanese version of the news one would believe that the Japanese had sunk the British navy and had taken down the American navy five times."[60] By decree, anyone with a shortwave set had to take it to a location where the shortwave coils were removed. Anyone caught with a shortwave set in working order could be summarily shot. Fortunately, this was not strictly enforced, so residents were able to keep informed about the progress of the war through people who had shortwave radios clandestinely. Some could make crystal sets and listen to the British Broadcasting Corporation or Voice of America. The Japanese were not at war with Soviet Russia at that time, and, despite protests from their Nazi allies, permitted an English-language Russian radio station to broadcast news from the Russian front.

Daily life was disrupted, but not fundamentally altered during the war. Petrol became very scarce. This led to innovative methods of fueling buses and other vehicles. Some inventive residents developed the "one-horse power" car, an auto with the motor removed and with tow bars connecting it to a horse. Others converted their cars to charcoal-burning motors. Gas produced in furnaces utilizing coal or charcoal mounted on trailers fueled modified engines. Vehicles began to appear on the roads with grotesque charcoal burners attached to the back. They spewed thick noxious black smoke into the atmosphere, generating steam compression which ran the motors. Desperate motorists soon realized that this was an alternative fuel and the use of such attachments spread fast, although it caused serious pollution. In stages, the owners of cars and trucks were obliged to cease using them. Shanghai's network of trams and trolley buses ran on electricity. But they were overcrowded and many who tried were unable to board. Rickshaws and pedicabs often waited to pick up those who were stranded.

---

59   Meyer, *Baghdadi Jews*, 159, 271.
60   Meyer, *Baghdadi Jews*, 271.

After 1943, three airports, dockyards, oil and coal storage facilities, military installations, and military troop concentrations around the perimeter of Shanghai became prime targets for bombing by Allied planes. By all accounts, parents shielded children from comprehending the seriousness of the situation. When they heard the air raid sirens, instead of crowding into the shelters, they brought out the binoculars to get a better view of the B-29 bombers and the P-51 fighter planes. The outskirts of the city were quite seriously damaged. The only destruction in the city proper was caused by ammunition from Japanese anti-aircraft fire falling back to earth.

After each bombing raid, Ellis Sassoon Jacob would rush up to the roof of their apartment building and see pillars of smoke surrounding the city and huge fires burning for hours, a few miles from them. According to him, the air-raid warning system was a bit of a joke. One long cycle of the siren was supposed to mean "Air raid imminent," two long cycles "All clear," and seven short cycles "Air raid in progress." But when they were bombed by B29s coming from the interior of China, the sirens invariably sounded at the wrong time or with an inaccurate message. By the time the sirens blew to warn them of an air-raid, the threat was usually over.[61] There were blackouts, and windows were taped to prevent them from shattering. The Japanese enlisted local Jewish residents, dubbed the Pao Chia, as assistant police. They patrolled the neighborhoods to ensure that no light could be seen from the windows. Long thick black curtains were rolled down at night. Occasionally, the Pao Chia would yell at residents from the street, and they would tuck the curtain down properly to prevent light from escaping.

Internment of "First-class Enemy Nationals"

On April 5, 1943 the Japanese, proclaiming that the war was a struggle to liberate East Asia from British and American imperialism, classified all Westerners, apart from Germans, the Vichy French, and the Italians, as "first-class enemy nationals." Among the British nationals rounded up were some 340 Baghdadi Jews. The Japanese requisitioned their homes and sent them to Civil Assembly Centers for the duration of the war. Internees could take a bed and a trunk each, which had to be delivered to a depot,

---

61   Meyer, *Baghdadi Jews*, 271.

some days before their departure. Dan Moalem's parents agonized for some time over what to do with their valuables. They finally decided to obtain a small stainless-steel box. At 3:00 a.m. on a dark moonless night, nine days before going to camp, his father and Dan buried it in the premises of the Ohel Rachel Synagogue. They later found it intact. Victor Reuben searched the shops for canned food: corned beef, Chinese-style meat, vegetables, and large tins of jam. Of the five trunks the family was permitted to take, two contained clothes and the other three canned food, which stood them in good stead during the two and a half years of their internment. Isaac Abraham's family were scrupulous in bringing in the special food required for the approaching festival of Passover.[62]

The Baghdadi Jews interned in camps were undernourished and lived in painfully cramped conditions. They showed resilience and ingenuity in adapting to deprivation. Notable were their painstaking efforts to accommodate their stringent religious requirements in these circumstances, which were respected by the Japanese. Lunghwa Camp, one of the largest in Shanghai, housed over 2,000 internees. Isaac Abraham recalls that Commandant Hayashi went to great lengths to comply with the Jewish internees' religious requirements, making a room available for prayer services. His father arranged a religious study program for his children and his son Abe celebrated his bar mitzvah in camp. Hayashi personally escorted Isaac's father, Moshe Hai Abraham, and brother David to visit his grandmother in the Old Age Home before she passed away. He then escorted three members of the family to attend the funeral in the city, stay overnight with a relative, and return to camp next day.[63]

Hayashi permitted facilities for kosher cooking. Part of the kitchen was assigned as the "Jewish Kitchen." Truckloads of provisions, meat, raw vegetables, cracked wheat, bread, and rice, arrived daily. Work rosters were set up to clean the vegetables, cook the meals, and keep the area clean. He allowed Baghdadi Jews still at liberty to send the internees their ration of kosher meat twice a week in securely packed wicker baskets with a double seal, when the food truck brought supplies for the whole camp.[64] The attractive appearance of the kosher cuisine prompted several non-kosher Baghdadis to ask to join, but the Commandant would not permit such religious opportunism. The daily menu of vegetable stew was only adequate

---

62 Meyer, *Baghdadi Jews*, 280, 318.
63 Meyer, *Baghdadi Jews*, 281.
64 Meyer, *Baghdadi Jews*, 280.

when supplemented by their own provisions. His benevolence probably cost him his job, as he was peremptorily moved after about eighteen months in Lunghwa Camp to a different theater of operations. He was in tears when he took his leave.

Internees were allowed a hot shower once a week. Lists on the notice board informed them when it was their turn. When the weather became warmer, they enjoyed daily cold showers. They were not allowed to use running water to wash their hands, but outside the toilets were communal basins of water with strong disinfectant into which they dipped their hands. Baghdadi Jews integrated remarkably well with the other inmates. Ezekiel Abraham set up a Boy Scout group. His sister Cecilia Abraham's training in the sick bay led to her career in nursing.[65]

Children attended an improvised school. Abe Abraham learnt shoe-making and attained a First class Diploma at his first-aid course. Matook Nissim, who wanted to be part of the medical team, learned how to test urine and assisted at operations, passing instruments. He arranged for a group of seven youngsters, the Mahouts (Hindi for elephant driver), to assist elderly people struggling with their luggage on arrival at the camp. He was appointed camp bugler and awakened the entire camp complex at 6:30 a.m. to 7:00 a.m. playing the Scottish entertainer Harry Lauder's "Oh, It's Nice to Get Up in the Morning." He organized various athletic programs, including calisthenics and relay races, and soccer teams. Internees set up a lending library and ran various classes, including art appreciation and bookkeeping. Internees spent many enjoyable hours organizing plays, concerts, dances, music appreciation groups and sing-a-longs, where everyone joined in the popular songs of the day.[66]

The brutal treatment of the Chinese shocked the Jewish internees. The Japanese provided sports equipment for various activities, including softball. Helen Reuben Bekhor recalls that the Japanese guards challenged the men's team to a game. On the morning of the game, the guards stripped and cruelly beat a Chinese man with sticks in full view of the camp. The internees cancelled the match, and, in retaliation, the Commandant cancelled the next Red Cross Parcel delivery.

Some in the Baghdadi elite were treated with extra care. Sir Elly Kadoorie was interned in the stables of his home, Marble Hall, where his

---

65 Meyer, *Baghdadi Jews*, 267.
66 Meyer, *Baghdadi Jews*, 84, 280.

son Horace looked after him. The house was well preserved, because the Japanese intended to use it for their puppet governor, Wang Ching-wei, after they won the war. The rest of the family were interned in Cha Pei Camp, where food was minimal: the equivalent of a ten-cigarette-sized tin of rice per person, which swelled to double the portion. When boiled, the weevils found in the rice were cooked and eaten for protein. Vegetables, which had been thrown out at the market, were served as an accompaniment.[67]

In 1944 D. E. J. Abraham was among the last batch of "enemy civilians" to be interned in the Lincoln Avenue Camp, where most inmates were elderly. The rest of the family in Lunghwa Camp were allowed to see him just before he died in camp, aged 82 in 1944. His body was taken to the Toegs' home, where the funeral rites were performed. Immediate members of the family were permitted to attend the funeral, then released from camp and placed under house arrest in the staff quarters of Marble Hall. They might have been given this special treatment because they used to spend holidays in Japan and were involved in various charities in Japan.[68]

Not Interned: "Second-class Enemy Nationals"

Italians, Germans, Vichy French, and some Asians were not interned. Neither were Russians (White, Red, and Russian Jews), because Japan had a treaty of neutrality with the Soviet Union. Russian Jews thus were able to play a key role in assisting refugees from Nazi Germany.

Roughly 450 Sephardim, who were either stateless or Iraqi nationals, were categorized as "second-class enemy nationals," and although not interned, faced considerable privation.[69] They were required to wear a numbered armband displaying the name of the country of their origin in Japanese, and their movements were strictly restricted. Foreigners with other than British passports suffered massive unemployment. Many Baghdadis employed in British and American firms lost their jobs or were obliged to work under Japanese management. With their assets confiscated and bank accounts virtually frozen, it became impossible to conduct personal business. Joe Jacob lost his job and had his car confiscated, then found odd jobs, rather than working under the Japanese supervisors now assigned

---

67   Meyer, *Baghdadi Jews*, 97.
68   Meyer, *Baghdadi Jews*, 240, 245.
69   This estimate of 450 from Joe Jacobs seems reliable, as he served as secretary to the SJCA during the Second World War. Interview with author, Jerusalem, August 20, 1998.

to every foreign firm. In striking contrast, Sasson Jacoby quickly adjusted to his new job at the Japanese Domei News Agency, with half of the staff being Nisei (second generation Japanese Americans).[70] Many sold their valuables to subsist. Teenager Rose Jacob Horowitz sold her father's coin collection on the black market, followed by her mother's jewelry, linens, crockery, cutlery, and crystal, for "gold dollars" (US currency), to get the best deals for food and necessities.[71]

Life became increasingly bleak for most of the "left-outs," as they called themselves. Food was scant, and electricity was cut off regularly. They could not afford to heat their homes and sparingly used the hot water brought into the home in buckets. Bicycles, rickshaws, and pedicabs became the primary means of transport. Fourteen-year-old Ritchie Jacob Safdie collected the family's rations—sacks of rice, flour, sugar and other sundries—on her bike each month. She also used her bike to transport her grandmother to her mah-jongg games. Her brother Saul Jacob bought old bicycles, renovating and then selling them. His brothers helped by scouring the streets to buy bicycles and scarce parts. David Jacob ventured into the peanut butter business. He acquired a stone grinder and ground the nuts by hand. It was not much of a success, but enabled the family to survive on the unsold stock, which tasted delicious. Leah Jacob Garrick's father and uncles survived the war years playing bridge, seemingly oblivious to the goings-on outside. They were unconcerned that all their neighbors were now Japanese officers and their families, who occupied the homes vacated by the interned British subjects. Maple Hardoon's family had to give their thumbprints, produce their identity cards, and bow to the sentry when they wanted to leave their stately home. There was a curfew at eight o'clock at night, so they rarely visited people or had visitors. Most of their staff was prepared to stay on, even if they were not paid wages. They asked only for leftover food. But the Japanese sacked all except the cooks, confiscated all shortwave radios, and took everything they wanted. The soldiers adored the family's vintage Renaults, pre-1919 model showpieces which they shipped to Japan.[72]

Religious services, football games, amateur dramatics, music and bridge circles preserved some sense of normality and cohesion. Rebecca Toeg, who was nine when the war began, rates the war years the best of

---

70   Sasson Jacoby, interview with Steve Hochstadt, Beijing, April 24, 1989, Shanghai Jewish Community Oral History Project, Muskie Archives, Bates College, Lewiston, ME.
71   Meyer, *Baghdadi Jews*, 159.
72   Meyer, *Baghdadi Jews*, 64, 119–120.

her life. She had a house full of children to play with, all the books she could possibly read, and the warmth of family affection. Her home became the hub of communal activity, assisting the less fortunate and maintaining the infrastructure and sense of community. Synagogue services were held there when the Japanese requisitioned the Ohel Rachel Synagogue. Food parcels were prepared to send to relatives and friends interned in camps, and Passover food supplies and *mazzoth* were distributed to community members. Several Baghdadi Jews became destitute. The Shanghai Ashkenazi Jewish Community made a room available in their synagogue for daily prayers when Japanese military authorities took over the premises of the Shanghai Jewish School and the Beth Aharon Synagogue, where they stored ammunition. They placed anti-aircraft guns in the Jewish cemetery.

The residents' movements were very limited. They had to wear red armbands, show their passes and were subjected to "blockades" each time some anti-Japanese act occurred. Troops would hoist their barbed-wire barricades and block off all the main streets, then conduct a house-to-house search for the perpetrator. Until they announced he had been found and executed, residents remained indoors. But the children would slip out and climb over fences until they reached a friend's home, where they talked, played records, played bridge and monopoly, poker for minute stakes, anything to break the monotony. Summers were great fun for some. Ellis Jacob would swim and play billiards or ping-pong at the YMCA, and there was always lots of activity at the Race Course. He was amazed at the White Russians' volleyball skills and was also introduced to the delicious fruit-flavored carbonated Russian drink called *kvass*.[73]

Wealthy Baghdadis in camps arranged with banks to continue to give money to maintain the poor who were not interned by the Japanese. Maurice Dangoor, the President of the Sephardi Community for the duration of the war, oversaw this transaction. He had to report to the Japanese every month with lists of donors and recipients as well as monthly statements of income and expenditure. He was called by various departments and subjected to searching questions about the community. Towards the end of the war the Japanese asked unpleasant questions: "We hear all Jews are rich—why collect money? If everyone says Jews are bad, there must be something in it."[74]

---

73 Meyer, *Baghdadi Jews*, 271.
74 Meyer, *Baghdadi Jews*, 259.

Rose Jacob Horowitz's father was now working at the Sassoon firm for a pittance under a Japanese supervisor. The business college Rose attended closed. One day a Japanese delegation called and made her father a proposition. By that time nationals of all allied countries had set up residents' organizations, which distributed cracked wheat supplied by the International Red Cross, passed out orders from the Japanese, and occasionally arranged aid for the needy. They suggested that he organize an Iraqi Residents Association to do much the same. They added, "We would expect you to work very closely with us, and we will remember you and will remunerate you very handsomely." He replied that he never had enough education to be involved with politics. He realized that they would not let him live through the war. He was picked up at his tram stop by Japanese gendarmes who worked in pairs with lists. They had a long discussion, finally returning his pass. Within weeks he suffered a paralytic stroke which left him bedridden for months.[75]

After February 1943, when the Japanese established what they called a "Designated Area" in the overcrowded Wayside and Yangze sections of Hongkou for all stateless refugees who arrived in Shanghai from 1937, connections between Baghdadi and German-speaking Jews were significantly reduced. Several Baghdadi families tried to assist the Hongkou refugees. Maurice Dangoor obtained passes to leave the "ghetto" for his children's German piano teacher, who spoke no English, and for his own Hebrew teacher, even if they found his Ashkenazi pronunciation painful.[76]

To this day, Ellis Jacob remembers June 6, 1944, when his father, with a beaming smile, informed the family that Allied troops had landed in Normandy. To celebrate the coming of the end of the war, his father opened a bottle of Napoleon-era brandy.[77] Of course, local stations told a different story, announcing that the Germans had devastated the Allied troops. Air raids, food shortages, and lack of gasoline continued.

Ellis Jacob recorded that residents heard on August 8, 1945, that an atom bomb had been dropped on Japan. A few days later the same thing happened again. Residents were shocked to learn that Emperor Hirohito had ordered Japanese troops to surrender to the Allied forces. The Japanese were crying in the streets, but, to their credit, they maintained law and order for the two weeks it took American and Chinese troops to take control of

---

75 Meyer, *Baghdadi Jews*, 159.
76 Meyer, *Baghdadi Jews*, 259.
77 Meyer, *Baghdadi Jews*, 130.

the city.⁷⁸ Over the next couple of months Japanese troops were repatriated to Japan, and a new era began in Shanghai. The foreign concessions of Shanghai were returned to China more than a century after Shanghai was occupied in 1842.

After the War

In August 1945, the first American occupation force entered Shanghai. A Jewish chaplain, Alvin Fine, asked permission for Jewish G.I.s to use the Ohel Rachel Synagogue following regular services on Friday nights. The US Army and the United Nations Relief and Rehabilitation Administration (UNRRA) supplied food and other necessities. The Army took over Lunghwa Camp, providing ample provisions. They set up their movie projector and showed one of the latest American movies, Judy Garland in "Meet Me in St. Louis," and a short documentary showing how the Allied Forces had put English words to the German song "Lili Marlene" and made it their own. They also played Frank Sinatra records. Goods began to appear in shops. Youngsters met again with their friends, went to the movies and began to interact with Russian and German Jewish youth.

Daniel Moalem recalls American naval vessels appearing in the Whangpoo River. American Army personnel were everywhere, and their military command operated in a mansion on Bubbling Well Road. In the evenings, youngsters sneaked in to watch their new movies. Ellis Jacob appreciated their optimism, exuberance, laughter, and *joie de vivre*. He remembers seeing an American sailor pulling a rickshaw along Bubbling Well Road, with the delighted rickshaw coolie riding in it, much to the amusement of spectators.⁷⁹ There was an abundance of American comics, movies, records and Coca-Cola. G.I.s travelling around in their jeeps, strange-shaped vehicles, handed out candies and chewing gum to children. There was a plentiful supply of chocolates, Western-style cheese, and jellies they had never tasted.

The US Army, Navy, and Air Force set up clubs for their servicemen, and social life in Shanghai again became quite hectic—sporting competitions, theatre, movies, cabarets, ballet, orchestras, and bands. Many American servicemen dated foreign girls and some, like Julie Abraham,

---

78 Meyer, *Baghdadi Jews*, 130.
79 Meyer, *Baghdadi Jews*, 130.

eventually married one of them. American Jewish soldiers were invited to a dance at the Jewish School and families extended hospitality to them. When a Jewish G.I. invited Helen Reuben Bekhor to a movie, she asked him to come home for Friday evening dinner with the family. It was a boring evening as they had nothing in common to talk about.[80]

After the initial euphoria, reality set in. To repossess their properties was not a simple matter. The Japanese had allocated the Abrahams' house to the German Consulate and maintained it in immaculate condition. The day the war was over, the German Consul suggested that the family reside there, before the Chinese Nationalist Government arrived to take it over. By contrast, Isaac Abraham's family did not immediately regain free access to their house in Seymour Road. The twenty-six-room building was divided into self-contained apartment units, virtually all of which, apart from their living quarters, were sublet. A period of legal shenanigans and much bribery ensued before the family acquired the entire house. Consequently, between September 1945 and their return home in January 1948, they were accommodated in a series of "Camps," first Chapei, subsequently Ash Camp, which was now under British Consular control.[81]

Daniel Moalem's family was dismayed that in their absence in Lunghwa Camp one of Chiang Kai-shek's generals had taken up residence in their home. There was nothing they could do to dislodge him. It took them a month to find accommodation. Not least, they had lost their business. Their partner, who had been looking after their material shop, had sold it a few months before the end of the War and absconded to Vladivostok with the proceeds. Italians from the sunken "Conte Verde" occupied Matook Nissim's home and all thirteen members of his family had to move into his aunt Miriam Jacob's home, where two Soviet families had been billeted. The Kadoories' Marble Hall became Allied Headquarters for the liberating forces. Later, Soong Ching-ling, Sun Yat-sen's widow, asked Lawrence whether it would be possible to give Marble Hall to the Chinese Government. His son deftly put it, "Of course, he said yes. My father didn't have much alternative."[82]

When the Japanese were expelled in 1945, Chiang Kai-shek triumphantly took control of Shanghai. But the struggle between Chiang Kai-shek's forces and the Communists continued without solving the real

---

80   Meyer, *Baghdadi Jews*, 274.
81   Meyer, *Baghdadi Jews*, 77, 281.
82   Meyer, *Baghdadi Jews*, 109, 162, 323.

problems of the country. Rampant inflation was devastating for the middle classes. Money in the bank depreciated daily, and many people withdrew it to invest in more liquid assets, such as gold bars, American dollars, or jade. An item which might cost 100 yuan rose to 500 yuan two weeks later. People brought home huge bundles of notes, which rapidly became worthless. Older people who had retired watched in horror as their assets dwindled. The government lost control of the economy. Speculation was rife. The black market flourished. "Pathetically, the authorities made a public show of arresting and executing black marketers and speculators. The poor soul earmarked for execution was taken to a busy intersection, blindfolded, made to kneel, and with crowds of people watching shot with a pistol in the back of his head. The pictures of these executions were emblazoned across the front pages of every newspaper as a warning to others. Unfortunately, the people executed were small fry in the scale of things. The big speculators and black marketers were never brought to justice. I am sure that in true Chinese fashion they bribed their way to the top. The worst transgressors were often government officials themselves who were siphoning large sums to overseas banks and making up for the shortfall in currency by printing more and more money."[83]

The Baghdadi Jewish community experienced its first substantial exodus. Sasson Jacoby's family had begun to disperse in 1945: his parents and two sisters to San Francisco, the brothers Jack, Ellis and Sassoon to Israel. After military service, Sasson married Hannah Levy and they settled in Jerusalem. Twenty-four-year-old Matook Nissim, in partnership with Red Symons, a friend from the Lunghwa Camp, sold practically everything ranging from apartments to toilet paper, and dealt in money exchange. He received a letter from Sir Victor Sassoon congratulating him on his release and welcoming him back. He had enclosed a check for about US $2,300 (roughly $29,000 in today's values), his back-pay for the two and a half years that he was in camp, and he was also given six months' home leave. He could not buy a passage as there were very few transport ships, so he went on board an American military ship and agreed to work in the galley, although he did not even know what it was. His *amah* had sewn gold bars into a vest, and when he arrived in Hong Kong, he deposited them with the National City Bank. There he also deposited US dollars, which he smuggled

---

83   Meyer, *Baghdadi Jews*, 235.

in a box of cigars for the Jewish Sephardi Association. Later, regulations and high inflation made it impossible to take money out of the country.[84]

Lawrence Kadoorie was anxious to return to Hong Kong, but the RAF refused to carry him as a passenger. To add to his misfortune, he tore his trousers on a nail in a jeep in which he was being transported. A passing jeep carrying several G.I.s took pity on him and they asked what was wrong. He replied: "Well, if you only had one pair of pants and you'd torn them, you'd also look fairly miserable." Within a few minutes, he found himself dressed in a G.I. uniform. He again approached the RAF who agreed that he could go as freight. Sitting in a Dakota on a pile of newly printed Hong Kong bank notes, which were to replace Japanese military currency, he was the first civilian internee to return to Hong Kong.[85]

Leah and Ritchie Jacob, aged eighteen and nineteen, left Shanghai for the United States on student visas on April 30, 1947, on the converted American army transport "S.S. General Gordon." Due to their Chinese National Stateless status, they were not allowed to disembark on route at Honolulu. The Jewish community greeted them with leis of flowers and the President of Honolulu even offered to put up a bond on their behalf, but to no avail. Similarly, when their parents and twelve-year-old brother Jack fled to Hong Kong with two suitcases each in March 1949, the British authorities did not allow them to stay for even a single day. Fortunately, Macau, an open Portuguese port on the China mainland, had no such restriction.[86]

A few people, notably the Dangoor family, left for Iraq. Renée married Professor Naim Dangoor, OBE, a scion of a distinguished Iraqi family and grandson of the Chief Rabbi of Iraq, Hakham Bashi Ezra Reuben Dangoor (1848–1930). She won the title of Miss Baghdad 1947.[87] The year 1948 saw an exodus of Shanghai Jewry to the newly founded state of Israel, where eventually about half the community settled. Others emigrated to Australia, Hong Kong, the Philippines, America, Canada, and Britain.

The civil war between Nationalists and Communists had insignificant impact on the community. They were unwilling spectators with no real interest in the conflict. Breakdown of everyday life preceded the downfall of the Chiang Kai-shek Nationalist regime, whose officials pocketed American aid instead of directing it to the civil war. Several Baghdadis

---

84   Meyer, *Baghdadi Jews*, 85, 250.
85   Meyer, *Baghdadi Jews*, 99.
86   Meyer, *Baghdadi Jews*, 121.
87   Meyer, *Baghdadi Jews*, 262.

became uneasy when officials from the Nationalist government departed for Taiwan with a huge amount of the country's wealth. A week before the Communist People's Liberation Army reached Shanghai, those with British passports had the option of evacuation to Hong Kong. Many who held foreign bank accounts, notably in Hong Kong, Canada, and the United States, had judiciously moved money out of China before 1949. Many chose to stay on, optimistically believing that the Communists would want to do business with them.

Maoist Victory

The Communist conquest of Shanghai in May 1949 brought an era to a close. Daniel Moalem recalls that in an overnight assault they occupied the entire city. Explosions and gunfire were heard during the night, but any pockets of resistance were rapidly overcome. By morning, all was quiet again. A Victory Parade began early and continued until late in the evening. There were hundreds of thousands of marchers, along with captured American tanks and cannons. Many soldiers carried American rifles, clearly captured from the fleeing Nationalists.

Biographical accounts describe how the city changed beyond recognition. After the Communist takeover in 1949, beggars and prostitutes were removed from the streets and placed in rehabilitation labor camps. The exciting liberal and cosmopolitan metropolis, where capitalism and Western influence had dominated for a century, gradually lost its vitality and appeal. The way of life Baghdadi Jews loved was being swept aside. All foreigners were classified as "foreign entrepreneurs," with the connotation of "despised imperialist parasites." Property owners were condemned as "exploiting capitalists." Chinese police supplanted the Indian Sikhs and Western police force. The Chinese populace became robustly antiforeign. Shopkeepers and street vendors served their Chinese patrons before foreigners. A Chinese youth accosted Ellis Jacob in the street, repeatedly calling him *ngahko peeseh* (foreign beggar). Maurice Dangoor's servant, a member of the Communist party, began to voice some of his objections to foreigners bossing the Chinese about in their own country. When ordered to do something, he reacted angrily, threatening his employer with a knife. Servants had to attend indoctrination meetings and were ordered to stop working for foreigners. Daniel Moalem's distraught *amah* offered to sneak into their flat before daybreak and leave after nightfall—a huge risk. People lost their servants overnight. Chinese employees took over some western firms, often locking supervisors in their offices until they extracted concessions from the management. The police and local authorities sympathized with Chinese workers, and when disputes occurred, they assumed the foreigner was in the wrong.[88]

The People's Republic of China was proclaimed in October 1949. Once in power, the Communist authorities assured residents that things would return to normal and their lives would not be interfered with. Stephen Sopher recalls that life under the new regime started on a good footing as foreigners were promised that business would continue as usual. There was an influx of Soviet Russians, to whom the Chinese referred as "elder brothers." Although the foreign imperialism of Treaty Port days characterized by foreigners living in their own enclaves was routinely criticized, now a super-enclave in the residential Hungjao was established for Russians. The residents of this "little Kremlin," and even some high Chinese officials, lived there in style and luxury. Limousines with their blue curtains drawn were their mode of transport. Intelligence soon revealed that the Soviet Union was supplying equipment, training, and advisers to the Communists. It was obvious that Stalin had China worked into his grand plan. For about four months not much happened, but then they noticed Chinese people being taken away for "reeducation." The first groups to go missing were employees of foreign companies and embassies, rickshaw pullers, and prostitutes. Residents never found out what happened to them. Affluent businessmen, professionals, and employees of foreign companies and embassies also began to disappear. The universities became a hotbed of agitation, and lecturers were taken off for "reeducation." Pagodas and temples were vandalized and Buddhist monks and nuns were rounded up. Worship was forbidden.

The situation rapidly deteriorated. Chinese businessmen were summarily charged, tried, and convicted for crimes against the downtrodden peasants. Many landlords and property owners were tortured and threatened with death. Stephen Sopher records that 1952 was a leap year. This had another connotation, as countless individuals were so humiliated, and panic stricken that they jumped to their deaths from apartment and office windows. He saw open trucks loaded with blindfolded men with their hands tied behind their backs followed by wagons full of coffins. By

---

88   Meyer, *Baghdadi Jews*, 127, 130.

comparison, life under Japanese occupation appeared to have been far less restrictive and threatening, although life became a nightmare for many Chinese.[89]

The exodus of foreigners accelerated. Those with passports had no problems being repatriated to their respective countries. However, the plight of the "stateless" refugees, especially German Jews and White Russians, was alarming. Although Stephen Sopher was only fifteen at the time of the takeover, he was convinced that Communism augured the doom of capitalism in China. Despite unmistakable evidence to the contrary, his father Arthur felt that the Chinese could never be true Communists owing to their ancient history of entrepreneurship and corruption, and believed that he and his brother Theodore would be able to continue to do business as they had done during the war under the Japanese. Most of the family's assets were in real estate, and their debts could only be paid if their property could be liquidated. Real estate transactions were no longer allowed, so they were unable to pay their debts, and business associates to whom they owed money litigated against them. The Communists imprisoned the brothers for thirty days. After a long delay, they gave up trying to squeeze them for money they assumed was hidden abroad and, in 1955, they were eventually allowed to leave Shanghai for Hong Kong.

The Sassoon firm reduced its property investment, selling at exceedingly low prices because of a lack of buyers. The Chinese staff became aggressively anti-"foreign imperialists." The rich property empire Sir Victor painstakingly built up was crumbling. The deterioration of his much-loved Cathay Hotel distressed him, as was reported in the *Scottish Daily Mail*: "The destruction of Sir Victor Sassoon's luxurious Cathay and other leading hotels. Chinese Nationalist troops set up machine-gun posts in rooms overlooking the waterfront. Guests were now living side by side with the garrisons. The manager protested in vain as soldiers, carrying full packs and wearing German-type helmets, clattered across the floors and trod the carpets. They carried in pots, pans, rice, vegetables, even firewood and asked where they could billet their mules?"[90]

Sir Victor Sassoon left Shanghai at the end of 1948, mindful that the commercial empire his grandfather Elias had established almost a century earlier was disintegrating. He set off in search of attractive investments and

---

89 Meyer, *Baghdadi Jews*, 202.
90 "Guns Set Up In Hotels: Shanghai is Preparing to Fight," *Scottish Daily Mail*, April 25, 1949.

switched his fortune from the sale of property from East to West, estimated at £15,000,000 (roughly £675,000,000 in today's values). He registered E. D. Sassoon Banking Co. Ltd. in Nassau in the Bahamas and took up residence there in 1949.[91]

Shanghai's Baghdadis found their circumstances untenable. Their attachment to Shanghai was replaced by an urgent desire to leave the Treaty Port as soon as possible, even at the cost of sacrificing their investments and business interests. Fraught by restrictions, they were relieved to hand over their assets in exchange for exit permits. Sir Victor Sassoon's cousin Lucien Ovadia, manager of E. D. Sassoon & Co., endured interminable bureaucratic procedures for two years. He received an exit permit only after he made final arrangements for paying the government a huge sum for the privilege of giving them the prestigious Cathay Hotel. The Communists returned confiscated British and Canadian properties once their respective governments recognized the regime.[92]

The Colonial Secretary, M. Morrison, enlisted the Kadoories' help in accommodating Jewish refugees in transit to Australia when they were held up in Hong Kong. There were considerable difficulties involved in obtaining visas. The refugees had to wait weeks, if not months, for their applications to be processed. Since the Hong Kong authorities refused to grant in-transit permits for more than a few days, it was pointless for the Jewish Agency to send refugees seeking admission to the United States to Hong Kong. Nonetheless, they appealed to the Kadoories to try to devise some means to shorten the period of waiting in Hong Kong. Lawrence was frequently called upon to find board and lodging for large numbers and generally put them up at the family's Peninsula Hotel.[93]

While postal connections between Shanghai and foreign countries were disrupted, D. Abzac, Chairman of the Migration Committee in New York, asked Horace Kadoorie to forward refugees' mail through his office, Horace accepted this role with his usual magnanimity, little realizing he was taking on a mammoth task. He graciously operated a free postal service forwarding letters to places as far afield as Shanghai, Australia, Haifa, San Francisco, New York, Seattle, Los Angeles, and Cleveland. One request was for five letters to be sent to Berlin, Frankfurt, Hamburg, Zurich, and Melbourne. With profound sensitivity, he assisted those in the depressing

---

91 Meyer, *Baghdadi Jews*, 220.
92 Meyer, *Baghdadi Jews*, 230.
93 Meyer, *Baghdadi Jews*, 105.

situation of having lost contact with their relatives. When grateful refugees sent Horace a reply coupon to cover the expense for the stamps, his standard response was: "It has been a pleasure to do this for you." He officially terminated his free postal service on January 19, 1950, when the US postal authorities began to accept airmail addressed directly to Shanghai.[94]

Departure from Shanghai was a hassle. The Chinese authorities sometimes scrutinized photographs, scrapbook albums, and other personal belongings. In a customs shed, uniformed men with lists of people permitted to leave checked passports, visas, and immunization records. Ellis Jacob's mother was cleared easily since her records were in order. He was stunned when he was told that he could not leave, because a financial claim had been made against him. This was too much for him and he started to cry loudly. Apparently, there were at least three other Ellis Jacobs in Shanghai and the lien belonged to one of them. Nonetheless, his father signed a statement guaranteeing payment of the claim, and Ellis was allowed to board. His father, having no means of income, left Shanghai in early 1953.[95]

Rose Jacob Horowitz and her mother managed to obtain temporary asylum in Canada. They left on a converted troopship sent by the State Department to evacuate personnel when the US Consulate in Shanghai closed, leaving no diplomatic relations between it and the new China. As they boarded the vessel, Nationalist planes flew in to bomb the docks, making her very first and very last impressions of Shanghai equivalent: bombing due to war. The ship docked in San Francisco and they were put on a sealed train which carried them "in bond" to western Canada to await their quota numbers allowing them to resettle in the United States. The quota numbers never arrived. However, they qualified under the new Displaced Persons law and received immigration visas stamped on one-time travel documents issued by the US Consulate in Vancouver, in lieu of their Iraqi passports.[96]

Some two hundred Baghdadi Jews and a thousand Ashkenazim, whose applications for entry permits to various countries were held in abeyance, remained in Shanghai and resigned themselves to the Communist takeover. Their resources dwindled, and many became dependent on Jewish charitable institutions. Faced with the heavy burden of taxation and fines, the Ohel Rachel Synagogue and Shanghai Jewish School were leased to the government in 1951, finally closed their doors in early 1952. The government also

---

94 Meyer, *Baghdadi Jews*, 107.
95 Meyer, *Baghdadi Jews*, 132.
96 Meyer, *Baghdadi Jews*, 160.

took over the Beth Aharon Synagogue. After 1958, only those waiting for exit permits and foreign visas remained in Shanghai.

Biographical accounts highlight the predicament of some sixty-five Iraqi Jews, who fell into the category of homeless, stateless people without legal or political protection from any government. The passports of the Iraqis in Shanghai were no longer valid after World War II, as more than five years had elapsed since they were issued. They were without any form of diplomatic protection and had no normal means of travel. Technically, they were in an anomalous position and were not entitled to the assistance stateless persons receive. The International Refugee Organization (IRO), which arranged the relocation of many thousands to the United States, rejected their pleas for assistance. Reuben Abraham's tireless efforts to help them cannot be overstated. His assurance that he would not leave Shanghai until all the Iraqi Jews had left exemplifies his remarkably strong sense of community, even to the very end.

The adopted Hardoon children settled as far afield as Argentina, Australia, and America. Leo, with help from the Jewish Agency, went to a kibbutz in Israel, where he met his Canadian wife and settled in Toronto. Maple went to the Channel Islands, where she married Melville Doron, and settled in Israel. Reuben had to remain in Shanghai to take care of Silas Hardoon's vast estate. It had not been confiscated, because the British Government was the first to recognize the Communist regime. Finally, he sold most of his share of the property to the Communists and raised enough money to get his wife and children out of the country and settled with George in Hong Kong. Catherine and Silah Charlie Hardoon left Shanghai in 1949 via Hong Kong to apply at the American Consulate for permission to go to the Philippines and acquire residency in Manila, where there was also an American Consulate. Fortunately, Charlie's brother, who lived in Paris, was able to renew their passports at the Iraqi Consulate there, which enabled them to travel to San Francisco.[97]

Ellis Sassoon Jacob applied for emigration to the United States in 1947. There were so many Westerners who were born in China that there was an annual quota of 105 for non-Chinese born in China. It was nicknamed the "White Chinese" quota. The typical waiting time was five years. His voyage to San Francisco on the "S.S. General Gordon" took about three weeks via Hong Kong, Tokyo, and Honolulu. Abraham Sassoon Jacob's family also

---

97 Meyer, *Baghdadi Jews*, 272.

embarked on the "S.S. General Gordon," on what turned out to be an excruciatingly circuitous journey of fifty-five days. It took about two weeks to San Francisco. On arrival in New York, they were confined at Ellis Island for six days to await their next connection. They travelled on a troop transport ship to Bari, Italy, then by train to the port of Trani, and eventually took a boat to Haifa. Eighteen-year-old Isaac was taken directly to serve in the army. The rest of the family was transferred to a transit center and later lived for a year in a *ma'abara* (transit camp) in central Israel. They eventually settled in the United States.[98]

As stateless citizens, Israel was the only place Rebecca Toeg's family could go and they applied for transit papers to Hong Kong, where she preferred to remain, because it reminded her of Shanghai. But six months later they left for the Philippines and took the plane to Israel.[99]

The Swiss Red Cross issued stateless Clive Jackie Levy an International Red Cross travel document in 1951. It took three days and two nights by train to Hong Kong via Canton. Finally, he walked a few hundred yards to the border between Communist China and the New Territories, and he caught another train to Hong Kong, where he had a memorable reunion with his *amah* Ah-say, who gave him some money, as he had left Shanghai with only five pounds in his pocket. He went on to Sydney where his brother met him at the wharf.[100]

Conclusion

In the heyday of the community, Baghdadi Jews complaisantly believed they were leaving a legacy for future generations and that they would continue to enjoy a privileged life in the Treaty Port. They were thus profoundly disillusioned by the terrible turn of events. Ironically, this community, which had acted as host to many Jewish refugees, themselves left Shanghai as refugees in search of new homes as far flung as Israel, Australia, Britain, America, and Canada, ending a community of three generations.

For some, like Joe Jacob, the lingering memory is one of squalor, war, and deprivation that engulfed the latter part of their lives in the embattled city. But most Baghdadi Jews remember the Shanghai of the halcyon days of their childhood and youth with a degree of nostalgia, with its comfortable

---

98 Meyer, *Baghdadi Jews*, 77, 133, 146.
99 Meyer, *Baghdadi Jews*, 253.
100 Meyer, *Baghdadi Jews*, 253.

prewar atmosphere, strong social infrastructure, and favorable conditions in the foreign enclave. They vividly recall the excitement of living in this fascinating, vibrant, modern metropolis, which offered wide-ranging facilities and where families of even modest means could afford servants. They regretted the necessity of leaving their cherished birthplace; it had been their home and their future. Angela Elias Phillips' father, Reginald Marcus Elias, remembered his childhood in Shanghai as the happiest time of his life. Despite Ellis Jacob's traumatic departure from the city, on his way to a new life in the Western hemisphere, he felt he would always be a "Shanghailander." Shanghai was his home for eighteen years and thus it remained a part of him. China was Catherine Levy's entire world, as she totally identified with Chinese culture and characteristics.[101]

The reality is that in the century of the Baghdadi Jews' sojourn, Shanghai was a Treaty Port in which they had the benefit of their privileged status. As Rose Jacob Horowitz wrote: "I was born and lived over a score of years in that very wonderful land; I was educated and exposed to the English language in all its glory, with ideas of freedom and justice, and I was brought up to be Jewish to my very core. Could anyone ask for more?" Leah Jacob adds, "*Jhah Jhah nu*!—Thank you!" She was grateful to China, where each of the three very diverse Jewish communities—Baghdadi, Russian, and the refugees fleeing Nazi persecution—found a haven: the first two seemingly providentially placed to assist the latter.[102] A deep affection for the past is evident, even to this day, with many people making frequent journey to China with their descendants, to recapture the memories.

Throughout its existence in Shanghai, the Baghdadi Jewish cultural heritage was perpetuated by the community elders who exerted a binding influence on the outlook and sentiments of its members. Jewish tradition appears to have undergone changes in the century of their domicile in Shanghai, due mainly to the prevailing British influence which overshadowed the small community. Given the British-oriented curricula in their schools, this is hardly surprising. Even so, their surnames for the most part have remained distinctively Baghdadi, easily identifiable within the wider community and seemingly an expression of their commitment to preserve their identity.

---

101 Meyer, *Baghdadi Jews*, 132, 136, 331.
102 Meyer, *Baghdadi Jews*, 48, 122.

A wealth of evidence confirms the extraordinary persistence and resilience of the community and the strong ethnic ties of this distinctive group with a common history, a shared ancestry and a uniquely rich culture. A community which grew and developed in a foreign environment could not have been expected to have responded more successfully to challenges both from within and without.

Anne Atkinson*

The Burak Family: The Migration of a Russian Jewish Family Through the First Half of the Twentieth Century[1]

The first half of the twentieth century consisted of unrelenting social, political, and economic turmoil. Some events were on a global scale, such as World Wars I and II and the Great Depression. Others were regional, for

---

*   Anne Atkinson was born in a small town in Western Australia in 1945 and educated in country schools. She worked as a nurse in pathology departments for four years. She married in 1966 and traveled though England and Europe for two years, before she and her husband moved to Papua New Guinea in 1971, where her two children were born. In 1976 she returned to live in Perth and completed an undergraduate degree with Honours in 1984. Anne commenced a PhD program in 1985 at Murdoch University in Perth, while working as a Community Education Officer in Multicultural and Ethnic Affairs for the state government for three years, and then teaching Australian Studies to overseas students. She earned a PhD in 1991 with a thesis on Chinese migration and settlement in Australia and taught migration and race relations at Edith Cowan University, Western Australia, until she retired in 2001. She has published *Asian Immigrants to Western Australia, 1829–1901* (Nedlands, Australia: University of Western Australia Press, 1988), and *Bough Sheds, Boabs and Bandages: Stories of Nursing in the Kimberley* (Perth: DB Publishing, 2008). She coordinated the project which published *Songs of Strength: Sixteen Women Talk about Cancer*, by the The Women's Cancer Group (Pan Macmillan Australia, 1997), that won a Western Australian Premier's Special Book Award in 1997. She is currently writing her family history through nine detailed biographies.

1   The basis of this family story comes from notes made by my mother, Dolores Gable, based on stories told by her mother Katya, the second daughter of Solomon and Bella Burak. Further research was conducted with a range of primary and secondary sources.

instance, the violent antisemitic activity in Eastern and Western Europe and socio-political revolutions in Russia and China. Other events were local, for example, the Japanese bombings of Shanghai in 1937, the ongoing encroachment of Japanese military operations in East Asia and outbreaks of the pneumonic plague in Manchuria. All these events, on whatever scale, resulted in population migrations, whether in barely discernable streams or in great waves, as people fled life-threatening situations.

Most common were simple journeys that involved groups or individuals moving to another country for resettlement. Others, caught up in repeated situations of turbulent upheaval, spent most of their lives moving from one country to another, from one region to another and from one location to another seeking safer and better lives. The journey of the Burak family provides an example of this latter, more complex, form of migration. Their multi-stage journey around the world was not exceptional for Jews in the twentieth century.

The Buraks, my family, were Jewish and originated in the Polish-Ukrainian region that was occupied by the tsarist Russian Empire in the nineteenth century. They lived in the Pale of Settlement, in an area specifically reserved by the Empire for Jewish settlement. My great-grandparents were both born in the Pale in 1878. Shulim Hainovich Burak, my great-grandfather, also known as Solomon, was born in Berdichev (modern-day Berdychiv in Ukraine). When Solomon was five, his parents and siblings were among hundreds of patrons who were killed in a fire that destroyed the theater his family owned. He was adopted and raised by his uncle, a jeweller.[2] My great-grandmother, Bella Lazarevna Haendler, was born in Sudilkov (modern-day Sudylkiv in Ukraine). Her father was a merchant.[3] Solomon and Bella married early in 1898 and had a daughter, Ida, shortly afterwards in Berdichev.

Throughout Solomon and Bella's early lives, Jews in the Pale were increasingly subjected to a regime of limitations on where they could live and what economic activities they could participate in. Jews were mainly

---

2   From Solomon's death certificate (1962/000290, Registry of Births, Deaths and Marriages, NSW, Australia) which recorded his birth names. Solomon's immigration application included *Khaninovitch* as an additional given name. The details of Solomon's burial from the cemetery records recorded his Hebrew name as Shlomo ben Chaim.

3   From death certificate (6000032T/1952, Registry of Births, Deaths and Marriages, Perth, Western Australia). Other versions of Bella's family name were Hendeer, Handeer and Gendler, the Russian version. Her Hebrew name on cemetery records was Baila bat Eliezer.

restricted to the smaller towns and villages, with few places available to them in larger towns or cities. Restrictions were also placed on their economic activities, limiting jobs to crafts and trades and excluding them from many commercial occupations. Increasing incidents of mob violence, known as pogroms, were directed specifically against Russian Jews. These resulted in the deaths of more than 100,000 Jews between 1881 and 1921, as well as looting, burning, and destroying Jewish property and livelihoods. They were conducted at first mainly in the rural areas of Ukraine, but later they were also experienced in Kiev (Kyiv) and other parts of the Pale.

The combination of antisemitic restrictions and violence resulted in the mass migration of two million Jews from the Pale to other parts of Europe, Great Britain and the United States in the late nineteenth and early twentieth centuries. With restrictions on Jews living in urban areas in the Pale, the Buraks continued to live in Berdichev, where they had their second daughter, Rebekka, in 1900. Another two girls followed: Fiera Esther in 1902, and Lucy in 1904. They lived a comfortable life in Berdichev, supported solely by Solomon's family. The older girls started school and then, in 1908, the young family left Berdichev to make the arduous journey to Harbin in Manchuria. The purpose of this emigration was twofold: to provide a safe and secure childhood for the girls far from the increasingly antisemitic activity in the Pale, and for Solomon to manage a button factory his family had established in Harbin.[4]

There are no reports of their journey, but it was most probably undertaken in summer to avoid the Siberian winter, and would have involved many weeks of travel by train, coach, cart, and sled, if there was still ice on Lake Baikal. It is impossible to guess just how difficult and uncomfortable the journey was, especially with four children aged between four and ten.

Harbin had been a small fishing village on the Songhua River for hundreds of years until it emerged as an important center during the construction of the Chinese Eastern Railway (CER) in the late 1890s. The Buraks arrived just when Harbin was rapidly expanding as a political, economic, cultural and communication hub in northeast Asia.

---

4   In 1904–5, one of Solomon's brothers was drafted into the Russian Army to fight in the Russo-Japanese War in Manchuria. On his return, he and one of Solomon's uncles, who were already running a button factory in Kiev, saw the potential to extend the business and open a button factory in Harbin. The "button factory" might also have come under the nomenclature of "haberdashery" as there are no references to a "button factory" in available data on Harbin.

Its growing population of Jewish and White Russian immigrants was attracted to the potential for political and religious harmony and trade and industrial possibilities. By 1913, Harbin had a multicultural, multiethnic, and multireligious population of 68,549 residents representing over 50 nationalities speaking 45 languages.[5]

We do not know how the Burak family were affected by global events in the first decades of the twentieth century, such as World War I. However, their daily lives would have been influenced by the outbreak of a highly contagious strain of pneumonic plague in Harbin in 1910. Within five months, the plague killed thousands of Harbin residents.[6] Although the plague surrounded them and touched their everyday lives, such as school attendance, food shopping, and mixing with friends and neighbors, the Burak family managed to emerge unscathed and to live a comfortable life.

My mother Dolores's notes of her mother Katya's stories describe the Burak household:

> with its indulgent father, strict mother and four vivacious girls and their pet Samoyed dog seemed a happy lot. Bella was a fanatical housewife—cooking, cleaning, polishing and dressing the girls in stylish outfits, a habit that lasted all their lives. They were a close family. The girls were all expected to help with work around the house—except Katya who refused point blank and locked herself in the bathroom where she spent hours reading.
>
> My mother [Katya] was angular, bright, and very clever. She was especially fond of reading, sport [playing basketball], maths and science in primary school. In high school she read the Russian novels and plays that were so popular then and excelled in her studies for which she was presented with a scholarship and gold medal. She was a defiant girl, with her outbursts and rebellious spirit a trial to her conservative orthodox mother, although I think her father rather approved of it all.

---

5   *The South Atlantic Quarterly* 99, special issue: *Harbin and Manchuria: Place, Space, and Identity* (2000).

6   The 1910–11 plague spread to Mongolia and other parts of Manchuria, eventually killing 60,000 people. A second bout of this plague occurred in 1920–21 and killed 9,300 people. However, by this time the Buraks had already moved to Shanghai. Jacob L. Kool, "Risk of Person-to-Person Transmission of Pneumonic Plague," *Clinical Infectious Diseases* 40 (2005): 1166–72.

The girls went to Russian school dressed in serge dresses, black stockings and high-buttoned boots with big, typically Russian, bows in their hair.[7]

Of the four girls, Katya, who had changed her name from the Jewish Rebekka to the Russian Katya, showed the most academic promise. At fifteen she was awarded a gold medal and entrance to any university in the Russian Empire to undertake her choice of study. Her scholarship also covered the expenses of a chaperone. Katya selected the University of Tomsk in Siberia to study medicine. Her older sister, Ida, accompanied her and studied law. They began their studies in the revolutionary year 1917. Katya reveled in the freedom of university life and did very well. Russia's political climate provided the strong-willed and spirited Katya and her student friends with material for vigorous debates and discussion. These helped shape the beliefs and values that she held throughout her life: communism, feminism, and atheism. Ida, however, retained her Jewish faith and ideals, which were cemented when she met her future husband Marçi Diamant, a Hungarian Hussar stationed in Tomsk, who was also Jewish.

Katya's and Ida's university education ended abruptly, halfway through their studies, when the Red Army closed the Trans-Siberian Railway to civilian passengers. Katya was bitterly disappointed that she could not complete her studies, and although she tried to make good use of what she had learnt, for the rest of her life she regretted being unable to qualify as a medical doctor.

The October Revolution led to the mass migration of White Russians across the border into Manchuria to escape Communism. Harbin's population was suddenly increased by 100,000 White Russian soldiers and refugees, which added to the 20,000 Russians already resident to make it the largest Russian enclave outside the Soviet Union. By the time the pressures of the increased population were felt in Harbin, however, the Burak family had already decided to start on the third leg of their journey and to migrate to Shanghai. Their reasons were mainly economic.

The button factory that Solomon had been managing ground to a halt. The family's financial situation was dire, and the request to Solomon's family for help had elicited a reluctant offering of some jewelry and a final letter

---

7 Although Bella ensured that Jewish rituals and traditions were maintained and there were several Jewish schools in Harbin, the girls attended a Russian school. This may have been the start of the gradual loss of Jewish identity for three of the four girls.

refusing any more appeals for financial assistance.[8] No doubt Solomon's family was extremely disappointed by the failure of a business that had shown such promise when it had first been handed to Solomon, and reluctant to continue to support him and his family. There is no evidence that there was any further communication between Solomon and his family in Berdichev and Kiev.

The economic situation in Shanghai appeared more encouraging and promised more job opportunities for the four girls. In the 1920s, Shanghai seemed an ideal place for four girls in their late teens and early twenties. Called the "Paris of the East" and the "New York of the West," it was an exciting cosmopolitan mix of cultures and traditions, both sophisticated and vulgar, with pockets of extreme wealth and poverty. It was the commercial center of Asia and the international center for opium, which was trafficked and traded relatively openly. It was considered "as much a Chinese creation as a Western creation," separate yet divergent.[9]

The Buraks arrived in Shanghai in 1920 and rented a simple two-storey attached house in the Jewish section of the French Concession. It was within easy walking distance of the synagogue and kosher delicatessens and cafés. At first Ida and Katya earned money teaching Russian to Chinese and other businessmen, but it was difficult for all four girls to find reliable work, even with English language skills and a comprehensive education. The Shanghai labor market was segmented by race, ethnicity, gender, and language, and Russian émigrés were treated with contempt. Russian men found it particularly hard, while Russian women were relegated to low-skilled work in hospitality and domestic service. Notoriously, 22% of Russian women aged 16 to 45 were engaged in prostitution.[10] Finding an acceptable job was partly determined by ethnicity, the ability to speak English, and the common perceptions of Russian women.

---

8   The jewelry was sent to Ida and Katya just before they returned to Harbin. It is not known what happened to the collection, but at least two diamond rings remain in the family.
9   Harriet Sergeant, *Shanghai: Collision Point of Cultures, 1918–1939* (New York, Crown Publishers, 1991), 2.
10 According to a survey by the League of Nations in 1935, cited by Marcia Reynders Ristaino, *Port of Last Resort: the Diaspora Communities of Shanghai* (Stanford: Stanford University Press, 2001), 94.

The Buraks in Shanghai in 1920. Back row from left: Lucy, Ida, and Fiera; front row from left: Solomon, Katya, and Bella.

One consequence of the Russian Revolution caused lasting problems for most of the family long after they left Russia. In 1921, a year after they arrived in Shanghai, the Soviet government revoked the citizenship of "political exiles," making them stateless, which limited the family's ability to seek better prospects overseas. It also meant that any child born to a stateless resident automatically became a Chinese citizen. This affected Katya and her three children, who were designated Chinese, making it almost impossible to migrate to countries with anti-Asian immigration laws, such as Australia.

Despite this, all four girls and Solomon eventually found work and became financially independent, either though employment or marriage. Ida married Marçi, who had followed her to Shanghai and became an accountant for a publishing house. Katya eventually used her medical knowledge to work in pharmacies, at one time even owning her own pharmacy. Fiera found secretarial work in the Russian Consulate, and Lucy worked in a hat shop in the French Concession.

Throughout the 1920s, the Buraks were involved, either intentionally or unintentionally, in seeking a solution to the problem of statelessness through marriage to nationals holding passports of acceptable countries.

Fiera married a Russian consulate officer and became a Russian citizen again. They moved to the consulate in Harbin and had a child in the late 1920s. Lucy married Pierre, a French national employed in the French Embassy. They had a child in the 1930s in Shanghai before moving to California.

Katya lived with Joseph Maria de Figueiredo, a comprador or merchant she met in Harbin, who had followed her to Shanghai. Joseph was twenty years older than Katya and a Portuguese Catholic, who was married with a twelve-year-old daughter. He and Katya had three children together between 1921 and 1926. They first lived together in a very smart detached two-storey house with a garden in the French Concession. They had a car, owned a pharmacy and employed several servants, including an *amah* for each of their three children: Dolores, born in 1921, Irene in 1923, and Edward in 1926.[11] Before Dolores and Irene attended school at a Catholic convent in Tientsin, a French governess tutored them. Katya and Joe spent their summers in a large rented house with wide shady verandahs on the beach front at Peitaiho, or Beidaihe, a popular beach resort near Beijing. Katya's and Joseph's relationship ended in 1926, and a few years later, Katya returned to Shanghai where she met and married English-born Thomas Henry Vickers, the Head Officer of the Ichang Fire Station, in 1931. The remaining members of the Burak family, Solomon, Bella, Ida, and Marçi, retained their stateless situation for the next thirty years, until they left China for Australia in 1951–1952 as refugees.[12]

There is little doubt that each member of the Burak family had a comfortable middle-class lifestyle, able to cushion them against any serious consequences of the Great Depression. There is no evidence that any of them lost their jobs, or were turned out of their rented apartments and houses, or were crippled by stock market crashes or poor financial choices. The Great Depression, which first impacted the USA in 1929, did not really affect China until 1933–1934, when it influenced the price of silver, China's

---

11   The evidence for Katya's and Joe's comfortable existence comes from the numerous photographs they took of their children, their accommodation, and their lifestyle.

12   Marçi, as a Hungarian citizen, became stateless because he had left Hungary for a period of more than ten years before 1929, when the Hungarian government declared that "in general those living outside of the present Hungarian borders lost their Hungarian citizenship and became citizens of the country which received the given territory (with some minor exceptions) after 1921." See the website of Consulate General of Hungary in Los Angeles, accessed March 8, 2019, https://losangeles.mfa.gov.hu/eng/page/hungarian-citizenship.

medium of exchange.[13] Katya took advantage of the price of silver when it depreciated after China dropped the silver standard, and bought enough to incorporate into an extensive cutlery set that she had made in Shanghai and which the family treasures to this day.

Of greater concern to the Buraks was the political uncertainty that accompanied the rise of the Chinese Communist Party, and Japan's military actions in Beijing, Shanghai, and Nanjing throughout the 1930s, including almost three months of Japanese air attack on parts of Shanghai in 1937. These factors triggered those Buraks remaining in China to seriously consider the fourth leg of their migratory path to permanent settlement outside China.

The first to leave was Fiera, although this had more to do with her husband's employment than conditions in Asia. They left Manchuria in the early 1930s for a period at the Russian Embassy in Paris before a permanent move to Moscow, where the Soviet Government employed them both. Fiera was an interpreter and translator in English and French, and after a little initial correspondence, gradually lost all touch with the family.

The second to leave China was Lucy, who moved with Pierre and their child to the French Consulate in Los Angeles. Lucy made several return trips to visit the family in Shanghai in the 1940s, and made one trip to Sydney in the late 1950s to see her oldest sister, Ida.

Katya and her husband Tom were the most affected by the rise of communism and the Japanese military activities. Both were socialists and claimed a sympathetic concern for the development of Chinese communism, especially in Shanghai. Tom, in particular, was interested, as far as his job would allow, in the activity of a workers' movement in Shanghai, and supported the union's efforts to "establish a new government and struggle against the oppression of the Nanking government."[14] However,

---

13 According to Richard Eberling, in 1933–34 in the United States, under Roosevelt's New Deal, silver was remonetized. The United States went on a buying spree and pushed up the price of silver not only in the USA, but also in China. It prompted the sale of silver throughout urban and rural areas of China. The resultant export of silver to the United States resulted in price deflation that severely affected China's agriculture and industry. China dropped the silver standard and bank notes became legal tender, leading to rapid inflation and eventually a steep depreciation of the yuan, crippling the Chinese economy and sending some regions in China into extreme poverty. Richard M. Eberling, "The Great Chinese Inflation," Foundation for Economic Education (2010), accessed March 22, 2018, http://fee.org/freeman/detail/the-great-chinese-inflation.

14 A copy of an undated Chinese proclamation and a copy of the English translation are pasted into Tom's photo album. The interest in socialism is noted throughout Dolores's notes used for this article.

the Japanese incursions into China affected them the most, especially the bombing of Shanghai in 1937. The Ichang Fire Station on Soochow Creek was responsible for the Chapei district, an industrial area that incurred significant bomb damage resulting in fires. Tom, as station chief, was responsible for fire services during the bombing and personally observed the extent of the damage that he recorded for insurance purposes.[15]

Katya, concerned for her three children, sent them to stay with their father, who was then living in Tientsin with his wife and children. After four months, Dolores, Irene, and Edward could no longer endure their estranged father, and caught a "cabbage boat" back to Shanghai, against Katya's wishes.

As Shanghai's foreign population left for safer places, including several close relatives, so Tom and Katya also planned to emigrate. After spending several years in Eastern Australia working on a dairy farm before and after World War I, and then in the NSW fire brigade, Tom had harbored an ambition to have his own dairy farm in southwestern Australia. It took two years to organize the move. One of the most important tasks was to adopt Katya's three children, who, as children born to a stateless mother, were defined as Chinese and would have been unable to enter Australia under the Immigration Restriction Act of 1901. They arrived at Fremantle in December 1940, leaving Solomon, Bella, Ida, and Marçi in Shanghai.

Thomas Vickers, head officer of the Ichang Fire Station, inspecting bomb damage in 1937

---

15   Tom's reports included photographs that he took to include in reports for insurance claims. His album contains about 30 of these photos, each one captioned and dated.

The foreign concessions in Shanghai had remained islands of prosperity during the Japanese control of Shanghai from 1941 to 1945, and even through increasing inflation after the war, until Shanghai came under the control of the People's Liberation Army. The founding of the People's Republic of China in 1949 pushed the remaining Buraks to leave China. By then most foreigners had departed, leaving those unable to get out because of statelessness, illness, poverty, or old age, or simply general reluctance. With the assistance of the International Red Cross and guarantees by Tom to provide accommodation and financial support, Solomon, Bella, Ida, and Marçi applied for entry to Australia. Solomon and Bella arrived in Perth via Darwin by plane, in June 1951. Ida and Marçi Diamant's departure was held up for another year, due to a request for Marçi to stay and train staff to take over his managerial role in a book printing business. They arrived by the same route in December 1952. Tragically, Bella died within months of arriving in Australia.

Bella Burak's grave

After Ida and Marçi joined Solomon at Tom and Katya's home in Western Australia, they soon decided that, after the metropolis of Shanghai, what seemed like desolate bush was not for them. They moved to Sydney to set up a business in the book industry and became involved in the Jewish community and in the Jews from China Association. Their first task in Sydney was to apply for citizenship, which after almost forty years relieved them of their stateless status. The Buraks became Australian citizens a few years later. Their journeys were over.

It seems that the long journeys of the Burak family were mainly to escape the threat of violence through pogroms, wars, or political disturbance. The exception was leaving Harbin, where the motives were economic and social, to give the girls a better future. Perhaps the most significant factor that determined when, how and why they would migrate, was the 1921 Soviet government edict that prevented Russian émigrés from retaining Russian citizenship, thus rendering them stateless. It could be argued that this encouraged the Burak daughters to seek marriage to non-Jewish nationals who could promise lives in safe countries. This led to the Burak family's dispersal, with each daughter settling in a different country or region, and for three of them, without strong family bonds, the loss of their Jewish identity.

Liliane Willens*

Russian Jews in Shanghai 1920–1950: New Life as Shanghailanders

In 1898, representatives from Russia and China signed a treaty to build the Chinese Eastern Railway (CER) in Manchuria, to be owned and administered by the Russians as an extension of the Trans-Siberian Railway. Tsar Nicholas II encouraged engineers, workers, and even Jews, the most oppressed ethnic group in Russia, to move to Manchuria for the five-year construction (1898–1903) of this commercial rail line. Subsequently, entrepreneurs helped develop the economy in the extraterritorial zone of the CER. Harbin was chosen as its headquarters.

During the last two decades before the Bolshevik Revolution of 1917, Harbin became a thriving city thanks to the CER, which linked the Russian border city of Chita in the west to Vladivostok in the east, as shown on Map 1. This line was shorter by 150 miles than the Trans-Siberian, which went north around Manchuria before reaching Vladivostok. During the Russian Revolution and the Civil War (1918–1920), waves of Russians from eastern Russia fled to Harbin. By the 1920s, the 15,000 Jewish Harbiners formed the largest Jewish economic and cultural community in the Far East.

---

* Liliane Willens was born in Shanghai to Russian Jewish parents. She graduated from the Collège Municipal Français there. She left China in 1951, spent a year in Japan, and then came to the United States, as did the rest of her family. She earned a PhD in French Literature and Language at Boston University and taught these subjects at Boston College and at Massachusetts Institute of Technology. In her book *Stateless in Shanghai* (London: China Economic Review Publishing (HK) Limited for Earnshaw Books, 2010), she wrote about her life in Shanghai during the Japanese occupation, the Chinese civil war, and the first two years of the establishment of the People's Republic of China.

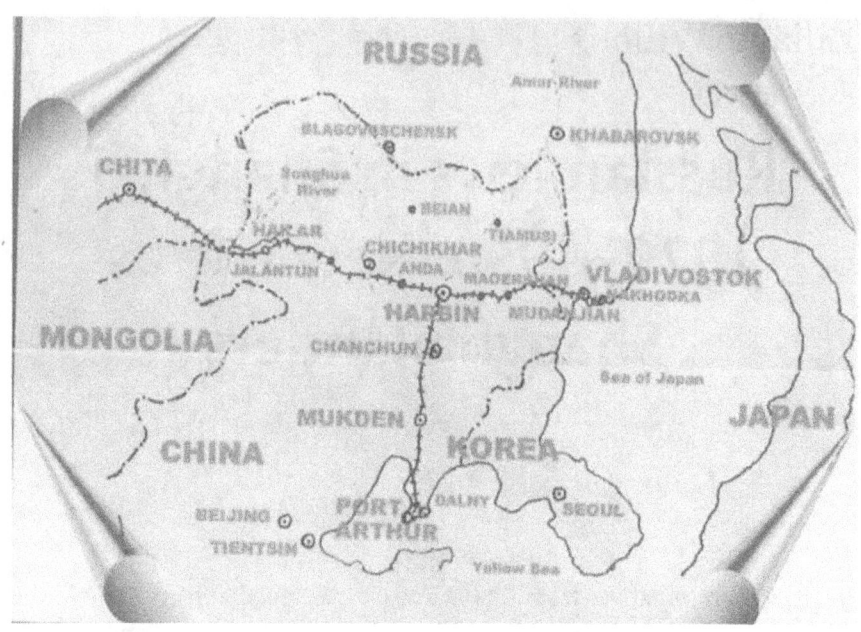

Manchuria and Chinese Eastern Railway

At the time of the Bolshevik takeover in October 1917, my parents were living in Russia's Far East—my father in Vladivostok, my mother in Siberia. My father Benjamin was born in 1894 in the small Ukrainian town of Radomyshl, close to Kiev. Because of the pogroms in Ukraine, Benjamin had taken the Trans-Siberian train earlier in 1917 to Vladivostok, having heard that foreign import-export firms were hiring Russian clerks. He found work in that city and in the process learned German and French, two languages which later would stand him in good stead in Shanghai. However, in 1919 when the Civil War was nearing Vladivostok, Benjamin left for Harbin. He tried to get a job with the Chinese Eastern Railway, the largest employer in the city, but that rail line did not hire Jews. After a one-year stay in Harbin, he took a ship from Dairen (Dalian) to Shanghai, where he believed that his linguistic skills would enable him to find work in the foreign concessions.

My mother Thaïs was born in 1902 in Novonikolaevsk (present-day Novosibirsk), Siberia, where she, her six siblings, and their parents led a comfortable and peaceful life until the outbreak of the Bolshevik Revolution. When I was in my early teens, I asked my mother why her family had lived in far-off "ice-cold" Siberia, which I thought was a region solely for criminals and political enemies of the regime. She explained that her grandfather was a *nikolaevskii soldat* (soldier of Tsar Nicholas I) at a time when Jews in their mid-teens were kidnaped to serve twenty-five years in the Tsar's army and in the process converted to Christianity. This forceful recruitment had been established early in the nineteenth century and lasted until 1856. As recompense for his long military service, my mother's grandfather did not have to live in the Pale of Settlement, a vast area in western Russia where most Jews were confined in villages (shtetls) to keep them out of the big cities. When her grandfather was discharged from the army (he never converted to Christianity), he went to the small town of Novonikolaevsk, where he bought land, built a house, and opened a bakery. The family in Siberia was far removed from the pogroms in Russia instigated by the Tsarist government whenever the economy was bad and the Jews were blamed for the ills of the country!

When in 1919 the Civil War approached Siberia, my mother's family took the Trans-Siberian eastwards to Manchouli (Manzhouli), where they transferred to the CER to Harbin. Thaïs's father was not successful in his business endeavors in Harbin, and within a couple of years he decided to move his family to Shanghai. Shanghai was an extraterritorial city administered and controlled mainly by England, the United States, and France after China had been defeated in the two so-called Opium Wars of 1842 and 1860. The British, the Americans, and several other European countries administered the International Settlement, the French had their *Concession Française*, while the Chinese government controlled two districts, Chapei (Zhabei) and Nantao (Nanshi), adjacent to the foreign concessions.

In 1921, all Russians in exile were rendered stateless by the newly established Bolshevik government. Although passport-holding foreigners in Shanghai enjoyed extraterritorial privileges, stateless Russians fell under the jurisdiction of Chinese laws.

The Russian Jewish refugees who went to Shanghai in the early 1920s were helped by the well-established and wealthy Sephardi community, who had arrived in Shanghai beginning in the mid-nineteenth century. They had made their fortune in commerce, often in the opium trade, and later, in the second decade of the twentieth century, in real estate ventures. Benjamin and Thaïs met and married in 1924 in Shanghai, where my two sisters and I were born and raised in the French Concession. My parents struggled financially during the first couple of years of their marriage, since they could only find poorly paid part-time work. They did not yet speak

English, the obligatory *lingua franca* for all foreigners working in Shanghai. However, thanks to my father's ability to speak French, he was hired in 1927 by Sun Life Assurance Company, a Canadian firm, to sell life insurance policies to French nationals working for the municipality in the French Concession or other French-owned businesses.

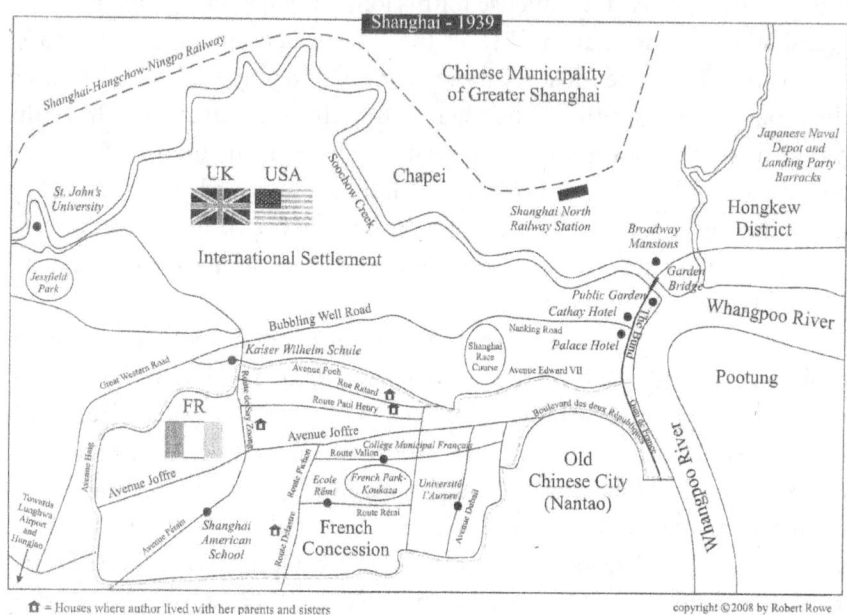

Map of Shanghai in 1939

That same year, 1927, General Chiang Kai-shek, the leader of the Kuomintang (Nationalist) Party, and Mao Tse-tung, head of the newly established Chinese Community Party, were on the verge of attacking Shanghai to put an end to extraterritoriality. However, Chiang Kai-shek, fearing a potential Communist-run joint government, did an about-face, secretly informing the Treaty Powers and wealthy Chinese businessmen that he had no intention of sharing power with the Communists. He told them that he would respect the *status quo* with regard to extraterritoriality, which would be discussed peacefully with the Three Powers at a later date. On April 12, 1927, Chiang's soldiers turned on his allies the Communists and up to 5,000 of them were massacred in a two-week bloodbath later known as "The White Terror." Chiang kept his promise. No change occurred, to the great relief of the foreigners in Shanghai, especially those who were stateless.

Within ten years of their arrival, many in the Russian Ashkenazi community had risen to middle-class status, owning small stores along the main street in the French Concession, Avenue Joffre (Huai Hai Zhong Lu), where the employees were Chinese and White Russians. The Jewish community established their social club and built in 1927 the Ohel Moshe synagogue in the Hongkou district of the International Settlement. Their children, whether Ashkenazi or Sephardi, attended the Shanghai Jewish School or could choose among the French or English public and private schools. During the summers, families went on vacation to the Mokanshan (Moganshan) mountain resorts or to the beach resorts of Peitaiho (Beidaihe) and Tsingtao (Quingdao) for respite from the heat and humidity in Shanghai, while some sailed to the Japanese cities of Nagasaki and Unzen. Passports were not required at that time to enter Japan, which allowed many stateless Russians to take advantage of these spotlessly clean Japanese resorts.

After Japan attacked Manchuria in 1931, many Russian Ashkenazi Harbiners moved to Shanghai in the mid-1930s because of the antisemitic activities of White Russians and the uncertain attitude of the Japanese towards Jews. The situation became especially dire for wealthy Harbiners, mainly Jews, when a number of them were kidnaped for ransom and several killed by members of the White Russian Fascist Party headquartered in Harbin. This was a signal for Jewish factory owners and merchants, including my uncle who owned a very successful pharmacy *Aptechnye Tovary*, to leave Harbin for Shanghai, where he and his fellow Harbiners were able to quickly reestablish their businesses.

Thanks to my father's success during the 1930s selling life insurance policies, our family's standard of living rose to upper middle class, with servants and even a car, which was rather unusual for a stateless Russian, since most foreigners took rickshaws, buses, or trolley cars. My parents attended balls and parties, socializing with their Russian Jewish friends as well as with Sephardim, since they now spoke English. In status-conscious Shanghai, our family had attained respectability thanks to my father's job at Sun Life Assurance Company. Because of Benjamin's relationship with his French clients, it is not surprising that we attended the Collège Municipal Français, where we were steeped in French culture and the glory of France during our entire education. My fluency in French language would later serve me well, as it did my father in China, when I immigrated to the United States and acquired advanced degrees in French language and literature and taught these subjects at several universities in Boston and Cambridge, Massachusetts.

Despite the Chinese civil war, the Japanese attack on Chapei on the outskirts of the International Settlement in August 1937, life continued as usual for the foreigners in Shanghai. Business was booming. This latest conflict between the Japanese and Chinese was generally considered "inconsequential" by the foreign community, since it was simply a war between two weak Asian countries. The fighting between the armies of the Kuomintang and Japan did not last long, for the Chinese were defeated by the overwhelmingly superior Japanese forces. The Japanese marine landing party remained in Hongkou and could not be dislodged by the Three Powers, now concerned, especially England and France, about Nazi Germany's increasing military strength and even the possibility of war in Europe.

During this conflict, Vladimir, the son of our relatives who had moved from Harbin to Shanghai, informed his parents that he intended to go to the USSR, where his professional skills would be in demand in the rebuilding of Russia. A graduate of the French Jesuit L'Aurore University in Shanghai, Vladimir could not, understandably, find a job, while the Japanese and Chinese were still at war in nearby Chapei. His parents tried to dissuade him, since in 1937 Stalin's bloody purges were at their height as thousands and thousands of Russians were arbitrarily executed or sent to the gulags. Although they reminded their son that his Harbin "bourgeois capitalist" background would surely be anathema to the Soviets, Vladimir left in 1938 for the USSR.

He did not know that on September 20, 1937, the Commissar of Internal Affairs had issued Operational Order #0059 with regard to the 25,000 former *harbintsy* (Harbiners) living and working in the USSR: "The overwhelmingly majority of them are agents of Japanese intelligence, which for a number years have sent them to the USSR [from Manchukuo] to conduct terrorist, diversionary and espionage activities."[1] These *harbintsy* were to be executed immediately, while the "less active" ones were to be imprisoned or sent to camps for eight to ten years. Vladimir was never heard from again.

The only group eager to leave Shanghai during those turbulent times were the young Russian Zionists trying to go to Palestine. Most

---

1   Mara Moustafine, *Secrets and Spies: The Harbin Files* (Australia: Vintage Books, 2002), 449–52.

Shanghailanders, whether passport holders or stateless, had no desire to leave the city, since in their opinion this "skirmish" between China and Japan would surely end soon, and business and social life would return to normal.

An interesting encounter occurred in Shanghai in 1937, when some members of the two Jewish communities were approached by Japanese officials. The latter felt Jews could be useful to Japan's plans of conquering all of Asia. They believed naively that some American Jews who had close contact with President Franklin Roosevelt could persuade the US government to stay out of their war with China. Japanese officials even toyed with the idea of giving refuge in Manchuria to the vast number of Jews fleeing Nazi Germany.

From 1933 to 1937, hundreds of Jewish refugees from Central Europe fleeing Nazi persecution came to Shanghai, one of the few places in the world where passports, entry visas, or work permits were not required. The Russian Jewish community learned first-hand about Hitler's vicious rantings against Jews, of Nazi laws denying their basic rights, and of concentration camps. After *Kristallnacht* (November 9–10, 1938) when 30,000 Jews in Germany were arrested and sent to concentration camps, and their stores, offices, and synagogues destroyed by rampaging Nazis, thousands of Jewish refugees fled to Shanghai. The Sephardi and Ashkenazi residents took care of these destitute people, setting up soup kitchens and finding rooms for them in Hongkou, where the rents were much lower than in the foreign concessions. My parents helped financially, also bringing clothes to the various refugee distribution centers. Most importantly, additional help came from the American Jewish Joint Distribution Committee, which opened an office in Shanghai to help the increasing number of refugees arriving on ships from Europe. By summer 1941, there were in Shanghai approximately 18,000 Jewish refugees from Central and Eastern Europe.

Although World War II had erupted in Europe on September 1, 1939, this event seemed very distant to the Shanghai Russian Jews. In summer 1941 they built the Shanghai Jewish Hospital staffed by refugee doctors and nurses, as well as the New Synagogue, which could hold approximately 1,000 congregants. However, when Japan attacked Pearl Harbor, life drastically changed for everyone in Shanghai, from the poorest Chinese to the richest *taipan* (member of the foreign business elite). At dawn on December 8, 1941, Japanese tanks rolled into the International Settlement, but not into the French Concession, because the Vichy government had sided with the Axis powers after France's defeat by Germany in June 1940. Our French school remained open, regrettably for many of us pupils, while the British and American-owned schools were closed. My father lost his job within a few months of the Japanese military takeover of Shanghai, when the Canadian Sun Life Assurance was closed as enemy property, as were other businesses belonging to enemy aliens, British, Americans, Dutch, and Belgians.

Starting in early 1942, life became very difficult for all Shanghai residents, when ration cards were issued for food. However, additional food supplies could be found on the black market, if one had the funds. My parents' savings was in gold bars, which they sold during the war whenever they needed cash to purchase food, coal, or medicine. In our home, electricity, gas, and water could be used for only a few hours a day. My father sold his car, and he and my mother started riding bicycles. Curfew from early evening to dawn was imposed, and windows had to be covered at night with black cloth because the Japanese feared bombing by American planes. They foresaw this correctly, because eventually enemy planes appeared nightly, then daily, to bomb Japanese factories on the outskirts of Shanghai.

One of the most frightening events for the Jews was the arrival from Tokyo in July 1942 of Colonel Joseph Meisinger, the head of the Gestapo in the Far East, who held discussions with the Japanese military authorities. He was known as the "Butcher of Warsaw," having directed the massacre of 100,000 Jews in Poland. Although there is no documentary evidence to date about these meetings, one can surmise that killing the Jews in Shanghai, especially those who had fled from Germany and Austria, was Meisinger's major priority. However, the Japanese did not appreciate any meddling in their affairs in China, and were also suspicious of their German allies, who had not informed them in advance of their attack on the Soviet Union in June 1941. Japan was also ill at ease with Aryan racism, since in the Nazi ranking of ethnic groups, Asians were only a few notches above the Jews. Most importantly, Japan had no intention of sharing power in Asia with their German allies. Japan's Greater East Asia Co-Prosperity Sphere plan was to conquer all Asian countries. Asia was for the Asians, but controlled by Japan.

In 1943, Allied enemy nationals in China were incarcerated in prisoner-of-war camps, including the Sephardi holders of British passports. Under pressure from Berlin, the Japanese military issued a Proclamation in February 1943 that "stateless refugees" (the word "Jew" was never mentioned) who had come to Shanghai after 1937 had to move within three months to a "Designated Area." This half-mile-long and three-quarters-mile-wide area in Hongkou became a kind of ghetto, which the refugees could not leave without a pass from the Japanese authorities. Since the American Jewish Joint Distribution Committee could no longer send money to Japanese-occupied Shanghai, and many of the wealthy Baghdadi Jews were incarcerated, the responsibility to help the refugees fell on the Russian Ashkenazi community. They decided to impose a tax on themselves, thus enabling them to purchase food and medication for the Hongkou, always in great shortage during wartime in Shanghai.

Most surprisingly, the 25,000 stateless Russians—20,000 White Russians and 5,000 Russian Jews—were not incarcerated during the entire war. Ironically, my stateless father was free, while his boss, an English *taipan*, lived in a prisoner-of-war camp, where food was barely above starvation portions. Having signed a Neutrality Pact with the USSR in April 1941, Japan did not want to antagonize the Soviets by sending Russians to prisoner-of-war camps. Japan did not want to open a second front along the Manchurian/Russian border, especially in 1943, when they were already losing islands in the Pacific to the Americans.

Although free, the stateless Russian Jews were nevertheless worried about their fate. There was great fear in their community in 1942, when six Jewish men were incarcerated and interrogated in Bridge House, a prison run by the *Kempeitai*, the much-feared Japanese military police. They were accused of spreading rumors, a serious offense that according to the authorities undermined Japan's security of the city. These men admitted that they were told secretly by a Japanese official that there were rumors the Japanese military, in collaboration with Nazi Germans, had plans to kill all the Jews in Shanghai.

The six men were found guilty of spreading rumors, but finally released, except for Boris Topas, a friend of our family. In the early 1930s, as one of the leaders of the Shanghai Ashkenazi Jewish Communal Association, he had led a delegation to Harbin protesting the treatment of Jews by the Japanese military in Manchuria. In addition, he had written many flattering articles about Sun Yat-sen and Chiang Kai-shek. Topas was tortured and finally freed, but as a man physically and mentally wrecked at the age of fifty.

The Russian Jewish community was also leery of the new president of China, Wang Ching-wei, a puppet of the Japanese, who had lived several years in Germany during the rise of Hitler and had become an admirer of Nazi Germany. The Jews had to contend with the the vitriolic antisemitic tracts emanating from the German Information Bureau located in the Park Hotel. The editor reminded the 1,000 German nationals, many now newly minted Nazis, not to associate with Jews or to buy anything from their stores. A similar barrage of antisemitic propaganda could be heard daily from the German radio station XGRS located in the German school, the Kaiser Wilhelm Schule. The Nazis collected intelligence for the Japanese on the activities of the Jewish community, checking whether they were in contact by radio or other means with the Kuomintang, the Soviets or Allied operatives.

The three and a half years before Japan's capitulation on August 15, 1945, were extremely difficult, psychologically and physically, for all residents in Shanghai. The Japanese soldiers became even more brutal towards the Chinese, slapping them or hitting them with their bayonets without cause. Only many years later could I appreciate how worried my parents and their friends in the Jewish community must have been during the Japanese occupation of Shanghai. England and the United States were no longer in charge, while the French authorities, although still administering the Concession, were in reality taking orders from the Japanese. People in Shanghai wanted desperately for the occupation to end, especially when they heard that Germany had capitulated in April 1945. But Japan continued to fight, despite enormous losses in men and materiel. However, the fateful blows of the two atomic bombs dropped on August 6 and August 9, 1945, brought Japan to its knees, and within a week Japan capitulated.

When the Pacific War ended, Chiang Kai-shek's army took control of Shanghai, followed by American armed forces, whose purpose was to disarm and evacuate the Japanese soldiers to their homeland. The euphoria following the liberation of Shanghai did not last long, because in early 1946 the civil war resumed between the Nationalists and the Communists. Foreigners, especially the "Old China Hands," realized there was no future for them in China, now racked by inflation and corruption by an autocratic regime and the civil war. Stateless refugees from Eastern and Central Europe were able to immigrate to the United States under the US Displaced Persons Act of 1948, thereby bypassing the quota system. That year, the exodus of foreigners with passports increased, followed by wealthy Chinese leaving for Hong Kong and Taiwan, while the stateless Russians waited for their immigration quota to the United States or Canada. However, tired of waiting, many Russian Jews opted to leave for Israel when it became a sovereign country in May 1948.

In our family, my older sister Rebecca married a US naval officer and left Shanghai in August 1948 with her husband under the non-quota War Brides Act enacted in December 1945 (which expired in December 1948). My mother, born in Russia, was able to leave in March 1949 for America, taking my younger sister Jacqueline, a minor, just before the arrival of the People's Liberation Army in Shanghai several months later. My father could not leave with them, because when he arrived in Shanghai he had registered as a Romanian national with the French police. He could not receive a quota number, because the United States had not yet signed a peace treaty with Romania, which during World War II had sided with the Axis powers.

I applied in 1947 to immigrate to the United States and was still waiting for a visa when the US Consulate General in Shanghai closed its doors in April 1950, six months after the establishment of the Communist People's Republic of China. I was in Shanghai when the People's Liberation Army marched victoriously but quietly into the city on May 25, 1949. I then lived two years under the newly established People's Republic of China and finally received an Exit Permit to leave China in April 1951.[2] I went to Japan, then under US occupation, and a year later received my immigration visa from the US consulate in Tokyo. When my father's national identity was "corrected" as a native of Russia and not Romania, he joined me in Tokyo where he received his immigration papers a year after I had left for the United States.

Why could I not receive a US immigration visa sooner, having applied for it six years earlier? I was indirectly affected by the 1882 Chinese Exclusion Act, which had banned Chinese immigration to the United States, but was rescinded in 1943. I was more directly affected by the 1924 National Origins Act (the Johnson-Reed Act signed by President Calvin Coolidge), which established a quota system based on one's place of birth and race. Quota numbers were calculated on 2% of each national group living in the United States at the time of the 1890 Census. This was obviously to keep America white, since most of the immigrants who had arrived in the US in the nineteenth century had come from western and northern European countries. Since I was born on Chinese soil, I came under the very small quota,

---

2   See chapters 26–31 of the author's eyewitness account of the first two years following the establishment of the People's Republic of China in her book *Stateless in Shanghai* (London: China Economic Review Publishing Ltd., 2010).

numbering 105 immigration visas a year, for both Chinese immigrants and non-ethnic Chinese born in China. As can be seen by the copy of my visa in Image 9, a distinction was clearly made that, although I came under the China quota, my ethnic background was white.

US Immigration Visa of Liliane Willens

When I left Shanghai in April 1951, there were very few Russian Ashkenazi Jews left in the city where they had first arrived as refugees in the early 1920s, later thrived, and then survived as Shanghailanders for the next three decades in a very chaotic era in China, a country beset by civil wars and a brutal enemy occupation.

Shanghai and the Holocaust

Jonathan Goldstein*

Desperate Hopes, Shattered Dreams: The 1937 Shanghai–Manila Voyage of the "Gneisenau" and the Fate of European Jewry[1]

This chapter is as much about the hopes, expectations, and disappointments of Jews fleeing Hitler as it is about actual historical events. After Hitler's takeover in 1933, many German and other Central and Eastern European Jews desperately sought places of refuge worldwide. Their primary choice of destination before, during, and after the Holocaust was always the United States. But immigration restrictions imposed by the US Congress in 1924 created a policy of "selective" or "approved" immigration with

---

* Jonathan Goldstein earned his PhD in East Asian History from the University of Pennsylvania. He has been a Professor of East Asian History at the University of West Georgia since 1981 and a research associate of Harvard University's Fairbank Center for Chinese Studies since 1985. He has published widely on Jews in Asia, most recently *Jewish Identities in East and Southeast Asia: Singapore, Manila, Taipei, Harbin, Shanghai, Rangoon, and Surabaya* (Berlin: De Gruyter, 2015), and has edited *The Jews of China*, 2 vols. (Armonk, NY: M. E. Sharpe, 1999 and 2000), and *China and Israel, 1948–1998: A Fifty Year Retrospective* (Westport, CT: Praeger Publishers, 1999).

1 Portions of this chapter are excerpted from the author's *Jewish Identities in East and Southeast Asia*. The author wishes to thank Charlotte Beahan, Charles Berlin, Iris Bruce, Richard Golden, Peter Hayes, Mel Johnson, Ber Kotlerman, Russel Lemmons, William Small, Casey Twist, Rivka Ulmer, and Bernard Wasserstein for their assistance with this research.

regional quotas, which effectively excluded Jews from open immigration to the *goldene medina* (Yiddish for "golden country"). After 1924 the only truly open immigrant destination worldwide was Shanghai. Neither that city nor China as a country had a self-conscious policy of welcoming refugees. Rather, "rescue" was a product of bureaucratic inertia. The metropolis was a hodgepodge of multiple jurisdictions with overlapping and conflicting administrations and no coherent immigration policy. Jews or anyone else who could physically reach Shanghai could simply walk ashore. Transportation to Shanghai was a problem, but official entry documents were not required.[2]

After the outbreak of Sino-Japanese hostilities in July 1937 even Shanghai's attractiveness as a refugee destination became problematic. Escaping the trials and tribulations of Europe for a war-torn city on the other side of the globe might well be going from one frying pan into another. Since the ultimate destination of virtually all European Jewish refugees was the United States, one possible alternative to Shanghai was escape to the American colony of the Philippines where, after a five-year residence, one could reimmigrate to the continental United States. An encouraging sign occurred on September 8, 1937, when the Philippines admitted twenty-eight German-Jewish refugees who had sailed from war-torn Shanghai aboard the Norddeutscher Lloyd steamship "Gneisenau." This was, significantly, a random contingent of immigrants. Their admission, however, proved to be an aberration in Philippine immigration policy. The episode was followed by a retreat to a policy of selective immigration, dashing the hopes of Jews still trapped in Europe. Thereafter, even amidst fierce Sino-Japanese hostilities, the open city of Shanghai became the exclusive Jewish "port of last resort." By 1941 approximately 18,000 Central and Eastern European Jewish refugees reached this haven via exasperating and circuitous routes, by land and sea. Wartime exigencies then effectively shut down all civilian transport to both Shanghai and Manila. As European Jews continued to reflect upon the differences between open immigration, selective immigration/rescue, and entirely closed doors in most parts of the world, they gradually realized that they were trapped on a war-torn continent, subject to bitter harassment and ultimately genocide. In order to

---

2   For a discussion of Shanghai's peculiar status as an immigrant destination, see the next chapter by Manli Ho, "Diplomatic Rescue: Shanghai as a Means of Escape and Refuge."

comprehend the desperate hopes of Jews who were intrigued by the possibility of immigration to the Philippines, some additional historical context is necessary.

The Jewish Community of Manila and the Rise of Hitler

In 1933, the Philippine Jewish community, only established after American colonization in 1898, amounted to some 1,000 individuals. They were of multiple national backgrounds and were overwhelmingly secular and intermarried. In 1920, Anglo-Zionist fundraiser Israel Cohen, who was impressed with Jewish institutional development in Singapore, visited Manila. He lamented that although

> there were several hundred Jews, they had not formed a synagogue. . . . Only those who still had a flickering of Jewish consciousness met together on the two most solemn days of the Jewish calendar . . . after which they hibernated for another twelve months. They were there twenty years [and] there was no Jewish organization or institution of any kind. If a Jew wished to get married, he took a day trip to Hong Kong. I left wondering whether all the fortunes of the rich Jews of Manila are worth the soul of one poor Jew of Zamboanga.[3]

In 1924 Emil Bachrach, a wealthy Ashkenazi businessman, helped establish a synagogue in Manila. Full-time, ordained clergy rarely serviced it. The community imported clergymen and lay leaders from Shanghai and elsewhere for short stints.[4] In 1930 an American journalist reported that the eighty Jewish families and fifty single Jews in the Philippines

---

3 Refers to a Syrian Jew from the southern Philippine island of Mindanao. That resident told Cohen that "we feel here in Galuth (exile) . . . soon we hope to get back to the land of Israel." Israel Cohen, *Journal of a Jewish Traveller* (London: John Lane, 1925), 108-14; Israel Cohen, *A Jewish Pilgrimage* (London: Valentine Mitchell, 1956), 193; Temple Emil "New Year's Card/ Calendar" for 1937-38, 1940-41, 1941-42, "Chanukah announcement 1939," "Program Chanukah-Party 1939," and "Program Simchath-Torah-Party 1941," all from Joseph Cysner Archive, Jewish Historical Society of San Diego; Ida Cowen, *Jews in Remote Corners of the World* (Englewood Cliffs, NJ: Prentice Hall, 1971), 141-47.

4 Jack Netzorg, *Manila Memories* (Laguna Beach, CA: Pacific Rim Books, 1990), 29, 66; World Jewish Congress, *The Jewish Communities of the World* (New York, 1963), 49; Lewis E. Gleeck, *History of the Jewish Community of Manila* (n.d., n. p., approx. 1989), 16-17; John Griese, "The Jewish Community in Manila" (MA thesis, University of the Philippines, 1954), 21-22; Cowen, *Jews*, 129-38; Frank Ephraim, *Escape to Manila: From Nazi Tyranny to Japanese Terror* (Urbana and Chicago: University of Illinois Press, 2003), 14-15. Ephraim's autobiography is the authoritative account about the Jewish refugee experience in the Philippines. It is firmly grounded in documents stored in

are all well established yet indifferent to their Judaism. They have no interest in a Jewish community. There is a handsome synagogue, but it is used only on the Jewish high holidays. There was a religious school, but it was closed on account of the scarcity of teachers. Thus, most of the children receive absolutely no Jewish education. The religious indifference of their parents plus the lack of knowledge of Jewish affairs of the children counts these families as a total loss to Judaism.[5]

The rise of Hitler mobilized some of Manila's most secular Jews into communal service. Minna Gaberman, the niece of the founder of the infrequently used Manila synagogue, asserted that "we only became Jewish conscious in a deep way when the terrible threat came out of Europe and suddenly there were Jews in desperate need of help."[6] The Holocaust and World War II, in short, gave the community an intensified Jewish consciousness. That transformation occurred within the context of the colonial relationship with the United States, which had begun in 1898.

That year the Philippines became an American territorial possession. On November 15, 1935, under the provisions of the Congressional Tydings-McDuffie Act, the colony gained self-governing status as "the Philippine Commonwealth." The US pledged to withdraw from the Philippines by July 4, 1946, at which time the "Commonwealth" would become an independent "Republic of the Philippines." In 1935 Manuel L. Quezon was elected the first president of the Commonwealth. The islands then received their first US High Commissioner.

Until the Philippines passed its own comprehensive immigration legislation on January 1, 1941, the immigration restrictions imposed by the US Congress in 1924 *theoretically* applied in both the continental United States and the Commonwealth. But *in practice*, the Philippines had some flexibility when it came to the implementation of immigration policy. One feature that attracted Jews fleeing Hitler was that there was no direct law forbidding immigration, which depended on the authorization of the local authorities

---

the US National Archives and Records Administration. Most documents originated with US Commissioner Paul McNutt, the US State Department, the US Army's Bureau of Insular Affairs, Philippine President Manuel L. Quezon, the Manila-based Jewish Refugee Committee, the Frieder brothers in Manila, the American Jewish Joint Distribution Committee (often referred to as "The Joint"), the New York City-based Refugee Economic Corporation, and the *Hilfsverein der deutschen Juden* in Germany.

5   "Jews in the Philippines Not Religious," *The Jewish Advocate*, Boston, March 25, 1930.
6   Minna Gaberman, Manila, quoted in Annette Eberly, "Manila? Where? Us? The Good Life Out There," *Present Tense* 2, no. 3 (1975): 60.

in Manila. A person could then reimmigrate to the continental United States without coming under a quota. Another factor which worked in favor of Jewish immigration was that President Quezon, exasperated by rampant corruption within the Philippine Immigration Department, dismantled that agency entirely, taking full authority into his own hands. Thereafter he relied increasingly on Manila Jews to help him vet the bona fides of potential immigrants, raising the hopes and expectations of the Jews of Europe.[7]

Varied Perceptions of Philippine Immigration Policy

The first two German Jewish refugees from Hitler to reach the Philippines may have been Karl Nathan and Heinz Eulau, from Offenbach. They arrived in Manila in June 1934 on affidavits of support from Eulau's cousin Dr. Kurt Eulau, who had lived in the islands since 1924 and would sponsor many other immigrants.[8] The admission of these Jews ignited optimism among others. The circumstances favoring the admission of additional Jews were noted in a December 24, 1936, letter from M. B. Shapiro, who moved from Tianjin, China, to Manila in 1935, to Meir Birman in Harbin, in Japanese-occupied Manchuria. Birman was an activist from the moderately socialist *Algemeyner Yidisher Arbeter Bund in Lite, Poyln, un Rusland* (The General Union of Jewish Workers in Lithuania, Poland, and Russia, often abbreviated as "the Bund").[9] By 1936 Birman had become, arguably, the social worker most involved in assisting Jews who were fleeing Europe for East Asia. His formal capacity was manager of the Harbin office of DALJEWCIB, the Russian-language acronym for "The Far Eastern Jewish Information Bureau." Shapiro informed Birman that, based on personal experience in immigrating from China to Manila, Philippine immigration policy was a sieve which could easily be penetrated, notably with the help of Manila's Jewish Benevolent Society, headed by M. Goldstein:

---

7 [Manuel E. Quezon], *Messages of the President*, v. V, part I (Manila: Bureau of Printing, 1941), 427; "Jews to Come in Gradually Says Quezon," *Manila Daily Bulletin*, April 24, 1940; David Wyman, *Paper Walls: America and the Refugee Crisis 1938–1941* (New York: Pantheon, 1985); Henry Srebrnik, "Why did the Holocaust go relatively unnoticed in America?," *Jewish Tribune*, Toronto, December 4, 2008, 4; Irene Eber, *Wartime Shanghai and the Jewish Refugees from Central Europe* (Berlin: De Gruyter, 2012), 62–63; Ephraim, *Escape to Manila*, 15–77; Griese, "Jewish Community in Manila," 18–28, 134.

8 Ephraim, *Escape to Manila*, 15–77; Griese, "Jewish Community in Manila," 28.

9 Meyer Eliash Birman was born in Ponevezh (Panevėžys), Russian Lithuania, in 1891, and died in New York in 1955.

There is no direct law prohibiting admission to the Philippine Islands (so far), this depends on the judgment of American consuls on the spot . . . a temporary or tourist visa is to be asked for. A tourist may not be in fear of deportation on the expiration of his visa for in such cases the Jewish Community or private persons with guarantees assist. Nothing to be afraid of. You may give this information to those who apply to you concerning the question of admission to Manila.

In case a visa is not given in Harbin, let him proceed to Tientsin [Tianjin], it is easier to get one there. A friend of mine, Mr. Kushner, is employed in the Tientsin American Consulate, and he will help him.

If you have in your files geologists or mining engineers out of work, these—with certain exceptions—will at once find work in the local goldfields. The salary is high. Generally, if there are such qualified specialists in Harbin, let them communicate with me beforehand, and then I shall send them a visa from here through the local consulate.

People arrive daily from Shanghai, so that it appears that visas are issued to everybody. 3d class tickets from Shanghai here cost 69.50 Mex. Dollars, European cuisine, berths for 2 and 4.[10]

On January 15, 1937, Birman forwarded Shapiro's suggestions to the Paris office of HICEM, yet another social service agency assisting Jewish immigration to East Asia. HICEM had been established in 1927 as a cooperative effort of three Jewish immigration assistance associations: HIAS, the Hebrew Sheltering and Immigrant Aid Society of America, founded in New York in 1881 and headquartered there; ICA, the Jewish Colonization Association, based in Paris but registered as a British charitable society; and Emigdirect, based in Berlin. Birman reminded HICEM that "residents of the Philippines after a 5 years' stay in the islands can emigrate to the United States freely, i.e. without a quota." But alongside Shapiro's optimism, Birman added a warning. He reiterated the gist of fundraiser Israel Cohen's observation of seventeen years earlier, that Manila's Jewish millionaires were by and large "indifferent to social work . . . distinguishing themselves in golf, tennis, races, and other kinds of sport." Most Jews who had firmly established themselves in Manila took "no interest in Jewish needs." Based

---

10 M. B. Shapiro, Manila, translation from Russian of letter to Meir Birman, Harbin, December 24, 1936, RG 245.4 XX D-2, HIAS/HICEM Far East, YIVO Institute for Jewish Research Library, New York (hereafter HI-HI, YIVO); Ephraim, *Escape to Manila*, 15–77; Griese, "Jewish Community in Manila," 28.

on Birman's evaluation, Dr. Kurt Eulau could be considered an aberration. Because of the weakness of Manila's "primitive benevolent society," Birman asked HICEM to proceed cautiously and keep Shapiro's advice confidential. Birman urged that "great care ... be taken in selecting suitable immigrants, for if *shnorers* ("obnoxious beggars" in Yiddish) are sent, they may be supplied with tickets and sent on to Shanghai or Harbin."[11]

The "Gneisenau" Episode: Open Immigration Raises and Shatters Hopes

Despite the optimism of M. B. Shapiro, as of January 1937 immigration officials like Meir Birman of DALJEWCIB felt that the Philippines held out only the prospect of selective, and not open and unfettered, Jewish immigration. Eight months later immigration officials and potential immigrants alike experienced a jolt of optimism when a relatively large group of randomly selected, and not carefully vetted, Jewish refugees arrived in Manila.

A set of bizarre circumstances underlay this arrival. On July 7, 1937, China and Japan went to war after what is commonly known as the "Marco Polo Bridge" incident near Beijing. Shanghai, with its four million inhabitants, became a major battleground. All German passport holders in Shanghai who were registered with their Consul were notified about the possibility of evacuation. This expatriate community included Jews and non-Jews. The Consul asked his Manila counterpart if asylum could be granted to German refugees from war-torn Shanghai. The German government would pay for transport aboard the Norddeutscher Lloyd steamship "Gneisenau," then in the region. The German Consul in Manila won approval from President Quezon and US High Commissioner Paul V. McNutt for emergency entry visas. The only stipulation was that the refugees not become a public burden.

The "Gneisenau" then touched at Shanghai. Uniformed Nazi storm troopers escorted a contingent of about fifty hastily assembled Jewish and non-Jewish German passport holders aboard ship. None of the Jewish travelers' documents were as yet inscribed with the large "J" stamp, indicating "Jude" or "Jew," a notorious provision subsequently requested by the Swiss government in its effort to restrict Jewish immigration. But Nazi officials

---

11   Meir Birman, DALJEWCIB, Harbin, letter to HICEM, Paris, January 15, 1937, Letter #52747, XV D-1, HI-HI, YIVO; Cohen, *Journal*, 108–14.

surely knew there were Jews among this émigré contingent. They were pragmatic enough to realize that the Americans would accept no refugees whatsoever if only "Aryan" Germans were included, while other Germans were excluded on the basis of Jewish ethnicity. At this time the German government was involved in a delicate balancing act in its relations with China and Japan. The last thing it needed was a diplomatic squabble with the United States, with whom it still enjoyed relatively good relations.

Hence, on September 8, 1937, twenty-eight German Jews from Shanghai disembarked in Manila along with an approximately equal number of non-Jewish Germans. Ethnically German Philippine residents assumed responsibility for their brethren. A hastily convened Jewish Refugee Committee (JRC), headed by American-Jewish cigar maker and Manila resident Philip Frieder, tended to the needs of the Jews. Significantly, this care was not meted out on the basis of kinship ties, as had been the case with the Eulaus. Rather, it was dispensed on a purely random and humanitarian basis by an energized Manila Jewish community. Thereafter, the JRC worked in close coordination with President Quezon and became, effectively, an ad-hoc board overseeing all Jewish arrivals in the Philippines.

We can only speculate on the motives for the benevolence of the non-Jewish officials involved. Quezon may have been favorably disposed toward Jewish refugees because of a recent visit to Nazi Germany, where he had seen antisemitism first hand. McNutt, for his part, was a Democratic presidential aspirant from Indiana with close personal ties to Jacob Weiss, the Jewish President Pro Tem of the Indiana Senate. In September 1937 McNutt had only been on the job as US High Commissioner to the Philippines for six months. As a shrewd politician, he doubtless knew the advantages he could reap stateside by assisting Jewish refugees overseas.

Refugee Frank Ephraim suggests yet another possible motivation. He asserts that "at the time, the committee assumed that the refugees would stay in Manila temporarily, until the situation in Shanghai had cleared." Jewish and non-Jewish rescuers alike may have felt that they were committing only to temporary immigration, a short-term palliative rather than permanent residency. If that were the case, in the final analysis their commitment would be minimal and could readily be handled by local assets. As events unfolded, the commitment turned out to be much longer lasting than originally envisioned.[12]

---

12 Ephraim, *Escape to Manila*, 23. On the overall diplomatic context which enabled the voyage of the "Gneisenau," see Gerhard Weinberg, "German Recognition of Manchoukuo (sic)," *World Affairs Quarterly* 28 (1957): 149–64; William C. Kirby,

Whatever the motivation of the Manila rescuers, back in Harbin, social worker Meir Birman harbored the faint hope that these two sympathetic officials might authorize the admission of relatively large numbers of additional immigrants. A random assortment of refugees as were aboard the "Gneisenau" was out of the question. But a significant number of Jews with special skills and who would not impose financial burdens on the local economy *might* be acceptable. In a July 5, 1938 letter, Birman expressed his enthusiasm to Philip Frieder. Birman argued that, over and beyond the group which arrived on September 8, 1937, "no difficulties are made at present by American consuls in Germany and Austria in issuing Philippine visas to [individual] victims of anti-Semitism. The latter have only to submit a friendly letter of invitation from a permanent resident of your islands in which it is stated that the persons in question would be able to establish themselves on arrival."[13] Birman also passed this upbeat advice to M. Asofsky of the New York office of HIAS.[14]

Birman's faint hopes were quickly dashed. On July 19 HIAS conveyed to HICEM, its sister organization in Paris, the affirmation of extant policy by Colonel Macdonald of the US Army's Bureau of Insular Affairs, which technically oversaw the Philippines. Macdonald reiterated to HIAS that there had been no change in long-standing immigration policy, despite hopes and expectations to the contrary. According to Macdonald:

> approximately 40 families of Jewish refugees who came to Philippine on own initiative or because of connections there have been absorbed. In order to prevent attempted entry of more refugees than can be cared for properly, it is unwise to give any publicity to the move. . . . No order has been made for

---

Germany and Republican China (Stanford: Stanford University Press, 1984); David Kranzler, *Japanese, Nazis and Jews: The Jewish Refugee Community of Shanghai 1938–1945* (New York: Yeshiva University Press, 1976); and Hsi-Huey Liang, *The Sino-German Connection* (Assen: Van Gorcum, 1978). On Quezon and McNutt, see Jonathan Goldstein and Dean Kotlowski, "The Jews of Manila: Manuel Quezon, Paul McNutt, and the Politics and Consequences of Holocaust Rescue," in *Between Mumbai and Manila: Judaism in Asia since the Founding of the State of Israel*, ed. Manfred Hutter (Göttingen, Germany: Vandenhoeck & Ruprecht, 2013), 123–37. On the "Gneisenau" episode in particular, see Ephraim, *Escape to Manila*, 20–25, 134.

13 Letters: M[eir] Bierman [sic], DALJEWCIB, Harbin, to P. S. Frieder, Manila, July 5, 1938; to HICEM, Paris, Letter #57095 (in German), July 8, 1938, both in RG 245.4 XX D-2, HI-HI, YIVO.

14 M. Birman, DALJEWCIB, Harbin, letter in Yiddish to M. Asofsky, General Manager, HIAS, New York, July 8, 1938, Letter #57009, XV D-1, HI-HI, YIVO. Birman mentions that Lazar Epstein is en route to Manila.

admission of any number of Jewish refugees, and merely these 40 . . . came on their own initiative.¹⁵

Macdonald's reiteration of policy put a damper on Birman's and Shapiro's optimism. It negated the possibility of unrestricted admission of large numbers of Jewish refugees. But it held open the faint possibility of a much smaller number of refugees with specific skill sets and financial guarantees. On August 1, 1938, Bruno Schachner, Assistant Secretary of the Refugee Economic Corporation, referred to this possibility when he admonished HICEM in Paris that "we have reached an agreement with the local committees regarding the immigration question. We would consider it extremely unfortunate if you were to send people to the Philippines who have not been selected in advance. In our opinion, this would tend to jeopardize seriously the success of a planned immigration scheme, and we are most anxious that you desist from doing so."¹⁶ In short, the policy of high selectivity would be as firmly enforced for Jewish entry into the Philippines as it was for admission to the United States itself.

Aftermath of the "Gneisenau" Voyage: Caring for Refugees, the Lazar Epstein Mission, the Mindanao Scheme, and Surreptitious Immigration

Later that fall Birman, HIAS, and HICEM received reconfirmation of long-standing Philippine immigration policy from yet another distinctly Jewish source. Meir Birman in Harbin sent Tianjin Bundist leader Lazar Epstein on a fact-finding mission to Manila and Shanghai. On October 10, 1938, Epstein reported back to HICEM and HIAS the important distinction between open immigration and selective rescue, not minimizing the importance of the latter form of relief. But he reiterated the same caution suggested in earlier reports, such as that of Israel Cohen, that the Manila

---

15 Macdonald makes apparent reference here to the September 8, 1937, group and a handful of other ad-hoc individual admissions. Colonel Macdonald, HIAS, New York, letter to HICEM, Paris, July 19, 1938, RG 245.4 XX D-2, HI-HI, YIVO. An appended telegram from HICEM to "Frieder, POB 423, Manille" [probably P. S. Frieder] notes forthcoming "Epstein Mission Re German Austrian Refugees" and asks "you and coreligionists extend him maximum help in difficult task." HICEM notes that the same text was sent to Manila ritual slaughterer [*shochet*] Israel Konigsberg and M. Goldstein of the Manila Jewish Benevolent Association.

16 Bruno Schachner, Refugee Economic Corporation, letter to HICEM, Paris, August 1, 1938, RG 245.4 XX D-2, HI-HI, YIVO.

JRC was "afraid to invite too many Jews as they are under the impression that it may affect their own status in the P.I." Epstein endorsed Frieder's suggestion that HICEM "send and support a secretary to direct and assist in the work of the Refugee Committee," to help those refugees who were "qualified and able to arrive." Shortly thereafter, the job was offered to Epstein himself, who, by then, had arrived in the United States and was wholly absorbed in refugee work from the American end. Epstein felt obliged to decline the offer and the Manila position was apparently never filled.[17]

Despite no formal change in Philippine immigration policy, pressures to admit Jewish refugees increased after the July 1938 Evian conference in France, which failed to alleviate the crisis of Jewish resettlement. The situation became critical after the November *Kristallnacht* pogrom in Germany and Austria, further energizing Jack Rosenthal and other American-Jewish friends of Quezon and McNutt.

These Philippine residents piggy-backed on a suggestion already afloat in the Philippine congress, arguing that large-scale Jewish immigration could contribute to the development of the southern Philippine island of Mindanao. Jews had already settled in Mindanao. Israel Cohen had encountered a Syrian Jew from Zamboanga eighteen years earlier. The island had a restive Muslim population, and there were about 14,000 Japanese in Davao province, where they dominated the *abaca*, or "Manila hemp," industry. Aware of both Muslim separatist trends and Japanese commercial threats, Philippine authorities had long considered elaborate schemes for colonizing Mindanao with patriotic, ethnic Filipino citizens. The Philippine Congress earmarked eight to ten million dollars for public improvements on the island.

---

17   Lazar Epstein, New York, letter to HICEM, Paris, October 10, 1938; Dr. James Bernstein, HICEM, Paris, letters to HIAS, New York, September 6, 1938, and to Lazar Epstein, New York, October 25, 1938, all in RG 245,4 XX D-2, HI-HI, YIVO. For an obituary of Lazar Epstein and a description of his work on behalf of refugees, see Moses Todrin, "Obituary for Lasar D. Epstein [sic]," *Bulletin of the Igud Yotzei Sin*, Tel Aviv, 239 (1979): 12 (in English); M. Klyaver, "Obituary for Lazar Epstein," *Bulletin of the Igud Yotzei Sin* 239 (1979): 28–29 (in Russian). For general biography, see Jonathan Goldstein, "Israel Epstein in China: A Case Study of Father/Son Conflict in Jewish Ideological Formation," in *At Home in Many Worlds: Reading, Writing and Translating from Chinese and Jewish Cultures. Essays in Honour of Irene Eber*, ed. Raoul David Findeisen, Gad C. Isay, Amira Katz-Goehr, Yuri Pines, and Lihi Yariv-Laor (Wiesbaden: Otto Harrassowitz, 2009), 295–311, and Jonathan Goldstein, "The Lazar Epstein (1886–1979) Papers in YIVO: Their Usefulness to Scholars of Asian Jewish History," *Journal of East Asian Libraries* 156 (February 2013): 1–10.

Rosenthal and his coreligionists now added geopolitical factors in favor of the establishment of a much larger Jewish presence: Jewish professionals could assist the national tasks of offsetting Muslim insurgency and Japanese commercial domination. These practical considerations reinforced the humanitarian argument on behalf of European Jewry. The "Mindinao scheme" could even relieve pressure on China caused by the arrival of penniless European Jewish refugees in war-torn Shanghai.

For all these reasons, in December 1938 Quezon issued an informal but widely circulated proposal to admit qualified European Jewish refugees who wished to settle Mindanao. Coming a month after *Kristallnacht*, this advice was quickly publicized in Berlin's twice-weekly information bulletin, the *Jüdisches Nachrichtenblatt*, a newspaper which the Nazis purposely left open to provide information about opportunities for emigration. With a print run of seventy-six thousand, this periodical was, according to historian Bernard Wasserstein, "like a prison bulletin with the difference that, until October 1941, the prisoners were being urged to escape."[18] On January 6, 1939, weeks after Quezon made his proposal, the newspaper advertised "planned immigration outlooks" in "the Philippines's Mindanao province as proposed by President Quezon in December 1938," triggering direct appeals to Quezon in German, English, and Spanish. In the Philippine National Archives, Israeli historian Ber Kotlerman has found pleas on behalf of forty beleaguered European Jews, as well as Alex Frieder's letter to President Quezon in support of the Mindanao scheme.[19] See one of these letters at the end of this chapter, along with a translation.

On February 15, 1939, Quezon sent a formal message to the Philippine National Assembly urging the admission of 10,000 German Jewish professionals. He also recommended the substantial investment of Philippine $300 million to assist Jews in Mindanao. The Mindanao project then encountered unexpected opposition within the National Assembly. Assemblyman

---

18 Bernard Wasserstein, *On the Eve: The Jews of Europe before the Second World War* (Cambridge, MA: Harvard University Press, 2012), 262.

19 "L. J. K. Geplante Wanderung: Aussichten." *Judisches Nachrichtenblatt*, January 6, 1939, reproduced photographically in Ber Kotlerman, "Philippine Visas-for-Jews from the Perspective of the Unanswered Letters of 1939 to President Quezon," *Darbai ir dienos / Deeds and Days 2017* [publication of Vytautas Magnus University of Kaunas, Lithuania] 67 [17] (2017): 278–79, accessed April 5, 2018, https://ejournals.vdu.lt/index.php/d-ir-d/article/view/1405. For a well-documented history of the Mindanao scheme, see Frank Ephraim, "The Mindanao Plan: Practical Obstacles to Jewish Refugee Settlement," *Holocaust and Genocide Studies* 20 (Winter 2006): 410–36.

Isidro Varmenta from Mindanao argued that the Jews had never engaged in farming and that their presence would add to the already vexing problem of unemployment. Arguably the most influential opponent was the renowned independence fighter Emilio Aguinaldo, who had publicly stated that needy Filipinos, rather than Jewish refugees, should be settled on Mindanao. Still others argued for Jewish settlement on Polillo Island, only an hour's sail from Manila, rather than in remote Mindanao. Paralyzed by ongoing resistance from the host population and its representatives, the project then fell into a morass of surveys and red tape, the final report being issued on October 17, 1939, one month after the outbreak of World War II in Europe. According to historian Henry L. Feingold, "not until the spring of 1941 was the site ready for the absorption of refugees. By then . . . it had become extremely difficult to get them out of occupied Europe. Moreover, almost before the project could get underway, the islands were occupied by the Japanese." Precisely one German-Jewish settler family reached Mindanao. They were forced to leave after about six months due to mudslides, snakes, and other adversities.[20]

While this grandiose scheme for extensive Jewish settlement on Mindanao, like a similar plan for Madagascar, never materialized, Rosenthal, the Frieder brothers, and other American Jews were able to persuade Quezon to independently authorize the admission of perhaps as many as one thousand other Jews carefully selected on an individual basis. For domestic political reasons, this number was cut down from the 10,000 immigrants originally envisioned for Mindanao. These drastically reduced admissions were codified under the terms of the Philippine Immigration Act signed into law by US President Franklin Roosevelt on August 26, 1940. Quezon was then able to personally admit Jews in coordination with the JRC. However, those reduced admissions, like all previous ones except for those on the "Gneisenau" voyage, remained based on fixed employment criteria. For that reason, Max Weissler, *éminence grise* of German-Jewish Philippine immigrants who ultimately settled in Israel, coined the phrase "selective rescue" rather than the somewhat misleading term "open door" to characterize Philippine immigration policy.[21]

---

20 Henry L. Feingold, "Roosevelt and the Resettlement Question," in *Rescue Attempts during the Holocaust*, ed. Yisrael Gutman and Efraim Zuroff (Jerusalem: Yad Vashem, 1977), 152–56; Feingold, *The Politics of Rescue* (New York: Holocaust Library, 1970), 97–99, 112; [Quezon], *Messages*, 427; "Jews to Come in Gradually...," April 24, 1940; Ephraim, *Escape to Manila*, 15–77; Griese, "Jewish Community in Manila," 28; *The New York Times*, April 23, 1939, 33; Ephraim, "Mindanao Plan," 411–12, 419, 429.

21 Max Weissler, Hod Hasharon, Israel, email to author, May 20, 2013; Joseph Berger, "A Filipino-American Effort to Harbor Jews is Honored," *Points East* 20, no. 2 (July 2005):

Some small groups of Jews may have slipped into the Philippines by wholly surreptitious means. The Philippines relied on US diplomatic personnel for the worldwide implementation of its immigration policy. In the blunt words of Jack Netzorg, son of Manila Jewish community president Morton Netzorg, "wherever the American consular staff was friendly to the Jewish people Jews got out, and where they shrugged their shoulders Jews did not get out."[22] American consular staff, like the personnel of many other countries, were not immune to bribes. City University of New York historian Abraham Ascher recalls that his father, in the then-German city of Breslau (now Wrocław, Poland), got a visitor's visa in exchange for a bribe to US Vice-Consul Stephen Bernard Vaughan of 500 marks, equivalent to $200 at that time or about $3,000 in 2019. Ascher concludes that, in return for financial inducements, Vaughan issued visitor visas "not only to the United States, but also to the Philippines, then an American commonwealth whose foreign policy was under the authority of the United States. . . . Apparently Vaughan issued quite a few visas to Jews claiming to be agricultural experts, much needed specialists in the Philippines."[23] The British Secret Intelligence Service uncovered at least three similar escapades involving US consular personnel in Warsaw. It is impossible to calculate the full extent of document-trafficking, outright forging of visas, and the long-standing practice of immigrants jumping ship and vanishing into the rabbit-warren of Manila's docks and warehouses. We are only left with euphemisms and justifications for such behavior, ranging from "self interested benevolence by consuls of many nationalities" to "the banality of virtue."[24]

Arriving by one means or another, virtually all Jewish refugees to the Philppines were poor and wound up with temporary two-year visas. Netzorg notes that although "the Jewish community was very small [it] practiced tithing to help the refugees. Five hundred were brought over in a three year period."[25] To his credit, President Quezon donated seven and

---

15–16; Dan Pine, "Poker pals in Philippines took gamble, saved 1,200 Jews," *Points East* 28, no. 2 (July 2013): 12–13; Goldstein and Kotlowski, "Jews of Manila," 123–37; Ephraim, *Mindanao*, 426.

22   Netzorg, *Manila Memories*, 3.

23   Ascher wrote that "I confess to having been mildly irritated to learn that [Vaughan] issued some visas for 80 percent less than he had demanded from us." Abraham Ascher, *Community under Siege: The Jews of Breslau under Nazism* (Stanford: Stanford University Press, 2007), 6, 138, 141–43.

24   Wasserstein, *On the Eve*, 366, 438; Ascher, *Community*, 142.

25   Netzorg, *Manila Memories*, 3.

a half acres of his country estate at Marikina for a working farm for Jewish refugees not destined for Mindanao. Marikina Hall was dedicated on April 23, 1940, and housed forty residents. Viewing Quezon's philanthropy from a worldwide perspective, the only comparable gesture from a head of state at that time was that of President Trujillo of the Dominican Republic. He set aside 26,000 acres of his personal estate for the resettlement of German Jewish refugees.[26]

The voyage of the "Gneisenau" and the mere suggestion of the Mindanao scheme ignited desperate efforts by European Jews to escape to the Philippines. We are left with the evidence of appeals made to no avail. Using records in the Israeli national Holocaust archive Yad Vashem, Professor Kotlerman has determined that, except for one fortunate escapee, all forty of the aforementioned Jews who wrote President Quezon for Philippine visas met their deaths in various Nazi extermination facilities. Their tragedy is compounded by the fact that all forty of these direct appeals to President Quezon went unanswered.[27]

Conclusion: Shanghai as a Port of Last Resort for Jewish Refugees

The voyage of the "Gneisenau," and the subsequent elimination of Manila as port with non-selective entry requirements, effectively steered thousands of Jewish refugees toward Shanghai, despite its war-torn status. Strictly by default, Shanghai, the city from which the "Gneisenau" sailed for Manila in the fall of 1937, became the port of last resort for Jewish refugees. A case in point is that of Ernest Heppner's family. Desperate to leave Germany, they lacked the luck of their fellow Breslauer, the visa-buyer Abraham Ascher. But fortune smiled on the Heppners in other ways. Ernest and his mother marveled that when they disembarked from the German liner "Potsdam" at the Shanghai Customs House on March 28, 1939, "it was difficult to believe that no one asked for our papers as we passed through.... Hundreds of thousands of Jews in Europe were trying to find a country permitting them entry, and here Jews could just walk ashore."[28] After the war fortune smiled on them once again when they achieved their goal of settlement in Indianapolis.

---

26 Netzorg, *Manila Memories*, 3; Ephraim, *Escape to Manila*, 68–69, 192–93; Feingold, *Politics*, 112, 121.
27 Kotlerman, "Philippine Visas-for-Jews," 273–91.
28 Ernest G. Heppner, *Shanghai Refuge: A Memoir of the World War II Jewish Ghetto* (Lincoln, NE: University of Nebraska Press, 1993), 40.

The Frieder brothers, Quezon, McNutt, and their allies must be credited for their contribution to an effort which ultimately brought about 1,200 Jewish refugees, selected on an individual basis, to the Philippines. However, with the bizarre exception of the "Gneisenau," the overall Jewish attempt at *mass rescue* was one of desperate hopes, shattered dreams, and minimal acceptances. Future Israeli President Chaim Weizmann summarized this tragedy in his observation at the time that "the world is divided into two groups of nations—those that want to expel the Jews and those that do not want to receive them."[29] The remnant of Jews left on the Continent experienced, in historian Bernard Wasserstein's words, "the agitated ineffectuality of flies sealed in a bottle, slowly suffocating. Wholly defenseless, largely friendless, and more and more hopeless, the European Jews, on the eve of their destruction, waited for the barbarians."[30]

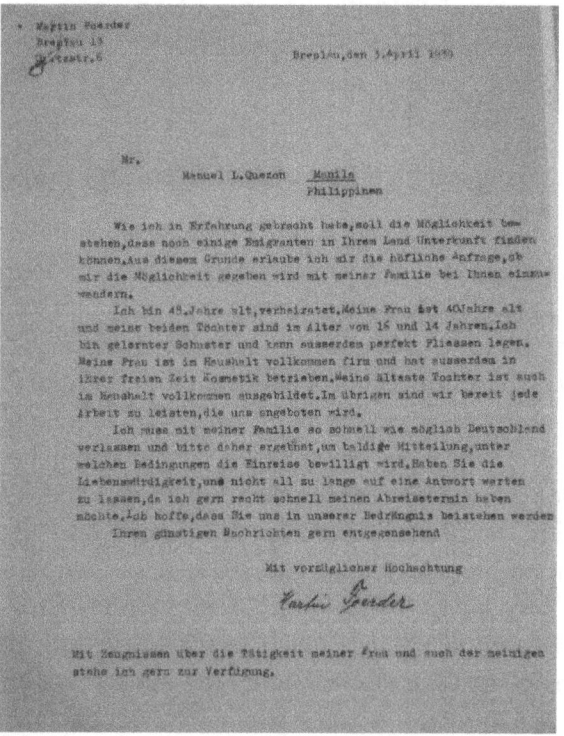

Letter of Martin Foerder to Manuel L. Quezon, President of the Philippines, April 3, 1939

---

29 Weizmann quoted in Laurie and Maurice Cowan, *The Wit of the Jews* (Nashville: Aurora, 1970), 71; Feingold, *Roosevelt*, 179–80.
30 Wasserstein, *On the Eve*, 436.

Translation of the letter's text:

As I have learned, there is a possibility that some immigrants can still find accommodation in your country. Because of that, I allow myself the polite inquiry whether I can be given the possibility to immigrate with my family to your place.

I am forty-eight years old, married. My wife is forty years old and my two daughters are sixteen and fourteen. I am a trained shoemaker and can also perfectly lay tiling. My wife is an excellent housewife and has also worked in cosmetics in her free time. My oldest daughter is also fully trained in housework. Additionally, we are willing to do any work that is offered to us.

I have to leave Germany with my family as soon as possible, and therefore sincerely request to be informed as soon as possible under what conditions the entry may be granted. Please have the kindness not to make us wait too long for an answer, because I would like to know my departure date very soon. I hope that you will assist us in our plight.

Waiting for your favorable news,

With highest esteem,
Martin Foerder

I am happy to supply testimonies of my wife's activities and of mine.[31]

---

31 Martin Foerder, his wife Margot, and their two daughters Henny and Lilly were murdered in 1941 at the Ninth Fort in Kaunas, Lithuania. Document courtesy of the Rare Books and Manuscripts Department of the National Library of the Philippines.

Manli Ho[*]

Diplomatic Rescue: Shanghai as a Means of Escape and Refuge

Over eighty years ago, the city of Shanghai, China, became a refuge of last resort from the Holocaust for 18,000 European Jews. The very use of its name as a destination provided thousands of Jews with a means of escape from the Nazis, and my late father, Dr. Feng Shan Ho, a Chinese diplomat in Vienna, Austria, played a pivotal role.

On April 21, 2015, I joined representatives of Israel and China to place a bronze plaque at the former Chinese Consulate General building in Vienna, where my father performed his lifesaving activities more than seven decades ago. It was fitting on the seventieth anniversary of the end of World War II that there be such a reminder in Vienna, because that city became the ground zero of mass Jewish emigration after the *Anschluss*, or union of Austria and Germany in March 1938.

Up until then, the Nazis' effort to render Germany *Judenrein* or "cleansed of Jews" had not gained much momentum. But with the *Anschluss*

---

[*] Manli Ho was born in Cairo, Egypt, daughter of diplomat Feng Shan Ho, and grew up in Mexico, Bolivia, and Colombia. After graduating from Smith College in 1972, she joined *The Boston Globe*, where she was on the reporting team that earned the paper a Pulitzer Prize in 1975 for coverage of the Boston school desegregation crisis. In 1981, she helped found *China Daily*, China's national English language newspaper in Beijing, and continues to serve as a consultant to the paper. She has also been a reference specialist for the executive search firm of Isaacson Miller in Boston. For the past two decades, she has written about her father's rescues as well as mounted the photographic exhibits "On the Wings of the Phoenix: Feng Shan Ho and the Rescue of Austrian Jews" and the Chinese-language "Visas for Life—Feng Shan Ho and the Rescue of Austrian Jews" in the US, Israel, and China. She is now working on a book about her father.

in 1938, antisemitic violence and persecution of Jews escalated, as the historian Saul Friedlander wrote in his book *Nazi Germany and the Jews*: "The persecution in Austria, particularly in Vienna, outpaced that in the Reich. Public humiliation was more blatant and sadistic; expropriation better organized; forced emigration more rapid. The Austrians—their country renamed *Ostmark*—seemed more avid for anti-Jewish action than the citizens of what now became the old Reich."[1]

The offices of Vienna's Jewish community and Zionist institutions were closed and their leaders put in jail. The activities of all Jewish organizations and congregations were forbidden. Jews were banned from any public activity, including participation in scientific and educational institutions and the arts. In May 1938, the Nuremberg laws, which forcibly segregated Jews in German society and deprived them of their livelihood, were officially enforced in Austria. According to SS Chief Heinrich Himmler's own figures, the number of Austrian Jews persecuted under these laws would reach 220,000. By mid-May, a Property Transfer Office with nearly 500 employees was actively confiscating Jewish property, businesses, and bank accounts.

In August 1938, Hitler dispatched SS Lieutenant Adolf Eichmann, later one of the architects of the Final Solution, to take charge of the so-called Center for Jewish Emigration in Vienna. Combining economic expropriation with the coerced expulsion of Jews, it became a "model" of systematic persecution and oppressive bureaucratic rules for emigration. This "model" was subsequently instituted in all Nazi-occupied territories.

As daunting as the Nazi-instituted bureaucratic emigration process was, it paled in comparison to the difficulties Jews encountered in finding a place to go. Those seeking to emigrate needed permission in the form of an entry or end destination visa from the countries they were trying to enter. Even the countries they would pass through required permission in the form of transit visas. In July 1938, nearly all of the thirty-two participants of the Evian Conference on the Jewish refugee question had anti-immigration policies and were unwilling to open their doors any further to Jewish refugees.

My late father, Dr. Feng Shan Ho, was posted as first secretary to the Chinese diplomatic legation in Vienna in 1937. A few months after his

---

[1] Saul Friedlander, *Nazi Germany and the Jews, Volume 1: The Years of Persecution, 1933–1939* (New York: HarperCollins Publishers, 1977), 241–42.

arrival, Japan launched a full-scale invasion of China. My father, who was fluent in German, became the face of the Chinese legation in speaking out against the Japanese occupation. His speeches and debates with his Japanese counterpart were published in a book *China Verteidigt Sich* (China Defends Itself) (Vienna: Michael Winkler Verlag, 1937).

Feng Shan Ho, Chinese Consul General to Vienna, c. 1938 (courtesy of Manli Ho)

At the end of 1937, when Sun Fo,[2] then the chairman of the Chinese legislature, passed through Vienna, he asked about the mounting political tensions Austria faced with Hitler. The head of the Chinese legation in Vienna downplayed the crisis. Hitler, he reported, only wanted to change chancellors in Austria, which was not a serious problem. My father disagreed. As a doctoral student at the University of Munich, he had witnessed the rise of Adolf Hitler. He likened the situation to a fire in a paper bag, which would soon burst into flames. Austria would lose its independence, he warned, with concomitant disastrous results, especially for Jews. Three months later, the *Wehrmacht* crossed into Austria.

In March 1938, my father watched in horror as Hitler marched triumphantly into Vienna. The Austrians, he recalled later, were delirious in their welcome of Hitler. The famous Vienna Boys Choir assembled under

---

2 Sun Fo, who name is pronounced Sun Ke in Mandarin Chinese, was the son of Dr. Sun Yat-sen and a Nationalist Chinese politician.

a banner that read: "We sing for Adolf Hitler!" My father told me, "The women were especially fanatical in their (Nazi) salutes." He would later write in his memoir, "Since the annexation of Austria by Germany, the persecution of the Jews by Hitler's 'devils' became increasingly fierce. The fate of Austrian Jews was tragic, persecution a daily occurrence."[3]

Less than a month after the *Anschluss*, the first Austrian Jews were sent to Dachau and Buchenwald concentration camps. They were told by Nazi authorities that if they emigrated from Austria immediately, they would be released. Many Austrian Jews wanted to emigrate to the United States. However, America not only required an affidavit of financial sponsorship, but had long ago filled its Austrian quota. Those who wished to go to Palestine found that Britain, under pressure from the Arabs, had severely reduced the quota for Jewish emigrants. In order to bar Jewish refugees from crossing their border, the Swiss demanded that Jews be identified by a red "J" stamped on their passports.

For Jews, obtaining emigration papers became a desperate and agonizing quest for survival. Here is how one refugee described it:

> Visas! We began to live visas day and night. When we were awake, we were obsessed by visas. We talked about them all the time. Exit visas. Transit visas. Entrance visas. Where could we go? During the day, we tried to get the proper documents, approvals, stamps. At night, in bed, we tossed about and dreamed about long lines, officials, visas. Visas.[4]

All the foreign consulates in Vienna were besieged by desperate Jewish visa applicants day after day, but most did not offer help. This led to some bitter black humor among Jews over their plight. One joke went like this: a Jew goes to a travel agency shortly after the *Anschluss*. He inquires about emigration. The agent brings up several countries, which are promptly discounted. One requires an exorbitant amount of money, another requires a labor permit, a third does not admit immigrants, and so on. While the two men are reviewing the options, they twirl a globe on the desk. Finally, the desperate Jew asks, "Haven't you got another globe?"

---

3   Ho Feng Shan, 外交生涯四十年 [Forty Years of My Diplomatic Life] (Hong Kong, Chinese University Press, 1990), 75-78.
4   Quoted by Leo Spitzer, *Hotel Bolivia, The Culture of Memory and a Refuge from Nazism* (New York: Hill and Wang, 1998), 35.

Jewish visa applicants in line at a consulate in Vienna

My father could not bear to stand by. He later recalled that "there was an American relief organization which was urgently trying to save the Jews. I kept in close contact with this organization. I spared no effort in using any means possible, saving who knows how many Jews!" That American relief organization was the American Jewish Joint Distribution Committee (called the "Joint"). However, unlike his fellow diplomats, my father faced a unique dilemma at that time: most of his home country and its ports of entry had been occupied by the Japanese since 1937. Any document or entry visa issued by a Chinese diplomat would certainly not be recognized by the Japanese occupiers.

In order to help Jewish refugees, my father came up with a way to use an entry visa as a means of exit or escape. The Joint became the major supporter of the Vienna *Kultusgemeinde* in providing emigration aid to Austrian Jews. After the war, it noted the predicament that Ho had faced at that time:

> ... virtually all the ports of entry into China and its principal cities, the places which foreigners came or were permitted by Chinese visas were in the hands of the Japanese. Surely this was only too well known to the Chinese Consul, a representative of the Nationalist government, who unquestionably knew or must be regarded as knowing that no representative of his government exercised authority at the ports to which the applicant could go.... In fact, the real and underlying purpose for the visa was to assist as an act of mercy and humanity these persecutees to escape from Austria.[5]

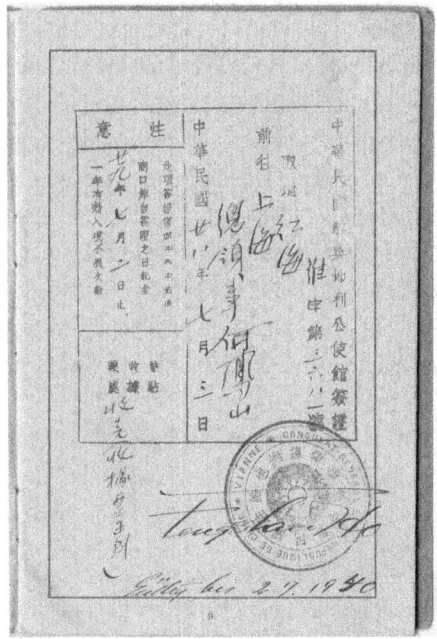

Shanghai Visa #3639 issued by Feng Shan Ho (courtesy of Manli Ho)

My father's entry visas were issued to only one end destination—the Chinese port city of Shanghai, a place unknown to most European Jews of that time. Soon after Hitler's rise to power in 1933, a handful of German

---

5   Affidavit of American Jewish Joint Distribution Committee General Counsel Jerome J. Jacobsen in the case of Egon Laufer with the US Department of Justice Immigration and Naturalization Service, July 1951, AJJDC Givat Joint Archives, Geneva III, Box L-24, File 426, p. 13.

Jewish doctors and dentists had answered an advertisement for medical professionals in Shanghai and had set up successful practices there in the foreign community. In the intervening years, there were few further arrivals until the mass influx of Jewish refugees into Shanghai at the end of 1938, following the *Anschluss* and *Kristallnacht*.

By then, Shanghai required no entry documents. In 1937, the Chinese sections of the city had fallen into the hands of the Japanese military. The Chinese Nationalist government had retreated to Chongqing, leaving Shanghai harbor unmanned and wide open, without passport control or immigration. As a result, anyone could land without papers.

My father was clear in his intent in issuing visas to Shanghai. They were meant to provide proof of emigration to leave Austria and a means to go elsewhere. He said: "The visas were to Shanghai 'in name' only. In reality, they were a means to help Jews to leave Austria and eventually find a way to the US, Britain or other preferred destinations."[6] These visas provided proof of an "end destination," so that refugees could legally obtain transit or temporary visas from countries which otherwise would not have allowed them passage. The majority of Shanghai visa recipients from Austria did not go to Shanghai, but used these visas to find their way to the Philippines, Cuba, Palestine, England and even the United States. Fritz Heiduschka, for example, was detained by the Nazis and was released only after his wife got him a Shanghai visa dated June 20, 1938. With Shanghai visas, the family weathered the war in the Philippines.

During the trial of Recha Sternbuch, a Swiss Jewish rescuer of Austrian and German Jews in 1938 and 1939, her lawyer explained how these visas were used in the illegal Palestine transports in the spring of 1939:

> . . . there were hundreds of passports that were equipped with Chinese visas, although the real goal was to land illegally on the coast of Palestine. These visas were used with the intention of fooling the countries where they passed through, because Italy, for instance, would never give a transit visa unless the final destination was indicated.[7]

---

6   Ho Feng Shan, oral memoir, 1988, tape #46B. At my suggestion, my father recorded his recollections of his childhood and his diplomatic career prior to writing his memoirs. These tapes were found after his death.

7   Joseph Friedenson and David Kranzler, *Heroine of Rescue: The Incredible Story of Recha Sternbuch Who Saved Thousands from the Holocaust* (New York: Mesorah Publications, Ltd., 1984), 31. Recha Sternbuch was put on trial by the Swiss authorities for helping thousands of Jews escape to Palestine via the illegal transports in 1938 and 1939.

Most of the passengers on these illegal Palestine transports were young, because their parents wanted to save the future of the Jewish community. Among those who escaped to Palestine on the transport ship "Sakaria" with Shanghai visas from my father's consulate in Vienna were the Lilienthal sisters: Ricarda, who was nineteen years old, and Lilith, twelve years old. As the sheltered daughters of a very prominent Viennese family, the two sisters came to board the illegal transport ship for the harsh and hazardous journey to Palestine wearing white gloves and toting their hat boxes.

Practicing what he called a "liberal policy," my father authorized the issuing of visas to any and all who asked. Having been turned down by other consulates, Jews soon discovered that they could get visas at the Chinese Consulate, and as word spread, long lines formed in front of the Consulate building. Even the passport of a pigtailed eleven-year-old child like Lotte Lustig bore a red "J," denoting her as a Jew. Her assiduous father obtained some American telephone directories and Lotte looked up every Lustig in the United States. She wrote to each of them asking for sponsorship, but was turned down by them all. The Lustigs obtained visas from my father's Consulate on October 18, 1938, a day when at least 106 visas were issued, and ended up in Shanghai.[8]

When I met the late Gerda Gottlieb Kraus, she told me the story of how her husband Hans Kraus obtained visas for himself and his family. She said: "He was nineteen years old at the time. There were long, long lines in front of the Consulate and while people were waiting, the Gestapo was outside harassing them and beating them up. There were so many people that Hans stood in line for many days, wondering when he would be able to get in. One day, when he lined up again, he saw the Chinese Consul General's car about to enter the Consulate gate. He saw that the car window was open, so he thrust his visa application papers through the open car window. Apparently, the Consul General received it because Hans then got a call and was told that visas were ready." Gerda Gottlieb met Hans Kraus in Shanghai, and they were married there and later emigrated to Canada.[9]

More importantly, in 1938 and 1939 the Shanghai visas were useful to gain the release of those jailed or in concentration camps, especially after *Kristallnacht*, a two-day rampage of burning, looting, and terror unleashed by the Nazis in Germany and Austria on November 9–10, 1938. Throughout

---

8   Lotte Lustig Marcus tells this story from her perspective in the next chapter.
9   Gerda Gottlieb Kraus, interview with author, Vancouver, Canada, October 19, 1999, and her subsequent written testimony to Yad Vashem.

Austria and Germany, synagogues, including the Tempelgasse synagogue in Vienna, were burned, 7,500 Jewish shops were looted, and nearly 30,000 Jewish men between the ages of 16 and 64, mostly heads of households, community leaders and businessmen, were arrested and deported to Sachsenhausen, Buchenwald, and Dachau concentration camps. The historian Sir Martin Gilbert called that infamous pogrom the "prelude to the destruction" of Europe's Jews.[10]

The Austrian physician Jakob Rosenfeld was among those arrested and deported to Dachau and then to Buchenwald. He was released in 1939 after his sister Sabine acquired the necessary documents for him—a passport, Shanghai visa, and ship tickets. He went first to Shanghai, but subsequently joined the Chinese Communist revolutionaries, becoming a general in the People's Liberation Army Medical Corps. He is considered a hero of the Chinese Communist revolution.[11]

In making Shanghai an end destination, my father had provided a failsafe to refugees not able to land elsewhere. After the *Anschluss* and *Kristallnacht*, Jews throughout Nazi-occupied territories knew that in China there existed a port which required no entry papers. This precipitated a mass exodus by ship and later by rail to Shanghai between 1938 and 1940.

In early 1939, following the plummeting of Sino-German relations, the legislator Sun Fo proposed that China's Yunnan Province be set aside as a special zone for Jewish refugees, in hopes of currying support from what the Chinese perceived as the powerful and wealthy American and British Jewish communities. However, the plan never came to fruition for lack of funds, and Shanghai remained the destination for Jewish refugees.[12]

As Evelyn Pike Rubin wrote in 2007 on a Rickshaw Chatterbox discussion:

---

10 Martin Gilbert, *Kristallnacht: Prelude to Destruction* (New York: HarperCollins Publishers, 2006) 15.

11 This information is based on extensive interviews with Margaret Rosenfeld Frija, Jakob Rosenfeld's niece, her detailed written, unpublished, family history, as well as Emigration Questionnaire of the Jewish Community Vienna (IKG) for Rosenfeld, Jakob, files 23065 and 23066.

12 For more on this Yunnan proposal, see the chapter in this volume by Xu Xin, "Chinese Responses to the Holocaust: Chinese Attitudes toward Jewish Refugees in the Late 1930s and Early 1940s."

I am from Breslau [now Wrocław] and all I can remember is that my parents seem to have heard about Shanghai from the Austrian Jews who needed to leave right after the *Anschluss*. I guess someone in Austria heard about Shanghai being an "open city" and the word spread and also got to us in Germany.[13]

By the outbreak of World War II on September 1, 1939, about 131,000 of the 206,000 Jews living in Austria during the *Anschluss* on March 13, 1938, had emigrated. Of those only about 5,800 went to Shanghai. Most of the Austrian Jews who were able to obtain visas from my father's consulate used them as a means to escape elsewhere.

How many Shanghai visas were issued by the Chinese Consulate in Vienna under my father's watch? We shall never know the exact figure. The best we can determine now is that they numbered in the thousands, based on the serial numbers of some still existing visas and the only surviving documentation from the Chinese Foreign Ministry, a report written by my father's successor as Consul General in early 1940. According to that report, the Chinese Consulate in Vienna issued an average of 400 or 500 visas a month to Jewish refugees in 1938 and 1939.

In this same report, my father's successor said that "the Foreign Ministry had long ago dealt with this issue (of visas to Jewish refugees)," leaving little doubt about what the official Chinese policy was. Therefore, he reported, when he assumed his post, he "adhered strictly to regulations" and "had curtailed the issuance of these kinds of visas." Desperate to salvage deteriorating diplomatic relations with Germany, Chen Chieh, the Chinese ambassador to Berlin, had ordered my father to desist from issuing visas to Jews. Angry that my father had disregarded his orders, he used the pretext that there was a "rumor of the selling of visas" to launch a witch hunt. He dispatched an investigator to Vienna who left no stone unturned, but could find no wrongdoing and left empty-handed.

On April 8, 1939, roughly a year after he began issuing visas, my father was punished with a demerit for disobeying orders. Just prior to that, the Consulate building at 3 Beethoven Platz, the same one on which the plaque was placed, was confiscated by the Nazis. The Chinese Nationalist government not only did not protest this breach of extraterritoriality, but refused to give my father funds to relocate. My father moved the Consulate to much

---

13 Evelyn Pike Rubin tells her family's story below in the chapter "Survival in Shanghai 1939–1947".

smaller quarters around the corner at 22 Johannesgasse and paid all the expenses himself.

My father was never reunited with any of those he had helped. He was unknown to most of them. After his death in 1997, it was only by chance that I began to uncover the extent of his mass rescue activities. During his lifetime, my father neither sought nor received recognition for his deeds. In fact, he rarely spoke of his tenure as the Chinese Consul General in Vienna.

Of his reason for helping Jewish refugees, he said simply this: "On seeing the Jews so doomed, it was only natural to feel deep compassion, and from a humanitarian standpoint, to be impelled to help them."[14]

---

14 Ho, oral memoir, Tape # 48B.

Lotte Marcus*

305/13 Kungping Road

Let me begin by saying I consider myself a fully recovered Shanghailander who has reflected on and edited (in oral and written forms) my Shanghai story for over seventy years. I am grateful both for the shelter that was given to us in World War II and for the lack of antisemitism shown by the Chinese. First of all, I'd like to honor my mother's and father's memory, and those of their generation, the older refugees who arrived in Shanghai at forty, fifty, sixty, seventy years of age, a generation that has been less recorded in today's recounting of our history.

To begin, let me take you into our single room at 305/13 Kungping Road in Hongkou, where we lived from 1943 to 1947. "It has a toilet and a bathroom," my father announced when he returned from his search for housing, in order to make our forced move to Hongkou in February 1943. "One toilet?" asked my blond and blue-eyed mother, whose eyes were growing larger daily at what was coming next. "Yes, and it will 'only' be shared by ten people. We're on the third floor."

By this time, four years into the immigration, my mother had stopped reminding my father of the five-bedroom flat we lived in at Schulerstrasse 20 in the inner city of Vienna. "*Sprechen wir nicht davon*" ("Let's not talk

---

* Lotte Marcus was born in Vienna in 1927. She and her parents escaped to Shanghai in 1939 on the "Conte Biancamano." Her father died in Shanghai at age forty-seven. She graduated from the Shanghai Jewish School in 1945. After the war, she and her mother came to San Francisco on a troop ship in 1947, and settled in Los Angeles, where she became a legal secretary for Metro-Goldwyn-Mayer. She married the writer Alan Richard Marcus in 1952. She graduated from University of California at Santa Cruz in 1962, and earned the master's in 1972 and the PhD in psychology in 1985. She taught English to immigrants and had a thirty-five-year career as a clinical psychologist in Monterey, California. With her husband, she founded AKTOS Inc., an educational company dedicated to producing and teaching video dramas for ESL classrooms. She was one of the founders of Monterey's Multiple Sclerosis Quality of Life Project. The Los Angeles-based Freedom to Live Foundation gave her its Spirit Award in 2003.

about it") had become the motto of our lives. My father was right: one toilet was not bad, when most of the Chinese around us were living in outhouses, where human waste was carried on two bamboo poles with ropes attached to buckets, then sold for manure for vegetable fields. "And you can cook on the roof garden." He didn't say we wouldn't have a kitchen, nor that the roof was flat and could accommodate one flower pot with coals, which had to be fanned for an hour until the coals were hot enough so a one-pot dish—a slice of chicken, Chinese cabbage, herbs—would stew in it. But it took a lot of fanning. As for the rest, we ate bread—bread for breakfast, bread for lunch, bread with dinner.

Oskar and Grete Lustig, parents of Lotte Marcus, before emigration

    No telephone. No refrigeration. We bought ice blocks and stuck them into a box, but the water dribbled, food got wet, and we spent time mopping floors. "Besides," my mother said, "the guy I buy it from spits each time he takes a breath. I'm afraid he has tuberculosis, I won't go there." So we gave up on ice. Our European down blankets are where we kept our cooked food warm. "*Fisch im Bett*" ("fish in bed"), my mother's note read when I came home from work earlier than my parents did.

"And we get hot water from the water carrier for bathing," my father promised us, continuing to gild the lily. "We will make a list with our other neighbors as to who gets the bath tub on what day." That is how it turned out. Monday was our bath day. My father sweated the most, so he got the first round of clean water, my mother the second, and I got the last. After all, I was the youngest. But, ah, the water flushed down, and we didn't have to carry it back! And we had an *amah* who came and washed our sheets in the river or at a communal wash site for servants only!!!!

Our rented room, 20 x 15 feet in size (was the landlord Chinese or Jewish?) became a marvel of adaptation: with windows on both sides "so fresh air can come in," my mother happily said, but soon they had to be covered with black air raid curtains, so the room was stifling. Clack, clack, clack, we heard the gunslinging Japanese soldiers march from lane to lane to check that no slit of light escaped, causing us to be on the alert night after sultry night. But we needed light, for it was at night that my father and I, seated by our one table, washed thousands of postage stamp sheets which my father purchased during the day, to be cleaned and reordered so as to resell them the next day. He had ingeniously rigged up a leather bag in which he put the stamps. Luckily, they weren't heavy, as he set out, with hand towels on the handle bars on his second-hand Japanese-made bicycle, pedaling 30 minutes across the Garden Bridge into the business section of town, one way, in 102-degree heat in the summer. A seven-towel bar meant the day was hot, humid, sweaty. It meant I had to run out and buy extra water, so my father wouldn't dehydrate.

9 p.m. was curfew time. I hated to come home. My parents slept kitty-corner on couches my father had hammered next to a table that was our stamp bench, a dining room, a catch-all table. The couch converted into beds at night. My half of the room was partitioned and I slept right next to the sink, the only sink, and my mother's Singer foot paddle sewing machine. She sewed American Indian suits for a Chinese store, a negotiation which she had proudly initiated, brought off much to my father's "macho" surprise. Next to that stood Didi's bassinet—Didi, all of four and a half years old, was my responsibility: son of a wealthy Chinese who wanted his son to live with us for 500 Yuen a month (not sure) so I would teach him German, so he could study German engineering at a university when it came time to study.

My father was against it, but I held my ground until Didi cried at the air raid signals, "*Weg, weg*" ("go away"), he cried, and I reluctantly returned him to his father and went back to work at the Jewish hospital, where the kitchen help often gave me a three-pack tin can full of food, which was a feast for house and a pride for me. I wanted so to ease it for my parents, for my mother whom I often heard crying quietly behind her cotton curtain.

So we managed to cajole this cramped space into a bedroom, a dining room, a pantry, a sewing room, my bedroom, a child's corner of a bedroom, my parents' bedroom, a storage room, a work room, a food-warming room, a room to cry in, a room to improvise our hopes, our fears.

Secondly, I'd like to honor the two communities, the refugees and the Chinese, with whom we lived door to door in Hongkou. I mention the issues of safety.

Let me walk you through the sparse mile and a quarter city area of Hongkou, half an hour by bicycle away from the business part of Shanghai and the European settlements, an area where squalid buildings collided with cobbled streets, bicycles, rickshaws, pedestrians, and where over 100,000 Chinese citizens lived huddled together, with and without plumbing. In February 1943, by Japanese military order, another 8,000 European refugees had to be accommodated.[1] Consider then, about 2,500 Jews were already living there in seven resurrected buildings ironically named *Heime*, surviving on welfare in cramped quarters, 10 to 50 in one large communal bedroom. Too hot in the summer, too cold in the winter, surviving on food dished out by soup kitchens. Another 5,000 were barely able to support themselves, selling off their belongings one by one, or, as I shall tell you later, marginally living and improvising.[2]

Which brings me to an important social subtext. How many of us refugees knew, uprooted and stateless as we were in 1943, that only six years earlier, in 1937, at a time when Nazism in Europe was growing, when German and Austrian families, who for years had been settled, accepted by their neighbors, had fought for their country in World War I, were suddenly being excluded, that *at the very same time*, thousands and thousands of miles away, Shanghai received hundreds of thousands of Chinese refugees, who fled for their lives from the Japanese attack in Nanjing and

---

1. Before the creation of the Designated Area, the 17,000 to 18,000 Jewish refugees had been split approximately equally between Hongkou and the rest of Shanghai.
2. David Kranzler, *Japanese, Nazis and Jews: The Jewish Refugee Community of Shanghai 1938–1945* (New York: Yeshiva University Press, 1976), 287, gives the figure of 2,500 for the total residents in *Heime*, and says about 5,000 to 6,000 needed the free meals provided by the *Heime* to survive.

other places.[3] Worse yet, in Shanghai and Hongkou, the same Hongkou that was forced to take us in in 1943, a second Chinese-Japanese war had been raging in 1937 with Japanese fighting the Chinese Nineteenth Army, in street battles, barricade by barricade. How many of us refugees knew of the bombings, the shellings, that the very same citizens into whose venue we now fell may themselves have been escapees from the countryside wars into Shanghai's foreign concessions. Shanghai's population had swelled to 4,000,000 in 1937. They, too, had participated in, witnessed, or been victims suffering from loss. Six years later, they received thousands of Europeans, who were forced into the Designated Area, stripped of all legal protection, designated as stateless.

So side by side, two communities existed, who for the last six years had been denigrated, victimized, lost homes. They shared a commonality of oppression, though from different causes, due to differing history and culture. The Chinese suffered colonialism, the Jews suffered from Nazi anti-semitism. But both endured hunger, disease, air raids, blackouts, inflation, bad hygiene, starvation—sharing in a daily struggle of uncertainty as to their survival.

At eleven and a half years old, I became an adult. Not only did I become my father's partner in cleaning, sorting, and pasting his stamp collection, our main source of income, I also started, with one of my boyfriends, "The Golden Star Paper Bag Co.," devoted to making bundles of toilet papers using the unwritten side of Chinese comic books. We sold them to refugee grocery stores, since during the diarrhetic hot summers the numbers of packages doubled from the number in the winter. I often was sent on my bicycle by our hospital, because I spoke English, to Chinese pharmacies in town, across the Garden Bridge, to secure drugs for diabetes, for respiratory and stomach infections. The Chinese store owners never treated me as a child, but validated our exchange with courtesy, with formality, a bow. We never shook hands. I also learned by chance that Chinese barbers valued human hair from which they made hairnets. So every three months, I sold my hair by the ounce and received a goodly sum of money, which I had determined by previously comparing prices from different barbers.

We were "free." We had no overseers. But, like refugees all over, we had no control over our situation. It was as if we were enclosed by a hum

---

3   Read Iris Chang, *The Rape of Nanking: The Forgotten Holocaust of World War II* (New York: Basic Books, 1997).

of weariness, which at any time could turn into a disastrous shriek, caused by hunger, illness, inflation. Or through hostile, random impulses, such as the mandate to move all 18,000 of us into a one-and-a-half-mile radius of houses in February 1943, with 100,000 Chinese already living there, some without running water, electricity, etc.

"Psychological trauma," writes Judith Herman Lewis in her groundbreaking book *Trauma and Recovery*, "is an affliction of the powerless."[4] Political refugees are in the front line to succumb to this affliction. It is, to me, a historic loss that interest in Shanghai refugees emerged in the last ten years, when the refugees who had come to Shanghai in their middle years, like my parents in their forties, had already died in their eighties and nineties. So, over the years, I have had the urge to apologize to those Chinese. I wished I could have helped. I wished we could have raised each other up, but instead, if the war had lasted longer, we would have sunk further into our despair. I have one regret: neither I nor most refugees chose to seriously study Mandarin Chinese. I spoke a few words of functional Shanghai dialect. We were there seven and a half years and never chose to study Chinese! Language, the great Separator!

I see nothing "harmonious" about those years—not for us, not for them. We were bound by hardships of war. We lived at "the outer edge" until the end of the war liberated us.

The Chinese have made enormous strides in this immense country. Shanghai today is nothing like the Shanghai then. But there is nothing shameful to say that both our communities lacked governing authorities, except for the military Japanese authority, who poked their loaded guns at us at whatever corner they happen to stand, who themselves were foot soldiers, country bumpkins, task-mastered from an imperial distance.

Shanghai, I've read, was a sanctuary, a safe haven. Let me correct: it was a haven, but it was not safe. From the beginning of 1938 to the fall of 1939, when the deluge of Jewish refugees poured in, according to Dr. David Kranzler's pioneering book, the Jews of Shanghai, in collaboration with the Municipal Council, formed committees: the International Committee for Assistance to Jewish European Refugees, the Paul Komor committee. They scrounged for assistance, while battling fears and rumors of crime waves that might cause a loss of face for the colonial communities vis-à-vis the Chinese, if Shanghai were overrun by refugees with no

---

4   Judith Herman Lewis, *Trauma and Recovery: The Aftermath of Violence—From Domestic Abuse to Political Terror* (New York: Basic Books, 1997), 33.

visible support. The local Baghdadi Jews actively collected moneys for our assistance, but were simultaneously working to stop the influx of Jews. After scary "negotiations" with the Japanese, it was only seven months after we landed in January 1939 that both a permit from the Japanese and a large sum of money was required of all arrivals, a sum, incidentally, which would have excluded my family.[5]

Religion, or being Jewish, was never an issue in my memory: with our round eyes and white skin, we were perceived as Whites—the majority of the population we came in contact with saw us as *nakojins*, as white-faced. We were treated orderly, correctly, politely—but there was no chance, in business dealings, to do more than that. And we, on our side, had no tour guide, no script to orient us. Neither were we really one community: we were never registered, never counted, as Irene Eber mentions in her book *Wartime Shanghai*.[6] We were Austrians, Germans, Poles, Czechs, bringing our different cultures into a strange land.

This is not a criticism. Shanghai, while we were there, was beset by political divisions. Anticolonialism, labor unrest, inflation, corruption were rampant. It's only a side bar, but based on readings and my memory there were no Chinese who volunteered to work on the above committees, except for those Chinese who were hired in our offices. We saw dead bodies carted away daily on the street. Bacterial and viral epidemics were endemic. My mother suffered from typhoid fever, and I had liver flukes every summer. Shanghai with its anarchy was a haven, but safe? Each of our steps were improvisations.

So it follows that we must praise and show our gratitude to those who did help. First, the Chinese official, Dr. Feng Shan Ho, who gave my

---

5   The new rules about entry to Shanghai were made public in August 1939. Entry was limited to the members of a Shanghai resident's immediate family, a resident's intended spouse, a holder of a contract for a job in Shanghai, or someone who could show a deposit of US $400 as "guarantee money." These applied to the areas controlled by the Western-dominated Municipal Council. The Japanese did not require the guarantee money, but gave out very few entry permits after that date. Kranzler, *Japanese, Nazis and Jews*, 272–73.

6   Irene Eber, *Wartime Shanghai and the Jewish Refugees from Central Europe: Survival, Co-Existence, and Identity in a Multi-Ethnic City* (Berlin: De Gruyter, 2012). Although there are no complete counts of the Central and Eastern European refugees who landed in Shanghai, there were several attempts made to keep track of their numbers. The German Consulate in Shanghai collected information about German citizens from the welfare committee set up by the Baghdadi Jews, which includes 5546 registration forms of refugees at least 16 years old. The Japanese took a census of foreigners in part of Hongkou in 1944, and counted a total of about 13,700 Jewish refugees, but there were many omissions. These counts are discussed in the Introduction.

parents and thousands of others our visa to Shanghai, as Consul General in Vienna, Austria.

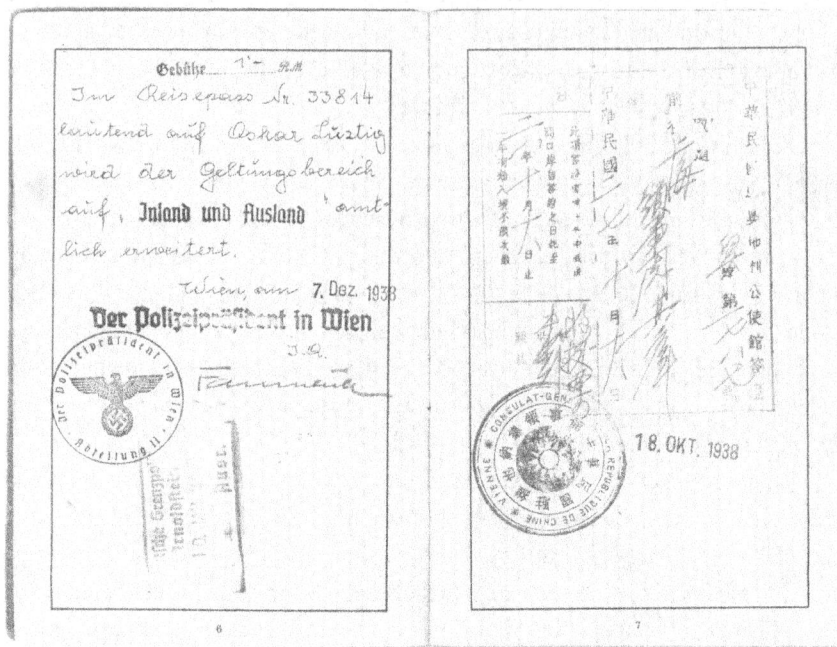

Chinese visa issued by Feng Shan Ho to Oskar Lustig

He was demoted for his activity by the government then, the very government that is now claiming him. He has been honored by Yad Vashem, thanks to the efforts of his daughter.[7]

It was the local Jews, the Baghdadi Jews, like Horace Kadoorie, Victor Sassoon, and the Abraham family, who contributed financially. As British subjects, they had become wealthy in Bombay, and saw new opportunities as the nineteenth-century treaties opened Shanghai to trade.

But for me, the heroine of our Shanghai story surely is Laura Margolis, the American social worker, and her partner Manuel Siegel, who were sent by the American Jewish Joint Distribution Committee to "investigate" the situation of the European Jews in Shanghai. I knew Laura personally, because I worked in 1944–1945 in the Shanghai Jewish Hospital where my father died of cancer and where she would make daily and weekly rounds: a big-boned woman with brown eyes, she exuded confidence. "That's a real

---

7   See earlier article in this book by Manli Ho.

American," I remember telling my mother. It was she who, in one afternoon, in a powwow with a Japanese overseer, arranged that the Japanese would accept from $30,000 to $100,000 per month to be used for food and shelter in Hongkou. She brought harmony by finding food to go through our hungry stomachs.

Laura Margolis, representative of the Joint in Shanghai

I see the gratitude that was been poured out at our conference by my fellow Shanghailander as the gratitude of *hindsight*—but also, justly, gratitude for a story of resilience and enterprise. There were cafés, theater, reconstruction of buildings with indoor plumbing. Ours was a triumph of good timing: the war ended when inflation and hunger were increasing.

Nevertheless, if a program such as the one I was honored to participate in is to have a larger meaning, I plead with you to retrace your steps and stand with the refugees as they lived through the uncertain present, the unknown future. That was at least until we knew that the war had turned in America's favor. Only in this way will you understand the formation of trauma today as it affects the generation of refugees circling the globe, be they Arab refugees who have been housed in camps for years, or the Rohingya boat people from Myanmar, or children from Eritrea who try to make it to Italy on capsizing boats, the new refugees from Syria, from Iraq, the busloads of Mexican or Guatemalan children who sit in detention camps at my own American borders, for whom, just like for us then, the earth trembles with uncertainty and fear. Trauma creeps in and each of us has a breaking point.

It's great to commemorate with museums. But the honor, the gratitude, in dark and evil times must go to those who took *risks* to help us: Dr. Ho, when he risked disapproval from his superiors; Laura Margolis, when she stuck it out in Shanghai and didn't leave after Pearl Harbor, and was subsequently interned; and, yes, my modest father, who risked to opt for the territory ahead.

Evelyn Pike Rubin*

Survival in Shanghai 1939–1947

I was born in Breslau, Germany (now Wrocław, Poland). When the Nuremberg Laws were promulgated in 1935, we started looking for countries we could immigrate to. A big red letter "J" was placed in our passports in 1938.

We attempted to go to Brazil, to Palestine, to Cuba, to England, to America, all to no avail. In 1938, my great-aunt, living in New York at the time, sent us an affidavit. However, under the existing quota system, we were informed that we were placed on the Polish quota waiting list, filled at the time, only because my father's place of birth had been ceded to Poland under the Versailles Treaty. It seemed there was no way out of Nazi-ruled Germany, till we heard about one little glimmer of hope. Shanghai, China, had been declared an "open" city. There was a good possibility one could go there without a visa, just for the price of a steamship ticket.

November 9–10, 1938, was *Kristallnacht*. My father was arrested and sent to the Buchenwald concentration camp, even though he had been a German soldier during World War I, and a prisoner of war of the French. During his incarceration, my mother purchased tickets for us to leave for Shanghai the following February. My father came home three weeks later. On February 9, 1939, we took the train to Naples, Italy, to board the "Hakozaki Maru" for the month-long voyage to Shanghai.

---

* Evelyn Pike Rubin was born in Germany and fled with her parents to Shanghai in February 1939. She attended the Shanghai Jewish School. She and her mother came to the US in 1947. She published her memoir, *Ghetto Shanghai* (New York: Shengold, 1993), lectures widely on her experiences, and is featured in the documentary film "Shanghai Ghetto." She is active in Jewish affairs in Jericho, NY.

Japanese ship "Hakozaki Maru"

We arrived in Shanghai on March 14, 1939. There were Baghdadi Jews who had arrived in the nineteenth century; Russians, Jewish and non-Jewish, who had fled there before, during, and after the 1917 Revolution; and business people from many other countries in Europe, as well as from the United States, who were in charge of branch offices of their respective firms. Also present were the American staff members of the American Jewish Joint Distribution Committee, who came with American funds to help the refugees settle in what was thought to be a temporary refuge. The Japanese occupied part of Shanghai as the victors of the Sino-Japanese War of 1937.

Aside from the culture shock, what greeted us were the horrific unhygienic conditions, very alien to a western European, which produced epidemics of wide proportion. We had to get inoculated against cholera, typhoid, paratyphoid three times a year and smallpox once a year. All drinking water had to be boiled at least five minutes past its boiling point and the same had to be done for all fruits and vegetables.

My mother sold the personal possessions we had brought with us to purchase an apartment in the French Concession. My parents established a typewriter business, with my father doing the repairs with a hired Chinese mechanic and my mother taking care of the business end. I continued my interrupted schooling at the Shanghai Jewish School. I learned English rather quickly, as well as French and Hebrew, which were part of the British curriculum that was followed by the School. My seventy-two-year-old paternal grandmother arrived in 1940.

1943 class at the Shanghai Jewish School

The subtropical climate, with cold, wet winters, monsoon rains that constantly flooded the streets, the summers with the high temperatures and humidity, wrought havoc with the refugees, already subjected to all the diseases around them. Then my father got ill and within a week he was dead, at the age of forty-three. The doctors figured it may have been a parasite he picked up in Buchenwald, where his war wound was left untreated, coupled with the unhygienic climatic conditions in Shanghai. I was ten, my mother was forty-nine and my grandmother was seventy-three years old. My mother continued running the typewriter business with the Chinese mechanic.

On December 8, 1941, we woke up to a tremendous explosion in the harbor of Shanghai and watched a parade of the Imperial Japanese Army and Navy. Soon thereafter, enemies of Japan and Germany were interned in camps where they were going to remain for the duration of the war. A tremendous food shortage developed, only slightly alleviated with sugar, flour, and rice rations. My mother now ran the typewriter business by herself. There was not much of a business, for her American and other foreign customers were either interned or had to liquidate their business and she could not afford the mechanic any longer.

On February 18, 1943, the Japanese issued a Proclamation to the refugee community stating that we had three months in which to "relocate to a designated area." In effect we were going to live in a ghetto in the slum Hongkou area. My grandmother died right before we moved. With three other families, we moved into a four-room house with one toilet, which we had to install, cold running water, and no heat. We did our cooking on a little Chinese stove on the rooftop, forming egg-shaped coals from coal dust mixed with cold water. The stove had to be constantly fanned to keep the flame going. We purchased hot or boiling water from the hot-water stand at the entrance to the lane.

The food shortage became even more acute and refugees were not just dying of disease, but of starvation and despondency. My mother was most innovative. She would buy 1 oz. of peanut butter and about 6–8 oz. of syrup and that would be a "great" spread. Little Chinese boys chased grocery trucks, slit the sacks, noodles would fall into the gutter and then be swept up and sold very cheaply. We would then separate the debris from the noodles. For the Sabbath and Chanukah festival, my mother fashioned metal into shapes that would hold some oil and then made a wick out of cotton threads.

A *t'ung*, special pass, to leave the ghetto area during the day (curfew for return was 6:00 p.m.) could, at whim, be obtained from Mr. Ghoya, one of the Japanese ghetto administrators, who promptly proclaimed himself "King of the Jews." My mother received a pass by applying as a typewriter mechanic. However, she used her pass for a different purpose. By visiting Chinese peddlers in parts of the city that westerners did not often frequent, she purchased sundries—scarves, sunglasses, belts, etc.—which she brought back to the ghetto peddlers who sold them on a consignment basis. It did not bring in much money, however, it kept us about one step above starvation.

My school was now out of the ghetto area. Our British teachers were interned, but we still had our British-trained Russian teachers. Even though there was a school in the ghetto area, many of us did not wish to transfer, even though it would take us up to two hours, each way, to continue going to the Shanghai Jewish School. We never had a problem obtaining a pass from Mr. Ghoya.

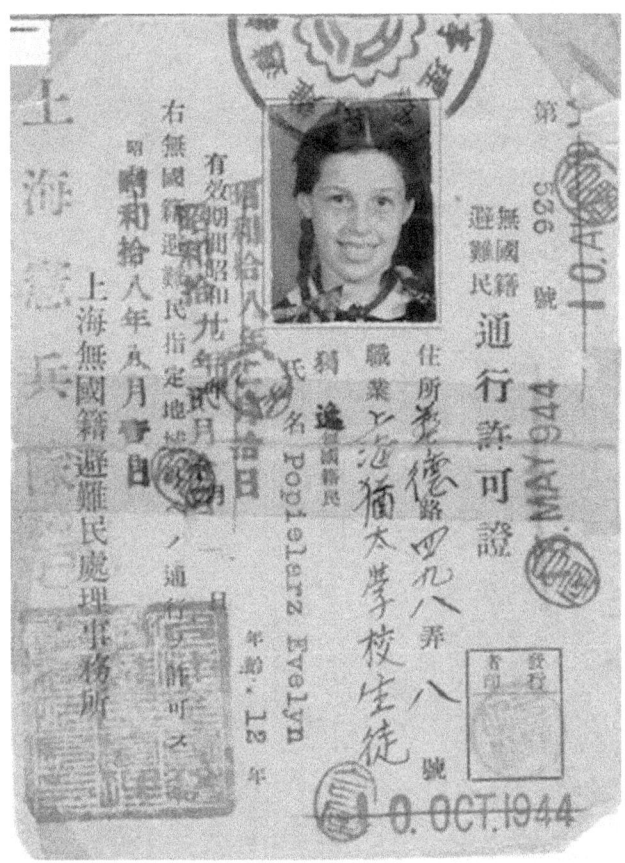

Pass issued to Evelyn Popielarz in 1944 to leave Designated Area

Germany's surrender on May 7, 1945, did not end the war for us in the Pacific Theater. A favorite pastime of us children was to bet with marbles as to who would shoot down whom, as we watched the American and Japanese fighter planes up in the sky. When we heard about the two atomic bombs that were dropped on Hiroshima and Nagasaki, we were really frightened, hoping that the Americans would not drop this bomb on us, in Shanghai. On July 17, 1945, American planes bombed the ghetto. Some thirty refugees were killed and hundreds more were wounded. Scores of Chinese inhabitants also were killed that day.

Our liberation came six weeks later, with the arrival of American soldiers and sailors. We were indeed fortunate to have survived in Shanghai. The Chinese population was most welcoming and very neighborly. They helped us whenever possible. My mother and I left Shanghai for the United States, this time on German Displaced Persons Quota, in March 1947.

Steve Hochstadt

What I Learned from Shanghai Refugees

I have been studying the Jewish refugees in Shanghai for many years, especially through interviews. I have recorded about a hundred individual stories of how families experienced the trauma of being expelled from their homes, traveling across the world, adjusting to a very foreign new home, surviving the difficulties of war, and then moving once more to another continent.[1] I have heard countless other personal stories in memoirs, diaries, letters, documents, and conversations. I have learned some lessons that are important to my understanding of the whole Shanghai refugee experience. Here are a few.

Perhaps the most important lesson is quite simple, but disconcerting for a historian: don't generalize. The problems with generalization were demonstrated to me in my first interview, with my grandmother. My grandparents, Josef and Amalia Hochstädt, enjoyed an upper-middle-class life in Vienna up to 1938. Amalia's brother Egon was the lawyer for the Vienna Symphony, and their musicians came to the Hochstädt apartment to play, with Egon on the violin and Amalia on the piano. When the Nazis marched into Austria during the *Anschluss* in March 1938, Josef, a gynecologist, was accused of assaulting a Christian patient, and jailed. An affidavit and visa were procured for their son, my father, who then traveled alone to the United States at age eighteen. They managed to get entry to England for their thirteen-year-old daughter on the so-called *Kindertransport*. Unable

---

[1] The interview materials are stored in the Muskie Archives at Bates College in Lewiston, Maine, as the Shanghai Jewish Community Oral History Collection: tape recordings, transcripts, and correspondence. Some of the transcripts are accessible at http://scarab.bates.edu/shanghai_oh/.

to obtain entry to these favored countries for themselves, they took an Italian liner to Shanghai in 1939.

That brief synopsis of a family's escape from the Nazis sounds similar to the many Shanghai stories I have heard, some of which I have used to create the books *Exodus to Shanghai* and *Shanghai Geschichten*, two different sets of oral histories of former refugees.[2] But my grandparents were exceptional in nearly every important respect. Their ability to place their children in countries which were difficult to enter represents unusual good fortune. That luck, created by both effort and money, characterizes their entire Shanghai experience. Although the Nazis confiscated the bulk of their wealth, including two apartment buildings in Berlin, the Hochstädts were able to bring a full set of fine china and silver to Shanghai. More unusual, my grandfather's entire office furniture was packed in a *Lift* and sent across the world.

While virtually every other refugee arrived in Shanghai with barely enough cash to buy a meal, my grandparents were able to rent a large apartment in the International Settlement at the corner of Bubbling Well Road and Seymour Road (now Nanjing Lu and Shaanxi Bei Lu). They hired a cook to make familiar Viennese dishes. When the Japanese issued their infamous Proclamation of February 1943, forcing all refugees into the newly created Designated Area for Stateless Refugees in the slums of Hongkou, the Hochstädts obtained permission from the Japanese to remain in the International Settlement, although they had to give up their sprawling apartment to a Korean who was working for the Japanese. A wealthy Indian named Lalcaca, presumably one of Josef's patients, allowed them to move into his house and set up medical practice there during the remainder of the war.[3] After the Japanese left Shanghai, my grandmother convinced the Korean to leave by threatening him with the imminent arrival of my father, by then a lieutenant in the US Army.

My grandparents certainly suffered downward mobility as they moved from Vienna to Shanghai and eventually to the United States. Arriving in New York at age sixty, my grandfather was not able to reestablish his full

---

2   *Exodus to Shanghai: Stories of Escape from the Third Reich* (New York: Palgrave Macmillan, 2012) is composed from interviews with former refugees who came to the United States; *Shanghai Geschichten: Die jüdische Flucht nach China* (Berlin: Hentrich und Hentrich, 2007) tells the stories of refugees who returned to Europe.

3   This might be B. P. Lalcaca, listed in the China Hong List of 1941 at 254 Gordon Road (now Jiangning Lu).

credentials to practice medicine, and had to take a position as the resident gynecologist at a mental hospital in New Jersey. They settled into a comfortable, but certainly not opulent, and anonymous existence. I never heard my grandmother play the piano. I know of no other refugee who had a Shanghai experience like this. The case I know best tells me little about other refugees.

A natural human reaction is to generalize from one's own experiences. Many former refugees do this as a matter of course, assuming that what they witnessed was general rather than particular. For example, Shanghai refugees from Vienna who did not obtain visas from the Chinese Consul General in Vienna, Dr. Feng Shan Ho, sometimes assert that such papers were unimportant or even useless. While it is true that no papers were needed to land in Shanghai, the thousands of visas that Dr. Ho issued in the few months after the *Anschluss* proved life-saving to refugees who used them to get relatives out of concentration camps after *Kristallnacht*, to pass through third countries on their way out of Europe, and to get entry papers to other destinations.[4]

So my advice to anyone wanting to understand the Shanghai refugee experience is: be careful about generalization. But historians must generalize, or we simply collect a series of personal stories with no connection and no context. I disregard my own advice to make several generalizations from the many stories I know about.

The first is that it was hard to become a refugee. It is certainly hard being a refugee, but it was also hard to get to that status. We know well that possible countries of refuge threw up obstacles to immigration. The quota system of US immigration provides a model of immigration obstacles and their origins in antisemitism. Not only was the quota for Germans and Austrians, established in the 1920s, much too small to meet the sudden demand of desperate Jews after 1933, but American consular officials in Europe used bureaucratic methods to make the process of getting a visa and an affidavit even more difficult and time-consuming.[5] Concerns about Jewish immigration into the United States were expressed clearly enough by State Department officials, right up to the notoriously antisemitic Secretary

---

4 See the essay in this book about Feng Shan Ho by Manli Ho, his daughter.
5 Among many books which treat the difficulties of getting permission to enter the United States, the most pointed is Bat-Ami Zucker, *In Search of Refuge: Jews and US Consuls in Nazi Germany 1933–1941* (Elstree, UK: Vallentine Mitchell, 2001).

of State Cordell Hull. Similar motivations led to restrictions in England, Canada, Australia, and other democracies.[6]

Sometimes the difficulties of getting from Nazi Germany into the United States are expressed through the metaphor of a closed door. Although many potential refugees were prevented from actualizing their desire to get to the United States, that metaphor is misleading. Neither the American "door" nor any other possible door was fully closed. In fact, more Jewish refugees successfully landed in the United States than anywhere else. During the key period between the *Anschluss* in March 1938 and the start of war in September 1939, about two-thirds of the 120,000 Jews who left Germany and Austria entered the United States. But by that time, about 300,000 had applied for visas to the States. A more complex metaphor is needed. Imagine the 525,000 German Jews and 200,000 Austrian Jews as an immense crowd being funneled through a partially open door. Many can enter, but more will wait in vain. Dozens of such doors existed around the world, even more narrowly open, allowing the lucky ones to trickle in, while the masses could not get through.

The only fully open door was in Shanghai, but like every other door, that one also shifted over time. It was open without restriction until August 1939, when the Japanese decided to restrict immigration to the sector of Shanghai they controlled, and the Western powers who shared control of the port through the Shanghai Municipal Council happily followed suit. The Shanghai door was not closed, but it remained open just a crack, allowing much reduced numbers to enter. Immediate relatives or the intended spouse of a Shanghai resident, someone with a contract for a job, or persons providing a deposit of US $400 could enter the International Settlement, with slightly relaxed rules applying to the sectors of Shanghai controlled by the Japanese.[7]

Every refugee had to first pass through another door at the borders of Nazi Germany. Even though the Nazis wanted Jews in the Third Reich to leave, they made it extraordinarily difficult. Besides a valid passport with a big red "J" stamped on the outside, Jews who wanted to leave needed

---

6 For example, Irving Abella and Harold Troper, *None is Too Many: Canada and the Jews of Europe 1933-1948* (New York: Random House, 1983).

7 For a fuller discussion of how this door was mostly closed, see Steve Hochstadt, "Shanghai: a Last Resort for Desperate Jews," in *Refugees from Nazi Germany and the Liberal European States*, ed. Frank Caestecker and Bob Moore (New York: Berghahn Books, 2009), 109–121.

many documents, most of which required a visit to police or Gestapo offices, where they were routinely humiliated. Jews had to prove that they had no criminal record and that they owed no taxes in order to obtain an *Unbedenklichkeitsbescheinigung*. They had to give up the great bulk of their possessions, including small items of personal value, such as jewelry and watches. They had to pay an emigration tax, and then leave behind the rest of their money, taking only ten Reichsmarks, the equivalent of four dollars.

Stripping all Jews of their incomes and possessions was a key element of Nazi policy implemented after 1933. An entire bureaucracy was created for this purpose, operating first on German-speaking emigrants and later on every European Jew who was brought into the concentration camp system. The Nazis collected millions of dollars' worth of cash, art, jewelry, clothes, and even gold teeth, before killing their victims.[8]

The best metaphorical representation of the process of becoming a refugee is two doors connected by a long hall. One door was controlled by the Nazis, allowing only those who had given up everything to pass. Refugees then entered a passageway, longer or shorter, depending on their eventual destination, clogged with thousands of others hoping to get through the next door, whose opening swung unpredictably wider or narrower. Many of those who got through the first door, but not yet the second, were later captured as Germany successively overran Czechoslovakia, Poland, the Netherlands, Belgium, and France. Some nearly reached the second door, only to be turned back, like the unfortunate passengers on the "SS St. Louis."

The many obstacles to becoming a refugee, the uncertainties attached to the eventual outcome, and the impossibility of imagining the ultimate fate of those who were left behind made the decision to become a refugee agonizing. Arguments broke out in countless Jewish families, even as late as 1939, about what to do. Alongside the difficulties presented by the Nazis, the decision-making process itself created obstacles.

Lotte Schwarz's husband was arrested and sent to Buchenwald in June 1938. They managed to leave Germany in August. She told me:

> My brother Berthold lived where I come from. My brother worked in a non-Jewish big men's clothing shop there. And when we left, he laughed,

---

8   Only recently has this financial side of the Holocaust become better known. See Frank Bajohr, *Aryanization in Hamburg: The Economic Exclusion of Jews and the Confiscation of Their Property in Nazi Germany*, trans. George Wilkes (New York: Berghahn Books, 2001).

it couldn't happen to him. But a few weeks later all the Jewish people left in Nordhausen were sent to concentration camp. He was three months in Buchenwald, too. So we got him a ticket to overseas, we helped with that. We wanted my mother to come before, and she said, she is not going before all her kids are out, that means my younger brother in Nordhausen. Then it was too late for her. She couldn't get out, you know. My mother stayed in Germany, and died there. It was terrible.[9]

Ilse Greening from Hannover said:

My boss, who was a lawyer, never expected Hitler to last. Even in November after *Kristallnacht*, my boss, who was a very intelligent, well informed person, said, "It's a pity you have to leave so soon, because Hitler is not going to last."[10]

Doris Grey of Berlin said:

Shanghai was the last place to go. They always said, only people who have been in prison, the worst people go to Shanghai. You were almost ashamed to say you go to Shanghai. When Hitler came to power, my mother said, "Oh, he will not last long, it's impossible, it couldn't be." My mother could have gone, but she didn't. She ended up in Auschwitz.[11]

Otto Schnepp of Vienna told me:

My mother also had an older brother, he stayed there. His wife was quite ill, and he didn't want to leave, she was not Jewish, it was complicated. It was probably to a great part because my grandmother did not want to leave that son there, that she didn't leave. So neither of them ever got out.[12]

We will never know what psychological and material obstacles were most significant in making Jews hesitate to leave the Third Reich. The fact that Shanghai was both the least desirable destination and the one with the least restrictions made the decision to go there more difficult.

A second generalization is that words are important. I don't mean long words or fancy words, but words which carry a big meaning. As soon as we move from telling detailed stories about people's behavior to using

---

9   Hochstadt, *Exodus to Shanghai*, 19.
10   Hochstadt, *Exodus to Shanghai*, 42.
11   Hochstadt, *Exodus to Shanghai*, 53, 55.
12   Hochstadt, *Exodus to Shanghai*, 45.

labels to identify historical subjects, we must exercise great care to pick the right words.

My interview partners, in describing their own histories of intercontinental travel, consistently used the word "emigration." I heard many versions of the German phrase, "*Wir gingen in die Emigration.*" Choosing to leave Germany for economic and political reasons was a familiar concept. By their use of this word, they offered some insight into how they perceived their actions, as a decision that some made and others didn't. What we have learned about the situation of Jews in Nazi Germany, however, makes the concept of emigration inappropriate for the extreme pressure of persecution, including the beginnings of mass murder, that forced Jews to flee if they could.

After the end of the war, official bureaucracies, like the United Nations Relief and Rehabilitation Administration (UNRRA), used the phrase "displaced persons" to refer to people who had been forced from their homes by persecution and war, another euphemism. In German, the best word refers to the beginning of the process, *Flüchtling*, one who flees. The best word in English is "refugee," a word hardly known to our refugees when they made their journeys.

Like all such categorical words, "refugee" covers a wide variety of experiences. The small number of Jews who left Germany before 1938 endured as a group much less trauma than the Austrians who suffered through the *Anschluss*, *Kristallnacht*, and the earliest deportations, leaving as late as 1940.[13] Families with wealth and connections, like my grandparents, might feel more like emigrants than those from whom the Nazis took everything of monetary value, and who sailed to Shanghai with tickets paid for by others. But my grandfather had been jailed, like the men in many families where the wife and mother desperately searched for ways to get them released. The generalization of words is necessary for our communication, but it covers up great differences.

Another such big word that I don't like to use in connection with Shanghai is "ghetto." The Holocaust, inextricably connected with mass death, changed the visual and cognitive images prompted by "ghetto." The

---

13 Lisbeth Loewenberg and her mother left Vienna for Shanghai in early 1940: Hochstadt, *Exodus to Shanghai*, 47–49. Deportations of Austrian Jews to Nisko in Poland had begun in October 1939. A fine study of that event is Jonny Moser, *Nisko: Die ersten Judendeportation*, ed. Joseph W. Moser and James R. Moser (Vienna: Edition Steinbauer, 2012).

first ghetto in Venice in 1516 was a place where Jews had to live, closed at night, but passable during the day. Nobody was killed, and Jews were free to worship as they wished inside the borders. As an area in the slums of Shanghai where some Jews, the recent refugees, were forced to live, the Designated Area that the Japanese created in Hongkou in 1943, fits that original concept quite well. It was natural for the refugee residents of Hongkou to think of their home as a ghetto.

Warsaw changed the meaning of ghetto. The Nazis created 1150 Jewish ghettos, an astounding number, the great majority of whose residents were eventually killed.[14] The particular circumstances in Shanghai make the use of "ghetto" inaccurate. The Japanese consistently refused to physically harm the refugees they forced into Hongkou. The outer limit of Japanese brutality toward Jews was reached and is still personified by Kanoh Ghoya, a bureaucrat charged with responsibility for granting daily passes out of the Designated Area's borders. He was notorious for emotional outbursts, sometimes accompanied by slaps to the faces of tall Jewish men in his office. Refugees whom I interviewed were anxious to tell Ghoya stories that they observed or heard about. They are the worst stories about persecution in Shanghai they know.[15]

I don't mean that I would correct a former refugee who says "emigration" or "ghetto." They must use the words in their own vocabulary that best express their meaning. So must we. Meanings have changed in the seventy years since the end of World War II. Generalizing labels are unavoidable, so we should use the best ones we can find.

Here's another lesson, one which was already a staple of antisemitism: Jews stick together, sometimes. Sticking together with people who are like you is usually seen as an admirable trait. The rise of nationalism in the nineteenth century led people who had felt akin mainly to localized groups to then see their connections to a much broader nation of people with a common culture and history. Ironically, the growth of European

---

14 A comprehensive guide to all the ghettos and the thousands of separate camps is *The United States Holocaust Memorial Museum Encyclopedia of Camps and Ghettos, 1933–1945*, in seven volumes, ed. Geoffrey P. Megargee (Bloomington, IN: Indiana University Press, beginning in 2009).

15 I discuss my understanding of the meaning of stories about Ghoya in *Exodus to Shanghai*, 242–43. Many of the refugees quoted in the book tell stories about him. Wei Zhuang, in his book *Erinnerungskulturen des jüdischen Exils in Shanghai (1933-1950): Plurimedialität und Transkulturalität* (Berlin: Lit Verlag Dr. W. Hopf, 2015), devotes a chapter to refugee memories and understandings of Ghoya.

nationalisms caused more antisemitism. Jews were criticized for sticking together because antisemites believed we had evil intentions toward everyone else. The more nationalist Germans emphasized the importance of sticking together with each other, and then lumped all Jews together and used that as proof of our wickedness.

In fact, Jews have a mixed record of sticking together, and the Shanghai story exemplifies both our unity and our internal differences. At every point in the process of becoming a refugee, journeying halfway around the world, surviving wartime Shanghai, and finding a new home once again, the Shanghai refugees were welcomed and helped by Jews across the world. Under increasingly threatening pressure from Nazi authorities, organized Jews in Germany began to promote Shanghai as a life-saving refuge in 1938. The largest Jewish periodical, the *Gemeindeblatt der Jüdischen Gemeinde Berlin*, advised readers about Shanghai as a possible destination, and the *Hilfsverein der deutschen Juden* helped prospective refugees with advice and money.[16]

Outside of the Third Reich, Jewish communities all along the route to Shanghai offered help. These spontaneous expressions of sympathy haven't left many records. I rely on a few stories I have heard to show what I believe was a more general phenomenon. Ernest Culman's family, sailing from Italy with a Dutch steamship company, had to change ships in Batavia.

> We had to transfer in what is now Jakarta, at that time it was called Batavia, where we had a one-week layover. In Batavia the Dutch Jewish community welcomed us, and they put all of us up in nice hotels. My father and his family, we were taken in by a major in the Dutch army, a Jewish doctor, and we lived like kings, you know, like the typical colonial British and Dutch people lived. We had a car for our disposal with a chauffeur, I mean, it was wonderful. A week later we went on board on this other ship that eventually got us into Shanghai.[17]

Eric Reisman told me a story which can stand for thousands of individual acts of generosity.

> The first port that we were able to get off ship was Aden on the Red Sea. One of the large stores along the waterfront dockside was evidently owned by an Arab Jew. We walked in, we had no money to spend, so we just looked

---

16 Hochstadt, "Shanghai: a Last Resort for Desperate Jews," 111.
17 Hochstadt, *Exodus to Shanghai*, 67.

around at all the beautiful things, they were mostly tropical things. We had winter suits on. So the fellow came up to me and he says, "Have you got a hat?" And I says, "No, I don't have a hat." "You need a tropical helmet." He gave me a tropical helmet, and I said, "I can't pay you." He says, "I don't want any money." And it was the first time in my life that I experienced the emotions of accepting a gift from a stranger. It made me realize that it is much easier to give than to accept a gift. It takes a lot more from a person to be able to gracefully accept a gift. Taught me a lesson. I wore that helmet during the tropical heat and exposure in China, until I couldn't force it on my head any more, [laughs] but I was very proud of that hat. It saved me probably a lot of heat strokes and so forth.[18]

The first steps off the boat in Shanghai were guided by Jews who were already at home in Shanghai. In August 1938, when perhaps only a hundred Central European refugees had arrived, the Baghdadi Jewish community organized a relief committee, headed by Paul Komor, the Honorary Consul General for Hungary. Rich Baghdadi families, like the Sassoons and the Kadoories, provided open trucks to bring the new arrivals to temporary quarters, often in the huge Embankment Building owned by Sir Victor Sassoon, fed them, and registered them as part of the Jewish community. Private housing and job interviews were arranged, a few loans were made, and some were given jobs with the committee, as it grew to deal with the arrival of thousands more refugees.

That was just the beginning of enormous and life-saving material support for thousands of refugees by the Baghdadi, and to a lesser extent, the Russian Jewish communities of Shanghai.[19] The most important institutions set up for and by the refugees were the Shanghai Jewish Youth Association School, the Ward Road Refugee Hospital, and the so-called *Heime*, barracks-like refugee camps for those without sufficient funds to live on their own.[20] The SJYA School was generously funded by the Kadoorie family, especially Horace Kadoorie, and was known simply as the Kadoorie School. Medical equipment for the Refugee Hospital was purchased by the Kadoories and by Sassoon. The *Heime* were supported by

---

18   Hochstadt, *Exodus to Shanghai*, 62.
19   These two communities are discussed in other essays in this collection.
20   The fullest discussion of the *Heime* can be found in the first scholarly treatment of the Shanghai refugees, David Kranzler, *Japanese, Nazis and Jews: The Jewish Refugee Community of Shanghai 1938–1945* (New York: Yeshiva University Press, 1976), chapter 5.

significant infusions of cash from the American Jewish Joint Distribution Committee.[21]

When refugees arrived in the United States, up to ten years after they left Europe, once again local Jews organized and financed the beginning of their new lives. Jews in San Francisco, where most refugees landed in the late 1940s, consulted with Jewish communities across the United States, trying to find places they could send a refugee who owned only a suitcase.

Without the direct aid given to the refugees by other Jews, many would not have survived. Other Jews saved the refugees. But other Jews also drove them crazy. The divisions among Jews are legendary, giving rise to the oft-repeated characterization: three Jews, five opinions. Some of these divisions are simply ethnic and cultural, because Jews existed in every national society. In the original Venetian ghetto, there were separate synagogues for the German, Italian, Iberian, and Levantine congregations.[22] Gérard Kohbieter, a sixteen-year-old from Berlin, traveling alone to Shanghai on an Italian liner, heard Jews talking about other Jews.

> I was attracted to the Viennese. The Berliners didn't like the Viennese, they were too polite for them, too gracious. They thought, *"Sie sind falsch. Sie schmieren Dir Rotz um die Backe."* They put honey around your cheeks. I figure everybody does that, only they do it more charmingly.[23]

Although the shared experience of being forced out of Europe and finding refuge in Shanghai appears to have moderated the differences between German and Austrian Jews, the more serious religious and cultural divisions among the Jewish communities in Shanghai remained. There was little social mixing among the Baghdadi, Russian, and German-speaking communities. While former refugees often speak with reverence about Horace Kadoorie's support of the Shanghai Jewish Youth Association School, at whose events he often appeared, none of my interview partners mentioned seeing other Baghdadi Jews in Hongkou. There are very few

---

21 Kranzler, *Japanese, Nazis and Jews*, is the best source on the hospital. On JDC support, which had to be sent in a roundabout way once Japan and the United States were at war, see Zhava Litvac Glaser, "Refugees and Relief: The American Jewish Joint Distribution Committee and European Jews in Cuba and Shanghai," PhD dissertation (City University of New York, 2015).
22 There is not much written on the ghetto in Venice. One suggestion is Fortis Umberto, *The Ghetto on the Lagoon: A Guide to the History and Art of the Venetian Ghetto (1516–1797)*, trans. Matteoda Roberto (Mira, Italy: Storti Edizioni, 1988).
23 Hochstadt, *Exodus to Shanghai*, 64.

references to any social contact with Russian Jews. On the other hand, both Liliane Willens and Rena Krasno recall refugees being invited to eat meals with their Russian Jewish families.²⁴

Although Jewish refugees from Central and Eastern Europe were both crowded into Hongkou, the traditional antipathy between more secular German speakers and more orthodox Polish and Lithuanian Jews continued in Shanghai. Ilse Krips told me of a visit to their room of a "red-haired Rabbi with a beard" who demanded that their new baby boy be circumcised immediately. When the Krips family hesitated, he spit into the room three times and said that the entire family would be cursed if he were not circumcised.²⁵ While such conflicts might have been unusual, there did exist a sense of competition for scarce resources between the two sets of refugees. The Orthodox yeshiva students from Eastern Europe received extra funds from American Jews, allowing them to eat better than the German-speaking refugees.²⁶

My final generalization is that this story, so important to Jews around the world, is also important to Chinese. Over the past twenty-five years, the Chinese have realized the value to themselves of telling the story of 18,000 European Jews surviving in Shanghai.

The first official interest in Jewish history in China was the founding of the Shanghai Judaic Studies Association in 1988. Right at the beginning, academic and economic purposes were combined: the group's constitution listed one of its purposes as "establishment of economic cooperation between Chinese and foreign industrial and business enterprises." Since then, intellectual, academic and historical interest in Jews has increased, alongside more practical political and economic connections between China and Israel.

In 1992, formal relations were opened between China and Israel. That same year, Chinese scholars traveled to Harvard to present at a conference on "Jewish Diasporas in China."²⁷ Alongside Xu Buzeng, who had

---

24 See the essay above by Liliane Willens; Rena Krasno, *Strangers Always: A Jewish Family in Wartime Shanghai* (Berkeley, CA: Pacific View Press, 1992).
25 Steve Hochstadt, *Shanghai Geschichten*, 153–54.
26 Sigmund Tobias, *Strange Haven: A Jewish Childhood in Wartime Shanghai* (Champaign, IL: University of Illinois Press, 2009), 79. The Tobias family were Polish Jews from Berlin, and his memoir provides the best discussion of the intersection of these two communities.
27 Jonathan Goldstein published papers from this conference in *The Jews of China: Volume One, Historical and Comparative Perspectives* (Armonk, NY: M. E. Sharpe, 1999).

been studying the contributions of Jewish refugees to Shanghai's musical history, two younger scholars appeared. Xu Xin, who had just established a Jewish studies program at Nanjing University, talked about the new development of Jewish studies in China. Pan Guang, formerly one of the four vice-chairmen of the Shanghai Judaic Studies Association and now the Dean of the newly formed Center of Jewish Studies Shanghai, addressed Zionism within the Shanghai Jewish community. Since then, Xu Xin and Pan Guang have become the leaders of Chinese Jewish studies.

In April 1994, Pan Guang organized the "International Seminar on Jews in Shanghai" in close conjunction with the Shanghai municipal government. Besides the scholarly presentations, a Monument for the Jewish Refugee Areas in Hongkou District was ceremoniously unveiled in Huoshan Park (formerly Wayside Park), perhaps the first physical public reminder that Jews had lived in Shanghai. The Shanghai Jewish Refugees Museum, founded in 2007, is the most significant government investment in the former Designated Area. That investment continues to expand: across the street from the Museum, a replica of the Weisses Rössl, a refugee-owned restaurant, has been constructed.

Xu Xin can be regarded as the godfather of university Jewish studies programs. His tireless fund-raising efforts have transformed the program at Nanjing into the Diane and Guilford Glazer Institute of Jewish and Israel Studies. His students have established programs all over China, notably at Henan University in Kaifeng, site of a medieval Jewish community which had long ago been gradually absorbed into the native Chinese population. Recently the government asked Xu Xin to serve as president of the Chinese National Institute for Jewish Culture, a consortium of Jewish studies programs, as they develop national curricula.

Chinese university programs study Jews in the widest sense. Although they began by focusing on the history of Jews in China, they now offer undergraduate courses on the Holocaust and encourage graduate study on the entire range of Jewish religion and history. Students learn Hebrew and participate in exchange programs in Israel.

The government's interests are both narrower and broader. Since establishing diplomatic relations with Israel (and possibly even before that), the Chinese government has benefitted from increasing economic and military exchanges. These are accompanied by the repetition of a particular form of memory about Jews in China. Official discussions of the history of Jews in China, including the exhibits of the Shanghai Jewish Refugees Museum, promote a useful message about China based primarily on the Shanghai refugee experience: 1) there is no history of antisemitism in China; 2) Jews have always been welcomed in China; 3) Chinese and Jews were friends in Shanghai. None of these ideas violates the historical record. But they can lead toward an exaggeration of the closeness of Jewish refugees and Chinese natives in Shanghai, which sometimes culminates in a conclusion which is not supported by history: "We saved the Jews."

Earlier I said that generalization is dangerous. That warning applies especially to an understanding of Chinese responses to and attitudes about Jewish history, in China and in the world. Certain Chinese use the history of Jewish refugees in Shanghai to make political statements, such as about the lack of antisemitism in China or the perfidy of the Japanese military assault on and occupation of China. As is true all over the world, the political use of historical information leads to exaggeration. Perhaps because the exact number of Jewish refugees who reached Shanghai will never be known, fanciful estimates can be found in official, semiofficial, and unofficial sources in China, which are then repeated in the Jewish media. The number 30,000 appeared on the websites of the Shanghai Jewish Refugees Museum and of the Center of Jewish Studies Shanghai.[28]

Even generalization about one institution can be untenable. In their exhibit which has traveled across the United States, as well as to Israel and Germany, the Shanghai Jewish Refugees Museum uses the number 18,000, which corresponds with the estimates of Western scholars.[29] I expect that all the output of the SJRM will soon use 18,000, and that eventually that number will become official across China.

The behavior of the Japanese in China toward Jews does not fit into a narrative of the Japanese as brutal war criminals. I would argue that Japan should be seen as a nation which protected the lives of foreign Jewish refugees, despite their alliance with Nazi Germany. Since that narrative clashes with the genocidal story of Japanese killing of Chinese civilians, it is and will probably remain a point of disagreement. Gao Bei of the College of Charleston argues that Chinese governmental discussions about creating a homeland for Jewish refugees in Yunnan province, which had no useful

---

28　http://www.shanghaijews.org.cn/English/, http://www.cjss.org.cn/a/English/Research_Achievements/2014/0306/177.html, and http://www.cjss.org.cn/a/English/Research_Achievements/2014/0304/176.html, accessed August 11, 2015.

29　See author's chapter "How Many Shanghai Jews Were There?" for a fuller discussion of this estimate.

outcome, demonstrate a better national attitude toward Jews than Japanese behavior in Shanghai during the War, which actually preserved thousands of Jewish lives.[30]

As in any nation, attitudes toward Jews are varied and complex in China. Government policy and academic interest in Jewish studies intersect and are both in flux. The story of Jewish history in China is being revised though a collaboration of former refugees and scholars from all over the world. In whatever form it takes, that story will always highlight the survival of thousands of European Jews in wartime Shanghai, a remarkable event which powerfully influences the continuing relations between Jews and Chinese.

---

30 Gao Bei, *Shanghai Sanctuary: Chinese and Japanese Policy toward European Jewish Refugees during World War II* (New York: Oxford University Press, 2013). My critical review of this book is in *American Historical Review* 118 (December 2013): 1499–500.

Xu Xin*

Chinese responses to the Holocaust: Chinese attitudes toward Jewish refugees in the late 1930s and early 1940s

Generally speaking, the Chinese public knew very little about the Holocaust. China is far away from Europe and there were few reports in China about what was happening to European Jews in 1933–1945. China was facing the invasion of Nazi-allied Japan and a full-scale war, and its people had too much to worry about themselves. However, that does not mean that China, one of the Allied Powers during World War II, ignored the suffering of Jews caused by the Holocaust. Major events in Europe could affect China or the outcome of its anti-Japanese War. This paper addresses Chinese responses to the Holocaust, especially the Chinese Government responses, by

---

*   Xu Xin was born in Jinan in Shandong province in 1949 and graduated from Nanjing University in 1977 with an English major, where he then began teaching. He is Diane and Guilford Glazer Professor of Jewish and Israel Studies and Dean of the Institute of Jewish Studies at Nanjing University. He has written many books in English and Chinese on Jews in China, and edited an abridged Chinese translation of the *Encyclopedia Judaica* (Shanghai: Shanghai People's Publishing House, 1993), which won many awards in China. His book, *A History of Western Culture* (Beijing: Beijing University Press, 2002), was named as National Planned Textbook in 2006 for Chinese colleges. He has translated many books about Jews in China from English into Chinese. He has lectured widely in the United States and was awarded an honorary doctorate by Bar-Ilan University in Israel. His most recent book is *Aliens in a Strange Land: Jews and Modern China* (Taipei: National Taiwan University Press, 2017). He serves as president of the Chinese National Institute for Jewish Culture, established by eight Chinese universities in 2015.

examining newspaper reports and documents from the Second Historical Archives of China. Those responses were little known outside of China, and are neglected components of the government policy towards the Jews. However, their very existence reveals Chinese attitudes and responses to the Holocaust. They show that the Chinese and their government were very sympathetic to the sufferings of European Jewry and tried to take actions to assist them, by proposing the establishment of a settlement in Yunnan Province in southwest China in 1939. Newspaper reports and articles show that Chinese intellectual circles denounced Nazi Germany's persecution against Jews.

Historical background

Chinese had very few direct contacts with Jews in history. But the great distance between China and Europe does not mean that Chinese, especially Chinese intellectuals, were ignorant about European Jews or the Holocaust. Dr. Sun Yat-sen, the founding father of the Republic of China, was a supporter of the Zionist movement. He wrote a letter to N. E. B. Ezra, secretary of the Shanghai Jewish Community, on April 24, 1920: "All lovers of Democracy cannot help but support the movement to restore your wonderful and historic nation, which has contributed so much to the civilization of the world and which rightfully deserves an honorable place in the family of nations."[1]

Chinese intellectual circles were aware of the persecution against Jews shortly after the Nazis came to power in Germany. A protest against Nazi Germany's persecution of Jews was organized in Shanghai on May 13, 1933, after the news that Germany burned books reached China, by the China League for the Protection of Civil Rights, a nongovernmental organization of Chinese intellectuals and social activists.[2] The League was headed by Song Qingling, wife of Dr. Sun Yat-sen.[3] A statement issued by Song says: "Organized persecutions against the Jews by the German government and Fascist Party and anti-Semite brutes are symbols of retreat of human beings

---

1   *The Selected Works of Sun Yat-sen* (孙中山选集), vol. 5 (Beijing: People's Press, 1985), 256–57. See also *Israel's Messenger*, a Jewish publication in Shanghai created in 1904.
2   The Chinese name for it is 中国民权保障同盟.
3   She is better known in the West as Madam Song. Some other members of the League were Cai Yuanpei (蔡元培), Yang Xingfo (杨杏佛), Lu Xun (鲁迅), and Lin Yutang (林语堂). They went to the German Consulate in Shanghai and protested against Nazi atrocities. See *Israel's Messenger*, June 2, 1933, 7.

and their culture to the Middle Ages and the darkest days of Imperial Czars."[4] This is the first recorded formal Chinese response to the Holocaust.

Shengbao (申报), one of the major popular newspapers in modern Shanghai, published many articles, including commentaries, about the Holocaust, representing public opinions of Chinese on the issue.[5] For instance, in three weeks from October 10–30, 1938, 41 essays or articles appeared in *Shengbao*, either reporting or commenting on antisemitic events in Germany, Italy, and Austria. Those articles occupied almost half of its international page during those days, which showed the level of Chinese concern. Quite a few local newspaper articles reported persecutions against the Jews in Germany by the Nazis.

Ever since Hitler came to power in Germany in 1933, Chinese, especially those who lived in cities such as Shanghai, Tianjin, or Hong Kong where Jewish communities had existed for many decades, began to hear about the ill treatment of German Jews. They learned about Nazi persecutions against Jews from news broadcast by foreign radios or through the arrival of Jewish refugees from Germany and other European countries. Quite a few Jews who wished to escape antisemitic persecutions in Germany came to Shanghai for a safe haven in the early 1930s. The very first groups of those Jewish refugees were professionals, such as doctors, lawyers, engineers, architects, editors, journalists, musicians, scientists, and professors. They brought with them horrors committed by the Nazis. From 1937 to 1941, when persecution got worse, about 18,000 Jewish refugees from Central Europe sought a haven in Shanghai. Chinese newspapers informed readers that they were Jewish refugees and were forced to escape from their original countries.

At the end of the war, quite a few publications provided information about the Holocaust. One of the earliest literary publications in Chinese about the Holocaust is the Chinese version of Soviet writer Vasilii Grossman's book, *The Years of War*. A Chinese translation from Russian of "The Treblinka Hell," one chapter of the book, was published in 1945, a year earlier than the English translation of the book.[6] The Chinese version was

---

4   Song Qingling, "Denounce Atrocities against Progress Personal and Jewish People in Germany," *Struggle for A New China* (Beijing: Foreign Languages Press, 1952), 49–50.
5   《申报》 was a daily Shanghai newspaper first created by Ernest Major, a British merchant, on April 30, 1872. It was considered an influential paper in modern Shanghai.
6   It was published by Time Press in Shanghai in 1945. Time Press was run by Russians, but published in Chinese. The English version is Vasily Grossman, *The Years of War (1941–1945)* (Moscow: Foreign Language Publishing House, 1946).

printed together with two cartoons and three pictures of Treblinka death camp, giving Chinese readers visual images of the Holocaust.

It is worth mentioning the attitude of the Communist Party of China (CPC) toward this issue, because within less than ten years the CPC took over the country from the Chinese Nationalist Party (KMT). The CPC, small in number at the time, denounced the fascism of both Nazis and Japanese. The CPC considered the Jewish people as an oppressed nation. In October 1941, a gathering on anti-fascism was held in Yan'an, where the headquarters of the CPC at that time was located. Ye Hua, a German Jewess who had married Xiao San, a well-known Chinese Communist writer and journalist, was invited to attend it as a Jewish representative.[7] Both she and Israel Epstein, another Jew supporting the war against Japan, were elected as members of an Executive Committee of the Anti-Fascist League after the gathering.[8]

In general, Chinese people as well as the Chinese government were very sympathetic to those refugees from Europe and tried to take actions to assist those helpless Jews in China. For instance, Jews in Shanghai were accepted in a friendly manner by their Chinese neighbors, who themselves were suffering from Japanese oppression at the same time. Later many Jewish refugees recalled that their life was difficult in Shanghai, but they felt free from the persecution and discrimination which were commonly experienced in Europe.[9] Many did business side by side with Chinese.

Official Response (The Yunnan Plan / 云南计划)

Having discussed briefly unofficial responses of China to the Holocaust, what were the responses of the Chinese government? In a sense, its response represented China's official response to the Holocaust. Under the pressure of the powerful advance of the Japanese army from North China to East China, on November 20, 1937, the Chinese central government announced that it was moving from the capital city Nanjing to a temporary capital at Chongqing, and set up temporary new offices there by December 1, 1937. However, at the

---

7   She was a photographer, whose real name was Eva Standberg. She met Emi Siao (萧三), a Chinese Communist journalist, and married him. After marriage, her name became Eva Siao (萧夏娃). She also took a Chinese name, Ye Hua (叶华), which is better known in China.
8   *Liberation Daily*, October 16, 1941.
9   For example, see Ernest Heppner, *Shanghai Refuge: A Memoir of the World War II Jewish Ghetto* (Lincoln, NE: University of Nebraska Press, 1993).

beginning all central government officials involved in the war effort against Japan moved from Nanjing to Wuhan, which served as a secondary temporary national capital for ten months, until it was captured by the Japanese in November 1938. The KMT finally moved their remaining central government and political party institutions to Chongqing at the end of 1938.

In Chongqing, the Legislative Yuan, the Chinese Parliament, held a session to discuss what China should do following the 1938 annexation of Austria by Nazi Germany. A new wave of antisemitic activity had erupted, causing European Jews to flee from their countries. On February 17, 1939, Sun Ke (孙科), President of the Legislative Yuan, personally made a proposal to set up a settlement in China for those who were suffering in German-occupied countries in 1939, sometimes named the Yunnan Project: "I am proposing the establishment of a Jewish settlement in the border region of Southwest China in order to receive incoming stateless Jews. I wish that this Legislature would examine it and make a final decision on this proposal."[10]

Sun Ke was certainly the right leader to present the proposal. He was the eldest son of Dr. Sun Yat-sen and one of most influential officials in the Chinese central government. He had just returned from a visit to Europe in 1938 and was well informed about the suffering of Jews in Central Europe. According to Manli Ho, daughter of Dr. Feng Shan Ho (何凤山), a Chinese diplomat in Vienna in late 1930s, Sun Ke had a meeting with Dr. Ho during his visit.[11]

Sun Ke cited the recent events of *Kristallnacht* in November 1938 to support the necessity for the settlement: "With the recent rise of fascism in Europe, the Jewish people have suffered even more merciless abuse, receiving the worst treatment in Germany. Following Hitler's annexation of Austria, and the massacre of Austrian Jews, the situation has further worsened. Recently, with the murder of a German diplomat in France by a Jew used as pretext, wide-scale antisemitic activity in Germany has begun, done with a level of cruelty never seen before."

Sun Ke knew the suffering of Jews in Europe and that a large number of Austrian Jewish refugees had fled to Shanghai seeking a safe haven since the annexation. He was fully aware of the new situation Jewish refugees heading for Shanghai might face. "Recently, Shanghai is to announce a plan to limit the number of people allowed into the city, due to its inability to deal

---

10 He is also referred to as Sun Fo in English. For details of the proposal, please refer to the English translation of the full text at the end of this essay.
11 Based on a conversation with Manli Ho in Shanghai in 2015.

with the large influx of Jewish refugees." The spirit of his humane attitude towards Jews became obvious.

In order to win his fellow members' support for his proposal in the Legislative Yuan, Sun Ke gave the following justifications.

1. With regard to our national policy, following the principles and wishes of our late Premier, we should unite with and assist disadvantaged and powerless nations.
2. With regard to policy towards England, by assisting the Jewish people, we can increase the sympathy that the people of England have towards us. Furthermore, English foreign policy towards the Far East is determined by the Far East's major businessmen and bankers. The initial obstruction and recent realization of English economic assistance was in each case controlled by the major businessmen and bankers. Furthermore, a large percentage of major businessmen and bankers are Jewish. Therefore, the implementation of this policy can lead to an improvement in the English attitude towards China.
3. With regard to policy towards America, American activities to assist the Jews have been at the center of attention for people in every part of the world and this has had a considerable influence on the efforts to assist the Chinese people. After the implementation of this policy, not only will we make a favorable impression on the American people, but we will also shift their attention towards us. This additional publicity will have enormous benefits.
4. With regard to the future path of the building of our nation, the Jewish people have a large supply of financial resources and talent. If we are able to foster goodwill with them, they can become our greatest ally and source of assistance.

The seriousness of the proposal can be seen by the following specific measures listed in the proposal.

1. At the Southwest region near the international border, we will designate an area of land that Jews may reside in.
2. The central government will create an organizing committee composed of officials from both the central and regional

governments; they are responsible for making arrangements regarding construction and management of this region.
3. The above mentioned committee is responsible for recruiting Jewish leaders of prestige, in China and abroad, to join with us in carrying out this project.
4. Another thing to consider is the establishment of a registry for unemployed Jewish technical specialists. We must, to the greatest extent possible, find employment for expert talents, who can then assist us with construction projects away from the front lines.

On March 10, 1939, the proposal was sent to the Executive Yuan for its inspection with instructions that "it should be examined and deliberated on." On April 22, 1939, the Civil Service Department of the government sent a letter along with a list of each department's suggestions to the section chief of government affairs in this government body, Jiang Ting Fu (蒋廷黻), for careful study. On May 3, 1939, after the resolutions to resettle Jewish refugees had passed and were approved by the Supreme Council of National Defense, Kong Xiang Xi (孔祥熙), President of the Executive Yuan, gave his order that the Nationalist Government should implement the resolutions. The proposal became a law.

Jacob Berglas, a German Jewish banker and a textile entrepreneur, had close contact with Chinese authorities over this plan. He visited China a few times and had some discussions with his Chinese hosts. He also kept updating Jewish immigration organizations on this issue, as well as Ellis Hayim, a local leader of the Baghdadi Jewish community in Shanghai, who expressed his support without any reservation. In order to solve the foreseeable financial problems, he even suggested that part of charitable funds for Shanghai could be used and that factories be established to hire those refugees and make the best use of their skill and knowledge. In this way they may be able to generate money as well as to solve unemployment problems.[12]

In July 1939, *Israel's Messenger* reported the plan.[13] *Die Gelbe Post*, a newspaper in German published in Shanghai from 1939 to 1941 by Adolf Josef Storfer (1888–1944), a German Jew, also reported the proposal and resolutions, and carried a number of introductory articles about Yunnan,

---

12 See *Israel's Messenger*, October 13, 1939, 16.
13 "One hundred thousand Jews may find home in China, Yunnan to be Promised Land of Refugees, German Banker Inspires Move," *Israel's Messenger*, July 14, 1939, 14–15.

where the settlement was supposed to be established, with discussions of job opportunities there, written by Jewish refugees in Shanghai.[14]

Though the resolution was not implemented due to the complicated developments of World War II, it is a strong evidence that the Chinese government and people did not stand by in silence and did try to provide assistance in time of need. The significance and importance of the response stands out if one takes into consideration the situation of China at the time. In 1939 when the persecutions of the Jews in Germany were intensified, the Chinese were also suffering a great deal from Japanese invasion and atrocities. Half of Chinese territory was already under Japanese occupation and millions of Chinese had died. The brutality of the Japanese war against China was beyond description. The Japanese fascism was no better than the Nazis as far as their brutality was concerned.

After the Japanese took over the city of Nanjing, then the capital of China, in 1937, they killed almost 300,000 within about six weeks. The death toll of the Nanjing Massacre exceeds that of the two atomic blasts at Hiroshima and Nagasaki in 1945 (estimated at 210,000) or the combined total of Jewish victims from Germany and Austria (also about 210,000). In these circumstances, the Chinese government still tried to make enormous efforts to give a helping hand to persecuted Jews in Europe.

It was a great pity that Sun Ke's proposal and the final resolution of the Chinese Central Government, which represented Chinese official response to the Holocaust, is not well known. Their existence, plus responses of Chinese intellectuals and people, shows that China as an Allied power acted as a friend indeed for the Jewish people.

---

14   See *Die Gelbe Post*, reprint edition, 1, 2, 3, 5, 6 (1939).

Documents relating to Sun Ke's proposal to settle European Jewish refugees in Yunnan, March to May 1939[15]

1. Official Letter from the National Defense Supreme Council for the Civil Service Department of the Nationalist Government, March 7, 1939

At the first standing conference of this council, council member Sun Ke proposed designating an area in the Southwest border region as a settlement for Jews who are wearied and have no home to go. We have drawn up a detailed statement of its justifications and a four-point plan of implementation. We request that the congress vote on this proposal. If it passes, it should be delivered to the Executive Yuan for discussion, so that procedures for its implementation can be investigated.

At the time of discussion of this proposal, every committee member is making arrangements for its widespread dissemination. The Executive Yuan should handle this bill; it should consider carefully how to word statements regarding its justifications when drafting. The corresponding record and copy of Mr. Sun Ke's proposal have been delivered together. After inspection, please forward these to Mr. Chen Mi and the Executive Yuan to handle. Thank you.

Respectfully,
Nationalist Government Civil Service Department

Attached manuscript of the original proposal:

Legislative Yuan President Mr. Sun Ke drafted a proposal to allocate a part of the Southwest border region as a settlement area for Jews who are wearied and have no home to go. We respectfully await a joint decision on whether or not this is feasible.

Justification:

The world population of Jews totals around 16 million, with the largest population in America, at approximately 4 million, the second largest

---

15 "Chungking National Government Programme for the Placement of the Jews in China," *Republican Archives* 3, 1993, 17–21; original Chinese edited and compiled by Bi Chun Fu and Ma Zhen Du; first draft of the English translation by Douglas Lerner.

population in Poland and Soviet Russia, at approximately 3 million each, and the rest scattered around various regions of the world. The Jewish people have suffered the profound pain of the loss of their country. With no home, they have been forced to wander from place to place for over 2600 years, facing oppression wherever they go. With the recent rise of fascism in Europe, the Jewish people have suffered even more merciless abuse, receiving the worst treatment in Germany. Following Hitler's annexation of Austria and the massacre of Austrian Jews, the situation has further worsened. Recently, with the murder of a German Diplomat in France by a Jew used as pretext, wide-scale anti-Semitic activity in Germany has begun, done with a level of cruelty never seen before. England and America have expressed outrage over this. England wishes to establish a permanent home for the Jews in Palestine, which has been met by intense opposition by the local Arab population. Troubles related to this have continued up until the present. America has expressed strong anger and resentment towards Hitler due to his heavy-handed oppression of the Jews. Because of this, there has been a surge in activities to assist the Jews, reports of which become the headlines on American newspapers. Recently, Shanghai is to announce a plan to limit the number of people allowed into the city, due to its inability to deal with the large influx of Jewish refugees. This proposal to allow Jews to live in the Southwest border region has the following justifications.

I. With regards to our national policy, following the principles and wishes of our late Premier, we should unite with and assist disadvantaged and powerless nations.
II. With regard to policy towards England, by assisting the Jewish people, we can increase the sympathy that the people of England have towards us. Furthermore, English foreign policy towards the Far East is determined by the Far East's major businessmen and bankers. The initial obstruction and recent realization of English economic assistance was in each case controlled by the major businessmen and bankers. Furthermore, a large percentage of major businessmen and bankers are Jewish. Therefore, the implementation of this policy can lead to an improvement in the English attitude towards China.
III. With regard to policy towards America, American activities to assist the Jews have been at the center of attention for people in

every part of the world and this has had a considerable influence on the efforts to assist the Chinese people. After the implementation of this policy, not only will we make a favorable impression on the American people, but we will also shift their attention towards us. This additional publicity will have enormous benefits.

IV. With regard to the future path of the building of our nation, the Jewish people have a large supply of financial resources and talent. If we are able to foster goodwill with them, they can become our greatest ally and source of assistance.

Plans:

I. At the Southwest region near the international border, we will designate an area of land that Jews may reside in.

II. The central government will create an organizing committee composed of officials from both the central and regional governments; they are responsible for making arrangements regarding construction and management of this region.

III. The above mentioned committee is responsible for recruiting Jewish leaders of prestige, in China and abroad, to join with us in carrying out this project.

IV. Another thing to consider is the establishment of a registry for unemployed Jewish technical specialists. We must, to the greatest extent possible, find employment for expert talents, who can then assist us with construction projects away from the front lines.

Proposal submitted by Sun Ke,
President of Legislative Yuan,
on February 17, 1939

2. Manuscript of the Nationalist Government Instructions for the Executive Branch, March 3, 1939

Instructions for the Executive Yuan:

According to the civil service department's petition: at the first standing conference of the Supreme Council of National Defense, March 7, 28th year of the Republic of China, council member Sun Ke proposed designating a part of the Southwest border region as a settlement for Jews along with other suggestions. After inspection, please forward these to Mr. Chen Mi and the Executive Yuan to handle. Attached is a copy of the original proposal. It should be examined and deliberated on. The suggestions attached to the original proposal should also be examined. We request that your governmental body acts in accordance with these instructions.

We have sent the complete investigation attached to the original proposal (there is also a duplicate for filing).

Republic of China, March 10, year 28.

3. Kong Xiang Xi's Petition to the Nationalist Government Draft, April 22, 1939

Presented respectfully to the esteemed government May 10, 28th year of the Republic of China, Chongqing confidential order 16, forwarded to the Supreme Council of National Defense regarding the plan to allocate land for the settlement of Jews. The recommendations endorsed by the Ministry of the Interior, the Ministry of Foreign Affairs, The Defense Ministry, Finance Ministry, and Transportation Ministry were sent to the section chief of government affairs in this government body, Jiang Ting Fu, for careful study. This summary of the request was drawn up and delivered to the 410th meeting of this government body for deliberation. They decided that the proposal had passed investigation and should be sent to the Supreme Council of National Defense. Apart from the resolution which has been delivered for investigation and deliberation, and the recommendations of each ministry delivered for reference and separate response, a copy of the original petition is attached for examination and deliberation. We respectfully present this petition to the Nationalist Government.

A transcript containing a summary of the petition, along with a list of each department's suggestions, is attached.

Summary

Jews that have a nationality possess the rights of and duties to their own countries. If they desire to come to China, they must meet the requirement of their country. Regarding their immigration procedure and living situation after immigration, current treaties and conventions should be followed. If they desire special consideration and they are obstructed by treaties, government policies, or economic or other hardships, this will cause problems for our domestic government, diplomacy, and other government functions. Therefore, no special procedures will be needed for Jews that have a nationality.

Jews that are stateless have special circumstances. Our national character highly values human sympathy. In addition, our former prime minister often told us that all humans are comrades, so we ought to aid one another to the greatest extent possible. However, the Jewish issue is complex. Though we wish to express our amicable feelings towards them, misunderstandings can easily arise. As far as domestic and international circumstances allow for, the following is our second three-part plan for assisting the Jewish people

I. Relocation assistance

Regarding Jews that the League of Nations, emergency relief organizations, or major international charities believe are decent and upstanding and are confirmed as stateless, our embassies and consulates stationed abroad may grant these people special passports which authorize them to enter our borders. We will present application forms to them declaring the following conditions for entry into China: 1. After entering our borders, they must abide by our laws and accept the restrictions set by our courts. 2. After entering our borders, they must not engage in any political or ideological activity, or criticize Sun Yat-sen's three principles of the people. If they disobey these rules, they will be deported.

II. Residence after immigration

After stateless Jews enter our borders, they will be temporarily stationed at an international treaty port, and should not move inland. If they wish to obtain Chinese citizenship, procedures will be conducted according to domestic laws. After receiving Chinese citizenship, they will enjoy equal rights and must not be discriminated against on the basis of race or religion.

III. Job placement assistance for Jews

Presently, stateless Jews are facing many hardships and so must be given assistance in job placement. Our nation is still in the process of development and so requires a large number every kind of technical specialist: scientists, engineers, doctors, mechanics etc. . . .

The government is responsible for investigating the scope of our needs for specialists and creating a detailed list clearly indicating which personnel are required and the wages that they will be paid. The Foreign Affairs Ministry will then forward the list to our consulates and embassies, which can then assist in hiring. We also request that the League of Nations assists in recruitment.

If suitable candidates are found and they can either pay their own travel expenses, or receive financial assistance from the League of Nations or international charity for travel expenses, after the relevant consulate or embassy receives permission from the relevant domestic government body, the candidates may sign employment contracts.

The National Government is not responsible for finding employment for other Jews that enter our country without signing an employment contract. However, the National Government can direct the provincial governments to hold registration for the unemployed and present job opportunities to them and to the extent that is feasible, present job opportunities to them.

If the above methods are approved, the government will issue orders to representatives at the League of Nations. We will issue an official notification to the League of Nations and at the same time, the Chongqing Government will issue a statement. The statement should be worded using this document as the basis.

I. Recommendations of the Ministry of the Interior

1. The Southwest border region demarked for Jewish residence should not be near commercial ports located along international transit routes.

    If many foreigners are allowed to live along these routes, inevitably, national secrets related to international affairs and national defense will eventually be leaked. In case adequate precautions aren't taken, this could lead to an unforeseen incident. However, we should also take into consideration treaty regulations regarding foreign residents (Limitations of Foreign Residents at International Treaty Ports). Also, in order to avoid religious conflict, large trading ports are most suitable for foreigners. In light of the above two view points, the most appropriate areas for Jewish refugees are the English controlled treaty ports near the border with Burma, at Tengyue and Tengchong in Yunnan province.

2. Government permission for construction of lodging in residence area

    Jewish people that are stateless, who do not receive the right to a trial, and are completely in compliance with our laws, are not bound by our laws regarding the land ownership rights of foreigners. They can receive special permission from the Nationalist Government to construct lodging, but should continue with naturalization procedures. Is it acceptable for them to either live in the refugee area or in a comparatively developed part of the southwest border region.

3. Regarding parts of the Southwest border region allocated for Jewish residence near commercial ports located along international transit routes

    If it is possible to avoid the problems outlined in item 1, then is it acceptable to place the Southwest border region designated for Jewish residence near commercial ports located along international transit routes. However, we must place emphasis on reinforcing national defense capabilities and determining our precise diplomatic situation. In addition, we must strengthen security bodies, especially the police force and must boost the powers of essential government officials. We can designate Hekou port in Yunnan province, bordering Vietnam, for dealing with matters pertaining to law.

4. Supervision of the living area

    The supervision of this area should be strengthened, with the police force serving as the backbone. It can be set up using the management of Mount Lu, Mount Gongji, and the three districts of Hankou City as models of organizational structure.

II. Recommendations of the Foreign Affairs Ministry

1. The problem of nationality

    Regarding Jews that come to China, the legal status is different for Jews possessing foreign citizenship and stateless Jews. Also, their situations regarding consular jurisdiction in China are different. For these reasons, managing stateless Jews is easy, while managing Jews possessing foreign nationality is difficult. Because of this, admittance to the living area should be limited to stateless Jews only.

2. The problem of consular jurisdiction

Regarding Jews that possess consular jurisdiction rights, if Italian Jews either move to the designated living area or move inland, they will not be subjected to our laws and court jurisdiction, so it would be highly inadvisable to allow large numbers of them into the country. Germany does not possess consular jurisdiction rights; however, if German Jews move inland, Germany can use diplomatic protection as a way of meddling with internal affairs.

3. The problem of residing inland

Foreigners residing in China are limited to living in international treaty ports. Foreigners without consular jurisdiction rights, for example, citizens of the Soviet Union or Germany, do not have legal permission to moving inland and live with the native population. If Jews from one of these countries move inland, their country will inevitably make demands on the basis of treaty conventions.

4. The living area problem

The Jewish people are hardworking and capable of overcoming adversity, and are also good at managing businesses. If the living area is excessively large, it may be easy to manage in the beginning, however, over time, there may be a call for regional autonomy. This will be difficult to control. Furthermore, if this area is near an international treaty port or international transit route, it will be easy for the Jews to attract international support for autonomy, which will be detrimental to China.

5. The problem of international propaganda

Enemies of China and fascist nations all have accused China of being communist. If at this time we take in large number of Jews, our enemies will inevitably use this for anti-Chinese propaganda purposes, because fascists often speak of Jews being connected to communism.

Recently the German Ambassador Secretary Kape has become aware of this proposal. Although he has stated that he is not currently able to express Germany's objections, there is a large amount of animosity between Germany and the Jews, so we must pay special attention to this situation, as there is already ample evidence that Germany is following the proposal closely.

The colonial powers of England and France will also not be pleased to hear that we are assisting downtrodden ethnic groups, so it would be inadvisable to further broadcast our plans to them.

If the proposal will be implemented during the scheduled time, according to the points described above, the following principle should be paid careful attention:

a) Stateless Jews should be granted residence in specially designated areas; these areas should be small in size. They should not be too concentrated, and they should be far away from commercial ports and international transit routes.
b) Jews possessing foreign citizenship should be restricted to international treaty ports.
c) When disseminating information regarding this plan to the international community, statements should be worded to emphasize humanitarian aid and emergency relief.

III. Recommendations of the Defense Ministry

1. We recommend against stateless Jews being given permission to reside in China. Permission should not be granted for residence in a specially designated area but rather, importance should be attached to the sovereignty of our territory.
2. If designating an area for Jewish residence is absolutely necessary, the area must be in a place where we can exercise sufficient authority, and should not be near an international border. (If Mengzi county, containing the Yunnan–Vietnam railway, is selected, we can provide reference material for choosing the best location.)
3. To facilitate easy implementation of this plan, Consulates stationed in foreign countries can handle explaining procedures to incoming refugees because their staffs are well versed in this kind of process. Another possibility is for relief organizations together with guest houses in our international treaty ports to assist in this process.

IV. Recommendations of the Finance Ministry

1. Determining a suitable region of land for cultivation
   If the above mentioned Jews originally were farmers or are knowledgeable about agriculture or forestry, then land should be selected near interior transit routes to be giving to them for cultivation. China previously has not allowed not-yet naturalized foreigners the right to

possess land for cultivation, so if their living area is near international transit routes, this would inevitably lead to abuse.
2. Flexible immigration procedures

Presently, large numbers of Jews are being forced to flee their homelands in panic. In addition, countries such as Germany and Austria are currently not authorized to handle emigration procedures for Jews. These people not possessing passports must be handled according to flexible procedures. A plan should be drawn up by the Foreign Affairs Ministry, so that this can be handled in accordance with the law.
3. Tax-free transport of goods when entering the country

Regarding ordinary Jews that are permitted to enter the country, apart from prohibited goods and large quantities of merchandise that should still be taxed, goods used in daily life and other small assorted items should not be liable to taxation when carried into the country. This is done as a show of goodwill.

V. Recommendations of the Transportation Ministry

Jewish people have been born and raised in countries with high-quality facilities, so it is unclear if they can accept the living conditions in the interior of China. We can first send staff to Shanghai and consult the Jewish organizations there for their opinions. Regarding the problem of location of and facilities within the designated living area, these matters should be further discussed before proceeding forward.

4. Official Letter from the Civil Service Department of the Nationalist Government for the National Defense Supreme Council Office of the Secretary, May 2, 1939

To the recipient: Respected office of the secretary, April 30, 28th year of the Republic of China, National Government official letter #1050. For the purpose of carrying out Mr. Sun Ke's proposal to allow Jews to reside at the Southeast border region in compliance with the procedures passed by the Executive Yuan, please forward the proposal to Mr. Chen Mi for thorough investigation and deliberation. In accordance with the decision of the standing conference of the Supreme Council of National Defense and after being review by Mr. Chen Mi, the proposal has passed the vote. Officially notifying the League of Nations is not necessary. After inspecting the record and transcript of the resolution, it should be passed on to Mr. Chen Mi in accordance with procedures. The plan has been ratified. In accordance with this, Mr. Chen has already given the Nationalist government secret instructions in accordance with the procedures of the Executive Yuan.

Respectfully presented to the National Defense
Supreme Council office of the Secretary
(Stamped by the) Civil Service Department of
the Nationalist Government

5. Kong Xiang Xi's Petition to the Nationalist Government, May 3, 1939

Presented respectfully to the esteemed government May, 28th year of the Republic of China, Chongqing, confidential file #49. Because the three resolutions to assist the Jews have passed the approval of the Supreme Council of National Defense at the 5th general assembly, in accordance with this, the orders are accepted. Apart from the handling of the separate instructions given to the Ministry of the Interior, Foreign Affairs Ministry, Defense Ministry, Finance Ministry, Commerce Ministry, Education Ministry, and Transportation Ministry, and the handling of the secret instructions given to the province-level and city-level governments, the state of affairs regarding the carrying out of these instructions should be reported back for investigation and auditing.

Respectfully presented to the Nationalist Government
(Stamped by) Kong Xiang Xi, President of Executive Yuan

Looking Back at Shanghai

Dan Ben-Canaan*

Imagined Geographies, Imagined Identities, Imagined Glocal Histories

The past is a foreign country: they do things differently there.[1]

This paper discusses stories of people's movements from one place to another and on to another, in an attempt to apply a better understanding to the study of identity and its relation to space and time, especially to ways identity, geography, and memory may intersect and change. It presents some cases of recollections, oral and written memories, diaries and publications based on motives, nostalgic remembrance, selective memory,

---

* Dan Ben-Canaan earned his bachelor's and master's in Mass Communication and Political Sciences from the City University of New York, his PhD in Political Information (Political Propaganda) from American University, a professional diploma in Television Directing and Production from R.C.A. Institutes in New York, and a journalism diploma from the Tel Aviv School of Journalism. He served as chair of the Sino-Israel Research and Study Center first at Heilongjiang University and now under the Harbin Jewish Culture Association, which he founded in 2014. He is Professor Emeritus of Research and Writing Methodology in the School of Postgraduate Studies at Northeast Forestry University in Harbin, Professor Emeritus at Heilongjiang University School of Western Studies, honorable research fellow at the Heilongjiang Academy of Social Sciences, and visiting professor for advanced postgraduate studies at the Heilongjiang Provincial CCP Party University. He is editor-in-chief of the English News at the Heilongjiang Television & Radio Broadcast Center and op-ed columnist for the "Global Times" in Beijing.

1 This paper was developed from an earlier short essay entitled "The Jews of Harbin: Nostalgia versus Historical Reality," *Mizrekh, Jewish Studies in the Far East* 1 (2009): 52–71. Quotation is the first line of the 1953 novel by L. P. Hartley, *The Go-Between* (New York: NYRB Classics, 2002).

psychological blocks and forgetting, or political manipulations. I call these "imagined history." Many attempts to tell the stories of individuals have transformed the pasts of Harbin and Shanghai into mental geographies, sometimes imagined. These pasts have been packed into suitcases that moved from one space and time to another, changing at each of the stations, creating new stories or hiding portions of old ones, while neglecting to note what was actually happening. A study of tellers' motives suggests a need for a new approach comprising not just historians, but other disciplines, among them psychology, law, anthropology, sociology, and literature.[2]

Glocalization, the adaptation of the global to the local in our case, is a portmanteau of globalization and localization.[3] And "portmanteau," coincidentally, means a "suitcase, chest, or trunk" used for traveling. Ergo, the title of this paper suggests that local memories, recollections, nostalgia, and remembrances are all stuffed into a glocal suitcase that moves from one geography to another, giving these other meanings or changing identities. Very few cities can be seen as truly "glocalized" spaces where transcultural crossroads converged. These cities were spaces where people brought their former geographies and merged them with others. In the process, changes were created not only to the characters and attributions of the old and new geographies, but to the identity of the travelers themselves. Harbin is one of these cities, and so was Shanghai to a lesser degree. Both were spaces into which human traffic streamed, but the reasons, structure, sense of belonging, hence, people's outlook of their future, were different.

---

2   According to Alexander B. Murphy, geographical thinking is vital for addressing some of the critical geopolitical, environmental, and socio-economic challenges. Yet the insights geography can offer are often overlooked because of the tendency to view geography in static, descriptive terms. It is important to understand geography's concern with spatial patterns and assumptions, mapping, and integrative place-based modes of analysis. This can enhance understanding of matters ranging from uprisings in the Middle East, to human alteration of natural systems, to the spread of disease, to the impacts of technology on contemporary society.

3   The term glocalization was developed from Japanese business practices. It comes from the Japanese word *dochakuka*, which means global localisation. Originally referring to a way of adapting farming techniques to local conditions, *dochakuka* evolved into a marketing strategy when Japanese businessmen adopted it in the 1980s. See B. Wellman, "Little Boxes, Glocalization, and Networked Individualism," in *Digital Cities II*, ed. M. Tanabe, P. van den Besselaar, and T. Ishida (Berlin: Springer-Verlag, 2002), 11–25. The term was popularized in the English-speaking world by the British sociologist Roland Robertson in the 1990s, followed by the Canadian sociologists Keith Hampton and Barry Wellman in the late 1990s, as well as Zygmunt Bauman. See B. Wellman and K. Hampton, "Living Networked On and Offline," *Contemporary Sociology* 28 (1999): 648–54.

A related idea about a globalized world is that "culture" and a space (global and local), added to it, are now a mixed entity and border-zoned, and an individual or a given community no longer lives in a world of discrete, located, identifiable, and historically grounded traditional bond.[4] Yet, just as the nation and the boundaries it sets around culture are being conceptually chased away, they come back, maybe in a different form. They do so politically, economically, legally, and symbolically, in mental geographies, constructed histories or imagined ones.[5]

The nature of Harbin as a local space transmuted into a global one creates a glocalized space where both spatial dimensions existed as one. This gives rise to glocalized memories that are a blend of facts and fallacies, misconceptions, mistakes, illusions, and delusions. Local memories are considered here in relation to their global placement, while considering problems of memory, recollections, nostalgia, remembrance, as well as motives of the storyteller.

The idea of transculturation was coined by the Cuban anthropologist Fernando Ortiz in 1940, to describe a process of transition from one culture to another in a context of (often forced) migration, out of which new cultural formations emerged. It has come to the fore once again, along with the idea of the transnational, within a conceptual framework that enables us to develop new interdisciplinary assertions of the global, the local, and the "glocal."[6]

Although history deals with recorded facts, what is written around these are interpretations that are open for arguments and debates. "Imagined history" means (re)constructed/recollected/imagined and sometimes invented or fabricated individual or collective accounts of events, which may have factuality behind them, but present a different reality because of the storyteller. Many of these illuminate, among other things, collective communal

---

4   B. Winter, "Imagined Transcultural Histories and Geographies," *PORTAL Journal of Multidisciplinary International Studies* 9 (July 2012): 1–8.

5   I especially like the way Andràs Gerö perceives the modern nation as the product of secular religion. This belief defines national identity and gives rise to symbolic politics, exemplified by the Hungarian case with its European roots. The result, Gerö argues, was an imagined history that did not reflect what really happened. Andràs Gerö, *Imagined History: Chapters from Nineteenth and Twentieth Century Hungarian Symbolic Politics* (New York: East European Monographs, 2007).

6   R. Wilson and W. Dissanayake, eds., *Global/Local: Cultural Production and the Transnational Imaginary* (Durham, NC: Duke University Press, 1996); Inderpal Grewal and Caren Kaplan, "Postcolonial Studies and Transnational Feminist Practices," in *Jouvert: A Journal of Postcolonial Studies* 5 (2000), accessed March 23, 2018, http://english.chass.ncsu.edu/jouvert/v5i1/grewal.htm.

membership that may share a local experience combined with a global wish. Both terms complement each other in that they present not what is or was, but something different—an assumed history. Recollections present a problem, especially in term of the editorialization of remembrance or "authoring the past" and their interpretation.[7] It is an ontological distinction between past and present—an access that no longer exists.[8] Recollections then become reconstructions and fall under the category of "imagined history."

Are memories, diaries, remembrance, and oral or written recollections products of a selective wish to record only a selected part of a whole? If so, for what purpose? To what extent can historians regard the information as valid? How and with which kind of history and memory do "local" attributes relate to more encompassing global communities? How do these glocalized entities influence one another? What, if any, are the differences and similarities in the relations between memory and history and do they influence the "creation" of new stories? Are historians equipped with the tools that are necessary to fully understand such cases? These are but some of the questions.

Each scholarly discipline tries to defend its domain, and by using its own methods, it locks itself into a narrower path. Thus, it may sound provocative when suggesting that the study of imagined history, memories, remembrance, and oral or written recollections should be carried out within a wider methodological framework, and a wider system of procedures, because one needs several keys to open a door to a past. In many cases a present perception of a past is influenced, among other things, by the experience of risks and threats, both personal and environmental, and these give rise to imagined history that tends to avoid memories of conflicts.

There are other considerations, among them personal motives and official state political manipulation of events and the "memories" that are attached to them. These influence collective communal memory and thus create imagined history. In using the term "historical reality," I refer to events of the past as they occurred factually, whether external or internal to the subject confronted with them. It deals with the actuality of existence in space and time. There is no concern with the prettification of its ugliness. It is a presentation of the past as it is, as it was, and it is very similar to court records and to journalistic accounts.

---

7   Alun Munslow, "Frontiers of history: Historical inquiry in the twentieth century," *Rethinking History: The Journal of Theory and Practice* 13 (September 2009): 283–85.

8   Pihlainen Kalle, "What if the past were accessible after all?" *Rethinking History: The Journal of Theory and Practice* 16 (September 2012): 323–39.

The many nationalities that existed in Harbin until the middle of the twentieth century created a rare kind of urban sphere that made it a truly international city created by foreigners on Chinese soil. Shanghai, on the other hand, a center to foreign conquered presence, was Chinese from its start. Shanghai is often referred to in contemporary histories as "antique modern" and presents a multiplicity of past/present/future. Shanghai was a free port which attracted global colonial powers, as well as well-to-do travelers and émigrés fleeing first the Russian Revolution and then persecution in Nazi Germany. In this way, it was a "global city" that offered cosmopolitanism in the Far East, and it is the memory of this that is mostly reflected today. The lauding of Shanghai by foreigners was in a sense self-congratulatory, as it was based on the belief that modern Shanghai was a Western creation.[9] However, "Shanghai was the leading commercial center of China long before the coming of the foreigner."[10]

In the years preceding the establishment of Harbin in 1898, China's northeastern region, known then as Manchuria, became a focus of global attention as well, when imperial powers, among them Russia, Japan, France, Britain, and the United States, made it a tool for their expanding national, political, and economic interests.[11] Harbin, the northeastern region's omphalos, is a unique example of where global and local interests assembled in a dynamic and complex way. This, to a much lesser degree, can be said about Shanghai, way down the eastern coast of China, which under foreign conquests and assertion of influence grew to be China's center of foreign influx and modernism.[12] Although there are similarities between these cities, the intention here is not to compare them, but to connect these unique spaces through the stories of travelers that left their original geographies, found themselves in Harbin, moved to Shanghai, and then to other destinations. Greater attention is given to Harbin, because the movements discussed came from there, and Shanghai was a middle ground where things started to change.

More than forty foreign nationalities speaking forty-five different languages gathered in Harbin to make the city an international cosmos. Among

---

9   Katrina Gulliver, "Shanghai's Modernity in the Western Eye," *East-West Connections 2009*, 120–21.
10 Gulliver, "Shanghai's Modernity," 121.
11 See Lin Huanwen and Zhao Dejiu, "Jindai Haerbin duiwai maoyi de lishi jiaoxun," *Haerbin yanjiu* (Harbin Research) 4 (1987): 42–45. Also in Soren Clausen and Stig Thogersen, *The Making of a Chinese City: History and Historiography in Harbin* (London: Routledge, 1995), 54–58.
12 Gulliver, "Shanghai's Modernity," 120.

them were Russians of several flags, Jews from different geographical locations, Japanese settlers and later invaders, Koreans, Poles, Ukrainians, Danes, Germans, Portuguese, Latvians, Lithuanians, Armenians, Georgians, Tartars, Italians, Greeks, Belgians, French, Swedes, Swiss, Americans, Britons, Indians, and others, as well as Chinese Hans from Shandong and Hebei. They brought their former spaces with them, created a new local existence, maintained global connections, and influenced global events, hence forming glocalized communities. And "by dwelling in the diasporic past, the global village create[d] its spiritual and intellectual theme park."[13] In this case, although Harbin (and Shanghai) was referred to as "global village," I prefer to label it a "glocalized space" with special spatial dimension. The suitcases that newcomers took with them on their journeys were full of memories of other spaces, some real and many imagined.

Upon leaving Harbin years later, they added another past to the suitcase which they brought to a new place. Over time, these pasts lost their boundaries and became almost one. This was the case, for example, with Ethel Clurman, who bought a small porcelain Buddha in a Harbin street bazaar in the 1920s and took it with her to San Francisco after she left China in the 1940s. She put the porcelain Buddha in the center of her living room, where it became a central reminder for the life in China and created a new glocalized space.[14]

"Big belly laughing Buddah," created by a porcelain artist in the south of China, brought to United States from Harbin by Ethel Clurman. Harbin SIRSC archives, Irene Clurman Files.

---

13 Thomas Lahusen, "Remembering China, Imagining Israel: The Memory of Difference," in *South Atlantic Quarterly* 99 (2000): 255.

14 Ethel Clurman was born February 20, 1900, in Odessa, Russia, lived many years in Harbin, and died April 4, 1994, in Reno, Nevada. Her granddaughter is Irene Clurman.

The case of Harbin is fascinating because it presents a blend of local memories, sometimes made of imaginary components, stuffed in a "glocalized suitcase." As Thomas Lahusen writes: "The memory of previous times was preserved, re-, and deconstructed elsewhere around the globe."[15] This is applicable to Shanghai as well. There were close relations between the Jewish communities of Harbin and Shanghai. In this sense, and depending on one's point of view, Harbin was the global and Shanghai the local.

Harbin was an inland port. As a railway hub, it drew human cargo from Europe, largely Eastern Europe, and Russia. Shanghai, on the other hand, was a Chinese port city for centuries, and its strategic location as an ocean gateway drew the major powers to colonize it and share its fortunes. Shanghai siphoned Jews and others from Harbin, as well as refugees by sea. It provided a temporary space for thousands of Jews, mainly from burning Europe in the late 1930s and early 1940s. Studying the stories that serve now as evidence to that era is very difficult, as these reflect traumas, nostalgic emotions and impaired remembrance.

Glocalized experiences and the memories or lack of them may present transcultural twists as in the following case. It is not only the geography that concerns me, but the background and character of individuals and the strange geographical journey they took in changing their identities and becoming something else.

Such is the case of Vera Dobrolovskaya, who was born Russian Orthodox on September 6, 1910, in Harbin and then moved to Shanghai in the 1930s, only to move again from one geography to another and another. Her father Alexander Dobrolovskii was from the Ukraine. Her mother Panna was from Vladivostok. Both were part of the antisemitic White Russian Orthodox community of Harbin. Vera's daughter, Rita Davies, said, "My Russian Orthodox grandmother was anti-Semitic as I heard her making comments about the Jews killing Christ. All this could not necessarily be reconciled and was buried instead."[16]

About her grandfather, Davies said, "Alexander Dobrolovskii was an officer in the Russian Tsarist military. Vera thought that her father was the Chief of Police for Harbin. She said that in 1928 a man he had put in prison shot and killed him following his release. . . . I have always found the story odd, even as a child. Perhaps the circumstances of her father's death were

---

15   Thomas Lahusen, "Introduction," in *South Atlantic Quarterly* 99 (2000): 2.
16   Rita Davies, communication to author, April–June 2015. Rita Davies, Vera's 70-year-old daughter who lives in Toronto now, has been trying to construct the early story of her family with much frustration.

difficult to accept, or it was his lifestyle of drinking that led to his death. Over time, she made it palatable by imagining a more noble reason and making him a heroic Dostoyevsky figure."[17]

In Harbin Vera attended a Russian school. Later she went to a convent and returned at the age of eighteen. She married in the late 1920s a wealthy Catholic Portuguese whose last name was Diniz. He had a much different cultural and economic background, and Vera looked for an exciting life and thought that he might fulfill her wishes.

She and her husband went to Shanghai sometime in the early 1930s in an attempt to resolve marital issues. Other than the fact that Diniz was physically abusive, there is no other information about this part of Vera's life. "She left Diniz at some point and later she met my Jewish father [named Jason Joseph Isaac] who by then had also left his first wife. My parents did not have a legal marriage because both were married to people who would not grant them a divorce. The Shanghai birth certificate of Rita Davies who was born out of wedlock to Vera and her new partner, shows the last name as Diniz."[18]

Jason Joseph Isaac, Rita's father, was born outside of Baghdad in 1908. After his father's death, he went with his mother to Hong Kong, where her grandfather's brother lived, Hacham Eliahu Isaac, the Hazan (cantor) of Ohel Leah Synagogue, who later became Hazan of Ohel Rachel in Shanghai. In his early twenties, he went with his mother to Shanghai. In 1930 he married another Baghdadi Jew, Mozelle Toeg. That marriage resulted in three daughters. The marriage broke up sometime in the early 1940s.

Jason Joseph Isaac and Vera Dobrolovskii-Diniz met in Shanghai and had three children. Rita was born in 1947. They left Shanghai in December 1949 on a cargo boat named "Wooster Victory" that carried refugees. It was a lengthy voyage until it reached the Israeli port of Haifa. Neither of Rita's parents had any citizenship, legal marriage certificates, or other form of documentation. They arrived in Israel as Jewish refugees sometime in 1950 and stayed there until 1959. They became an Israeli Jewish family by now and the legality of their marriage and the status of the children were taken for granted. The family left Israel for Canada in 1959. Soon after that,

---

17 Rita Davies, communication to author, May–June 2015. By 1926 the Chinese had already taken control of the city council and of all other governing posts including the police. Although there were a few Russian policemen that remained part of the force, the head of police and officers were Chinese.

18 Rita Davies, communication to author, May–June 2015.

Jason Joseph Isaac (right) and Vera Dobrolovskii-Diniz (center) with friends at a Shanghai night club, c. 1944. Vera wears an Orthodox cross necklace. Harbin SIRSC archives, Rita Davies Files.

the father changed his family's name to Davies from Isaac "because he was afraid of Canadian anti-Semitism."[19]

Their Shanghai photographs reveal a style of life untouched by the Japanese occupation of the city. There was no mention of refugees nor of hardship. In the photos, their lives looked like an endless party and nightclub dances. "Their generation was secretive. I was not told much of their or my past."[20]

A past has its twists. In this case it starts with antisemitic Russian Orthodox background in Harbin, entangles a wealthy Portuguese Catholic, finds a Jewish connection in Shanghai, continues west to Israel and ends in Toronto, Canada, after a long year in Italy. It presents several geographies and problems with memories and imagined pasts, motives, and identities, and the connection among them. The three daughters Jason Joseph Isaac had from his legal marriage, and the three daughters that were born to Vera

---

19　Rita Davies, communication to author, June 8, 2015: ". . . my parents were 'married' on the ship by a cousin of my father's, Eziekel Zion, who was a *Hacham* [sage]. I don't think that gave him the authority to perform a marriage. In any case, my parents were both still married to their first spouses. They needed this 'marriage' to get into Israel and these were desperate times. . . ."

20　Rita Davies, letter to author, May 2015.

from her relations with him, have been living a confused life, because what was left for them were only imagined pasts and assumed identities. The Jewish connection was coincidental, but helped to form a new dimension to the identities of the players and especially of their descendants.[21] And while the three out-of-wedlock daughters practice Judaism, their Jewish stepsisters consider them to be "others."

A past may be also a hidden place, if the main actors wished to keep it so, or, as in the case of the Hardoon family's adopted children, the past of each child is a "black hole." We know where it may have started, but we do not know what it contained. This saga of the Hardoon family of Shanghai starts in Harbin, develops in Shanghai, and finds itself far behind vast oceans in the United States. The journey and transformation of space and identity here has to do with economic reasons.

In 2010 I received a request for information about a Cherniavsky family photo I had placed on the Jewish Harbin web site.[22] The letter said, "My mother's parents met and married in Harbin; they had two daughters. My grandfather died suddenly, and my mother was adopted by a Shanghai family due to financial hardship after my grandfather's death. My grandfather's name was Jan Czyrkowski-Czerniawski. He worked in a Russian bank. I know very little about him. My grandparents were married in a Roman Catholic church; their daughters were baptized Catholics. However, my mother was adopted by a Jewish family. Cherniavsky sounds the same as Czerniawski (Polish spelling). I thought perhaps there might be a connection between the Cherniavsky family and my grandfather, Jan Czyrkowski-Czerniawski."[23]

A document I received on July 31, 2010, confirmed assumptions that the adopters were the Hardoon family. "A Jewish adoption agent took my mother to a Jewish home in Shanghai. . . . Mother was legally adopted in 1930, when contact with birth family ended. My adoptive grandfather died in 1931, and adoptive grandmother died in 1941 in Shanghai."[24]

---

21 When mental geographies are all that exists, and when an individual's space is being replaced by another, it may create an impaired identity that results in cultural transformation.
22 http://kehilalinks.jewishgen.org/harbin/. In July 20, 2010, I received a letter from a Mrs. Kathleen X of Fort Myers, Florida. She asked for privacy in this matter, therefore I am referring to her given name only.
23 Kathleen X, communication to author, July, 2010. All information is stored at the Sino-Israel Research and Study Center in Harbin.
24 Kathleen X, communication to author, July 31, 2010.

CERTIFICATE OF INQUIRY: I, Vtoroff, notary public of Harbin, whose office is at No. 34 Central Street of the said post now issue to the Catholic priest Antoni Janovich Leszczewicz residing at the premises of the Catholic Church of Malaya Aptekarskaya Street this Certificate as follows:

My book of record for the 19th year of the Chinese Republic [1930] shows the following matter under the date of 13th December of the same year: "Now appears Czerniawska-Czyrkowska Maria, whose father's name is Jan, residing at 68, Koikovsky, Harbin, as evidenced by Residence Permit dated 6th August of the same year produced to me, and applies in writing for registration (of document) and the contents of the said document are that Czerniawska-Czyrkowska expresses approval of the adoption by a British subject of her own-born daughter Janina Cyrylla, who was born in Harbin on the 18th of March 1927 as evidenced by birth register No. 148 issued by Harbin Catholic Church on the 9th December 1930, and who was given the name of her adopted father Hardoon.—Paid judicial fee $ 2. Prison fee $ 1. Procedural fee $ 3. Register No. 203. Maria Czerniawska-Czyrkowska.

This Certificate is issued for the use of Leszczewicz, catholic priest, and based on the declaration produced to me by Czerniawska-Czyrkowska and the said Declaration has been registered with the Representative in China under No. 5/23 on the 23th March 1932, believed to be true and signed by said lady.

Dated the 2nd day of April, 1st year of Dah Tung. Paid judicial stamp fee $ 2. Register #13947. Notary Public Book #857.

Janina Cyrylla was adopted by Silas Aaron Hardoon and his wife Liza Roos, also known as Luó Jiālíng, and was brought up, without official Rabbinic conversion, according to the Jewish faith.[25] She later migrated to the United States. Hardoon's grandson David, who lives in Singapore, confirmed my findings: "I am familiar with this person, and her mother has been indeed adopted by Silas Hardoon. I am in contact with a handful of descendants of the adopted children although I believe much of the history has been lost."[26]

---

25 Chiara Betta writes of Hardoon's wife that "at the turn of the twentieth century she adopted a number of Chinese children. . . . It should then be added that after 1919 the Hardoons also adopted together foreign children who were brought up according to the Jewish faith. . . ." Chiara Betta, "Silas Aaron Hardoon (1851–1931): Business, Politics and Philanthropy in Republican Shanghai, 1911–1931," *The Scribe* 75 (2002), accessed March 23, 2018, http://www.dangoor.com/75060.html.

26 David Hardoon, communication to author, August 9, 2010.

The now Jewish daughter's attempts to find her mother's past in Harbin were unsuccessful. There was no connection to the Jewish community, and Harbin could not provide answers about her grandmother and natural siblings. She could only imagine her mother's early life, because Janina did not remember or refused to tell.

Both Jewish communities of Harbin and Shanghai had long established symbiotic relations. And each needed, at times, the help and assistance of the other. Shanghai helped provide security for the Harbin Jewish community. The relations between the two communities were almost dependent and the following case shows Shanghai as glocalized distant geography and a source for support.

The protocol of the December 9, 1925 session of the China Eastern Railway Employee Strike Committee states:

> To safeguard its members, the Jewish community of Harbin began to look for the possibility of purchasing weapons for a self-defense force against bandit attacks and could-be pogroms by White Russians. This possibility never officially materialized, although some members of the community did manage to possess guns.[27]

Secret communiqués were sent to Shanghai requesting guns for protection against the growing White Russian antisemitism in Harbin. It also brought about the formation of Betar, an active Jewish youth organization, who engaged in sporting, communal relief activities, body combat, and self-defense practices.[28]

While many elected to hide or forget, some told their stories in a factual manner. In a 1982 audiotape made in Reno, Nevada, Ethel Clurman tells the story of her family in Harbin: "Isak Grigori, my husband, carried a pistol when walking the streets of Harbin. . . . In May 1938 he disappeared while on his way to our lumberyard. . . . No one ever saw him again. The Harbin Jewish community believed that the Japanese secret police had

---

27 Information regarding Jewish self-defense steps can be found in the protocol of the December 9, 1925, session of the CER Employee Strike Committee: GARF (Gosudarstvennyi arkhiv Rossiiskoi federatsii) 211:1,3/905.

28 Mordechai "Modka" Olmert, father of Israel's former prime minister Ehud Olmert, gave an interesting account on the start of the Betar youth movement in 1923 Harbin, in his autobiography titled "דרכי בדרך הרבים" [*Darchai b'Derech Rabim*, My Way among others] (1981). He was born in 1908 in Russia and died in 1998 in Israel.

tortured him to death and buried him in a mass grave. . . ."²⁹ Two official documents issued by the Jewish community in Shanghai and Harbin, and one by the Manchukuo government confirmed the unfortunate death of Isak Grigori at the hands of the Japanese police.

Isak Grigori on a pile of coal at his lumberyard in Harbin in the 1930s. The Harbin Hassidic synagogue (known as the New Synagogue) is behind him. Harbin SIRSC Archives, Irene Clurman files.

Ethel Clurman's account stands contrary to many diffuse memories or conceptual beliefs that override realities and create an imagined past with new contexts and new "facts." Harbin was not a paradise as many elected to tell. It was sometimes a violent space, similar in a way to the experience families had in their "old" geographies.

From its foundation, Harbin experienced turbulent times: two devastating plagues in 1910–11 and 1929, two global economic crashes that impacted local businesses, White Russian fascism that burned the old synagogue to the ground in 1932, overt antisemitism in the streets and in newspaper articles, clans of Chinese gangs that kidnaped and killed for ransom,

---

29 Ethel Clurman received an official document from the Shanghai Ashkenazi Communal Association and the Manchukuo government stating that the deceased Isak Grigori Clurman was her husband. The document was translated to Chinese and Russian. Dates differ because of Manchu, Russian Orthodox, and Gregorian calendars used by the translators.

the cruel Japanese occupation, and the postwar atrocities of the occupying Soviet Red Army.[30] We therefore must try to understand the storyteller's outlook of life, motives and circumstances, in order to put his/her tale into perspective. Can we take any testimony for granted or should we search for more informational avenues?

Despite Harbin's turbulent past, many of its foreign inhabitants chose to describe the city as paradise and safe haven. In 1929, when many of Harbin businesses were crashing in the midst of the global economic crises and the Japanese army was getting ready to invade Manchuria, seventeen-year-old Alexander Galatzky was about to pursue his university studies in Paris. He had spent his childhood and teens in Harbin, having escaped from Russia with his family in 1919. For five long years, between 1926 and 1930 this young man wrote detailed diaries about his life, friends and school in Harbin, avoiding any mention of possible hardship or concerns by those who are around him.[31] His parents left for New York sometime in the next decade.

Many years later Galatzky's daughter, who was born after her father's relocation to the United States, tried to follow his life in Harbin and decipher his diaries: ". . .so far, in my reading of his life in the years of '26–'30, this boy's writings do not reflect any of the angst or foreboding that his parents may have been concerned about given the shifting political sands. . . . After all, he was not confined to his home." That is why, "I find the diary that I am reading a piece of the puzzle of analyzing the period. . . . [There are] no references to any impending turmoil affecting his daily life, of friends moving, of parents' anxiety, etc."[32]

Why was the teller, in this case Alexander Galatzky, creating another space and story? Was the picture he painted an attempt to shield an unpleasant reality?

It is both the willingness and the ability to "think globally and act locally"[33] that may give rise to such contradictions. It takes a particular decision

---

30   Lin Huanwen and Zhao Dejiu, "Jindai Haerbin," 42–45.
31   The hand-written diaries, from 1926 to 1931, are stored at the Sino-Israel Research and Study Center with the Harbin Jewish Culture Association. The diaries are currently being translated from Russian.
32   Bonnie Galat, Washington, D.C., letters to author, December 27 and 31, 2010.
33   The original phrase "think global, act local" has been attributed to Scots town planner and social activist Patrick Geddes. See D. Barash, *Peace and Conflict Studies* (London: Sage Publications, 2002), 547. Although the exact phrase does not appear in Geddes's book *Cities in Evolution*, the idea as applied to city planning is clearly evident: "'Local

to alter the reality of life. It may come with a view of what should be known in the future. This is a global thinking. And the action taken by concealing facts is the local one. To cling to the past by wishful thinking is not a presentation of historical reality, but of "imagined history."

In considering an individual's past identity, the case of Chinese Air Force General Lin Hu, a decorated national hero, may demonstrate the complexity of historical investigation in determining a motif or reconstructing a past when facts are manipulated, imagined, or lacking.[34] This case is especially difficult, because the Chinese General Lin Hu has a European complexion, and because his geographies, spaces, and time are confused and guarded in a locked box that military authorities refuse to grant permission to open.

Lin Hu claims that he was born in Harbin in 1928. He says that his father was Chinese and his mother was Jewish Russian. His father died of unknown causes a few months after his birth. The mother died in 1932 or 1933 and was buried in Harbin. The boy and his older sister, whose name he does not remember, were put in an orphanage located near the Harbin train station. At some point the sister was taken by someone and her whereabouts are not known. The boy was taken by a family who lived near the station. After a year or so they sent him to Shandong province to another family, where he was treated very badly. They gave him his name: Lin Hu.[35]

General Lin Hu has no recollections of his past. He does not remember the name of his mother, although he says that he went to visit her grave twice, first at the age of seven, and a second time in the early 1950s. He claims that

---

character' is thus no mere accidental old-world quaintness, as its mimics think and say. It is attained only in the course of adequate grasp and treatment of the whole environment, and in active sympathy with the essential and characteristic life of the place concerned." See P. Geddes, *Cities in Evolution* (London: Williams, 1915), 397. The phrase "Think globally, act locally" or "Think global, act local" has been used in various contexts, including town planning, environment, and business.

34 Lin Hu's personal story told by his two daughters, Lin Li and Lin Ying, who contacted me via telephone at the end of 2010 and visited my home in Harbin in March 2011. His plane was shot down during the Korean War. When he fell into the hands of the North Koreans, they mistook him for an American because of his Caucasian features. Lin Hu lives with one of his daughters in Beijing. The younger daughter lives in Toronto, Canada. They have an older brother who lives in Beijing as well. His CV was provided by his daughters. Some information including a photograph came from WordPress. See "Lin Hu: Growth in the People's Liberation Army major general school," accessed February 18, 2010, http://www.9xgo.com/2010/02/lin-hu-growth-in-the-peoples-liberation-army-major-general-school/.

35 There is no reference to his birth name anywhere.

his mother's tombstone had a Star of David engraved on it, but cannot say in which cemetery it was. This "remembrance" has led his two daughters, now middle-aged Chinese-looking women, and their offspring to believe that they are Jews.[36] One may wonder how a person like General Lin Hu finds himself in a predicament such as this. A high ranking military pilot, who remembers details of military and air maneuvers, fails to recollect his own past.[37]

History is viewed sometimes as a progressive and gradually changing process. It is especially so when the storyteller moves from one space to another, forming glocalized memories. When the storyteller leaves to a new space, the old spaces go there as well. The local becomes global, hence glocalized, and many of the memories come to be imagined. In Teddy Kaufman's words: "We, who were either born in Harbin, or came to live there for some time . . . still bear in our hearts the memories of our Harbin, because each of us has a Harbin of his own."[38]

How then can one decipher facts that are held in many different hearts? What interpretation would be accepted? And who will decide which history will prevail? Irene Clurman writes, "My Aunt once told me [that] no one could write the history of Harbin Jews, because no matter what the person wrote, a dozen other people would jump in and say, no, it wasn't that way at all! And I know, because I was there."[39] Wayne Mellon suggests that presenting Harbin as a "paradise" for the Jewish community is a fiction: "I believe that my great-grandmother was interred in a Japanese concentration camp. . . ."[40] His statement shades light on a time that many other residents

---

36 Lily Lin, to author, April 4, 2011: "Do you think DNA test can prove if my dad's mother was a Jewish or not?"

37 There are many difficulties in determining the truth, partially because Lin Hu does not know either his birth name, or the names of his parents. Further investigation, including advanced psychological hypnosis, was refused by the PLA on the grounds of "national secrecy."

38 In the preface to the 2006 album edition "The Jews in Harbin" published by the Heilongjiang Academy of Social Sciences, and in Theodore Kaufman, *The Jews of Harbin Live on in My Heart* (Tel Aviv: The Association of Former Jewish Residents of China in Israel, 2004). Teddy Kaufman was born in Harbin, from which he moved to Israel in 1949. He served as president of the Association of Former Jewish Residents of China in Israel for many years. He passed away in 2012 at the age of 88.

39 Irene Clurman, letter to author, August 12, 2006. The subject of the letter in her words was "Remembering Harbin." Her grandparents, parents, and other members of the family had roots in Harbin.

40 Wayne Mellon, who lives in the United States, email to the author, October 14, 2006. It is possible that his grandmother was brought to Unit 731, the notorious Japanese secret "Medical Experiments camp" in Ping Fan, Harbin.

of Harbin elected to hide or forget, because there are but few accounts pertaining to the Jewish community under the Japanese occupation.

A detailed study of Harbin, from its inception through the Russo-Japanese War of 1904–1905, the end of Tsarist rule and the Bolshevik revolution, the Japanese invasion and occupation of the city and the region in 1932, the brutal Soviet occupation in 1945–46 and the formation of the People's Republic of China, reveals a picture quite different from many of the accounts, oral or written memoirs. Charles Clurman, who was born and grew up in Harbin, attempted to paint a realistic picture of the Japanese invasion of the city. In a letter to his daughter dated June 16, 1997, he described the difficulties of life in Manchuria:

> I was thirteen years old and Johnny [his younger brother] was three. I stood on the street corner and watched Japanese mechanized army units roll into the city.... We were totally defenseless and had no one to turn to for help and protection.... Gradually, like the Nazis, the Japanese tightened their hold on Manchuria and then the atrocities really reared their ugly heads.... They just wanted to eliminate the ruling class and Jews and Chinese merchants were it.... The White Russian remnants ... went to work for the Japanese and made sport of denouncing Jewish people to the Japanese Kempetai [sic]. Father had good connections with the Japanese since we traded with them before the occupation. He used to help our people when they were taken by the Kempetai. Unfortunately, when he was taken, there was no one to help him.[41]

There are not many accounts that describe a past as it was. Charles's memories, which confirm the story told also by several others, stands counter to others that diffuse memories and change realities.

If history lacks reality, it may give rise to mistakes, controversies, and intentional or unintentional misguidance. Nostalgia, like displaced memories, describes a feeling of longing for the past, often idealized and unrealistic, generalizing or omitting many aspects of existence.[42]

---

41   From interviews and information provided by Charles Clurman to his daughter Irene Clurman in 1997. Charles, who was born in Harbin, was sent to the United States by his father, Izko Chaim Gershowitz Clurman, for a new and secure life. One should not forget, however, that this letter was written more than half a century later and the "realistic picture" was that of a thirteen-year-old boy.

42   "An important function of nostalgia may be in providing a link between our past and present selves—that is, nostalgia may provide us with a positive view of the past and this could help to give us a greater sense of continuity and meaning to our lives." See

Nostalgia, in fact, may depend precisely on the irrecoverable nature of the past for its emotional impact and appeal. It is the very pastness of the past, its inaccessibility that likely accounts for a large part of nostalgia's power. . . . . This is rarely the past as actually experienced, of course; it is the past as imagined, as idealized through memory and desire. In this sense, however, nostalgia is less about the past than about the present.[43]

Memory is a strange and sometimes dangerous box to open. One may not know what will be found there, because the process of remembering an experience or an event that took place under certain conditions of time and space has to be considered. One should be "using positive reminiscence as part of a cycle that also includes savoring the present and looking forward to the future."[44]

For eighty-two-year-old Paul Agran, who was born and married in Harbin and lives with his wife and family in Chicago, nostalgia is a key word when he attempts to recall his personal experience in the city of his birth. "I look at everything here with nostalgia. Everything was great. Life was good. . . ."[45] How reliable are his words? What was he thinking about when he altered historical reality in his testimony? Does he remember the "good times" only?

Daniel Schacter, a Harvard professor of psychology, sees memory as a deformed mental representation of past events and facts. This deformation makes it difficult to reconstruct recollections.[46] He refutes the notion of "recovered memory," arguing that false memories can be easily created. Paul Agran's recollections are an example.

A study of history and memory should also be linked to the age, character, and motives of a storyteller.[47] The notion "that memory is a

---

Barbara Isanski, "The Psychology of Nostalgia," accessed March 23, 2018, https://www.medicalnewstoday.com/releases/132971.php.

[43] Linda Hutcheon, "Irony, Nostalgia, and the Postmodern. Methods for the Study of Literature as Cultural Memory," *Studies in Comparative Literature* 30 (2000): 189–207.

[44] Marina Krakovsky, "Nostalgia: Sweet Remembrance," *Psychology Today*, May 1, 2006, accessed April 21, 2018, https://www.psychologytoday.com/us/articles/200605/the-art-remembrance.

[45] Video interview with Paul Agran, Shangri-La Hotel, Harbin, June 2005, the Sino-Israel Research and Study Center, at the Harbin Jewish Culture Association.

[46] Daniel Schacter, *Searching for Memory: The brain, the mind and the past* (New York: Basic Books, 1997).

[47] Scholars of Holocaust studies have been leading the way in memory studies.

reconstruction of the past, not a reproduction"[48] and that the reality of history is in the mouth of the teller, may facilitate the adoption of a method with which the examination of the past by historians is just one part of a much larger equation.

Emily Rayson of Montreal presents many of the concerns: "My father, Alan Rayson, formerly called Lucia Resnikov, was born in Harbin in 1919 and he and his family were a part of the city's vibrant Jewish community. I grew up hearing all about the Hotel Moderne, his ice skating escapades and what a privileged and sheltered life he led there especially during the 2nd World War. . . ."[49] Altered memories are not necessarily nostalgia, but they do become so when one longs sentimentally for a certain past or tries to hide it.[50] Lucia Resnikov spoke of his Harbin pleasures only. And, in order to leave the past where it was, he changed his name to Alan Rayson after relocating to his new geography.

For most descendants of emigrants, their ancestors' past remains unclear and often a mystery, because only few agree in their later years to tell their stories. It is a phenomenon that makes the unveiling of past accounts difficult and in many cases inaccurate. Nevertheless some first-hand accounts do exist, as in B. F. Adams:

> Between 1921 and 1931 life was not as comfortable in Soviet-dominated Manchuria as it had been before 1921. Unemployment remained higher than it had been. The levels of prosperity reached between 1907 and 1920 did not return, and there was considerable tension between Soviet and non-Soviet Russians who lived as neighbors. During those years the city's population declined considerably from its post-civil war peak.[51]

---

48 M. Gallicchio, ed., *The Unpredictability of the Past: Memories of the Asia-Pacific War in U.S.-East Asian Relations* (Durham: Duke University Press, 2007), 5.
49 Emily Rayson, communication to author, May 11, 2011.
50 R. Douglas Field, "Making Memories Stick," *Scientific American* 292 (2005): 74–81, cited by Mariya Simakova, "The Neurobiology of Nostalgia: A Story of Memory, Emotion, and the Self," accessed March 23, 2018, http://serendip.brynmawr.edu/bb/neuro/neuro06/web3/msimakova.html: "When most of us think about memory, we imagine a grand neural library, with complete records filed away at particular locations, ready to be pulled off the shelf when the correct stimulus is introduced. Current neurobiological research, however, challenges this model of memory and suggests that there are no complete 'records' stored anywhere in the brain. Instead, both long- and short-term memories arise from the synaptic interactions between neurons."
51 Bruce F. Adams, "Re-emigration of Russians from China (1921–1960)" (paper presented at conference at Novosibirsk, Russia, December 9–11, 2002).

But economic hardships were not the only concern. Harbin became, in a sense, a mirror of Russian society as a whole—an arena for political, religious, economic, and social conflicts, as well as fertile soil for extreme Russian fascism.

> The new message of the Black Hundred (*chernosotentsy*) was that the fundamental confrontation of the contemporary world was 'Russia versus Jewry'. The idea of a Jewish conspiracy against Russia was gaining ground among Russian nationalists mainly as a result of the appearance of the notorious *Protocols of the Elders of Zion* (*Protokoly Sionskikh Mudretsov*), an infamous forgery attributed to the tsarist secret service.[52]

Jews and others came to Harbin for various reasons, among them economic opportunities as well as the perception of a "safe" environment. In this regard, Mara Moustafine sheds additional light on life in Harbin.[53] She collaborates, in part, with Clurman's testimony:

> The division into White émigrés and Soviets would have far-reaching consequences for those who remained in Manchuria during the 13 years of Japanese occupation under the guise of the Manchukuo puppet regime. Life for Jews in Manchuria deteriorated seriously after the Japanese occupation. The Japanese . . . associated closely with militant anti-Soviet Whites, such as the Russian Fascist Party (RFP), whose ideology of anti-Bolshevism and nationalism was laced with virulent anti-Semitism. For many of those who stayed on in Harbin during the Japanese occupation, life was a frightening experience. Starting in the early 1930s, Russian fascist hoodlums associated with the RFP terrorized the city in campaigns of kidnappings, extortion and murder of wealthy businessmen, among them Jews. These campaigns were masterminded by the *Kempeitai*. Faced with a declining economy, the rise in banditry, anti-Semitism, the takeover of their businesses by the Japanese and political intimidation, many Jews left Manchuria.[54]

---

52   T. Parland, *The Extreme Nationalist Threat in Russia: The Growing Influence of Western Rightist Ideas* (New York: Routledge, 2005), 22. The term "Black Hundred" refers to the paramilitary groups that belonged to the Union of Russian People (*Soiuz Russkogo Naroda*), the most important rightist party that had emerged before the first Duma elections in 1906.

53   Mara Moustafine, "My family and its city: fifty years in Harbin" (paper presented at the International Seminar on the History and Culture of Harbin Jews, Harbin, China, August 30–September 2, 2004).

54   Mara Moustafine, *Secrets and Spies: The Harbin Files* (London: Vintage, 2002).

These accounts shed a different light on the reality of Harbin, which most other writers elected to ignore or hide. The question is why they did so and for what purpose. It is natural that if the past is to matter at all, one must be aware of its nature, its shifting meanings, and its vulnerability to adjustments, causes, needs and alterations. "Materials that have to do with history, culture, society, and many other subjects that humanists and social scientists teach . . . are bound to generate controversies because no two audiences are alike. . . . Many chose to edit history but which edition is a correct one."[55] "What we remember from the past has a lot to do with what we can learn in the future."[56]

"Creation" of history is another problem, and Harbin, like many other cities in China, has several good examples of it. For China, history is a fluid process that can be, and sometimes should be, manipulated in order to achieve certain political, economic and social aims in a particular present. In such cases, the creation of history serves a new agenda, and ties everything to a past that in many instances was different or did not exist at all. In turn, it becomes a historical reality. These "histories" are easily erected and can disappear at a whim when an order is given.

An example of this is the "cemetery for the fallen Russian heroes" who died in the vicinity of Harbin while fighting the Japanese in 1945. The cemetery was constructed in 2006, just before the signing of a strategic treaty between China, Russia, and India. The ceremony took place in Harbin and the Russian Foreign Minister gave a speech in the cemetery. The fake cemetery holds newly made tombstones and no graves. Among the tombstones are those of persons who died here in the 1950s and were taken from the neighboring new Russian Orthodox cemetery. These present a problem, because history does not remember any Russian soldier who died on Chinese soil, near Harbin, in the late 1940s and in the 1950s.

---

55 Prof. Jing Wang, "Further thoughts on the MIT controversy," H-Asia, May 5, 2006, accessed April 21, 2018, http://h-net.msu.edu/cgi-bin/logbrowse.pl?trx=vx&list=H-Asia&month=0605&week=a&msg=ES3gm4QRAVCUFL6Az244/g&user=&pw=%3E.
56 Ashish Ranpura, "How We Remember, and Why We Forget," Brain Connection, accessed April 21, 2018, https://brainconnection.brainhq.com/2013/03/12/how-we-remember-and-why-we-forget.

Workers construct the cemetery for fallen Russian soldiers at Huangshan Public Cemetery in Harbin. Photo: Dan Ben-Canaan, 2006.

Political maneuverings influenced by interests and needs of a particular time have put forth new sites as symbolic gestures. But beneath the symbols one can find signs that suggest that even a cemetery is part of the game and that the dead or their tombstones may be an ever changing temporary space. "Place defined not simply in terms of location and topography, but of the memories enshrined in myth and rite which render it unique, the center of the world for those whose place it is," or those who made it their new home. "In being lost—often long lost—these places have also lost their particularity; the nostalgia is no longer for places, but for place imbued with an

Edenic innocence."[57] The Harbin fake military cemetery has a history now. And the Harbin municipal government proudly announces its existence by recommending a visit.[58]

Many so-called historical accounts, official and private, are edited to suit the writers' goals and wishes. In his autobiography, Mordechai-Modka Olmert opened a small window into the daily existence of a young person and his family in Harbin and Qiqihar.[59] "In Harbin, my mother opened a small store where she sold milk. . . ." Later, when the family relocated to Qiqihar, a small town northwest of Harbin, Modka writes, "Every family in the small community of Qiqihar had a few chickens for eggs and a cow for milk. . . ." His writings, however, were manipulated by Amram Olmert, his elder son, who reconstructed his father's memoirs to fit a certain personal wish.[60] He claims that his family was the first to establish a dairy farm in China over a hundred years ago. Passages from his fictional story have already been included in at least one academic paper.[61]

The most popular nostalgic accounts about Harbin published in recent years have been several photo albums, memoirs, and autobiographies. Some were published in China in order to paint a picture that aids the attainment of particular political or economic goals,[62] and others either drew material from incomplete reports or were based on nostalgic and selective recollections.

Karl Schlögel suggests that "It would be . . . fascinating to map Harbin or the many different and conflicting Harbin textures . . . and to create a cultural topography which demonstrates and visualizes the social, political,

---

57 M. Featherstone, "Global and local cultures," in *Mapping the Futures: Local Cultures, Global Change*, ed. Jon Bird, Barry Curtis, and Tim Putnam (London: Routledge, 1993), 177, cited in J. Beckett, "Against nostalgia: place and memory in Myles Lalor's 'Oral History,'" Oceania 66, no. 4 (1996): 312–22.
58 See Harbin Municipal government's list of suggested sites (in English).
59 Olmert, *Darchai b'Derech Rabim*.
60 Amram Olmert, *My China* (Tel Aviv: Saar Publishers, 2008). Israeli-born Amram Olmert served as Agriculture Attaché at the Israel Embassy to China in Beijing.
61 Jonathan Goldstein, "Not Just Another Country: The Olmert Family Sojourn Through China as a Case Study of the Role of Travel in Jewish Identity Formation," in *Jewish Journeys: from Philo to Hip Hop*, ed. J. Jordan, T. Kushner and S. Pearce (London: Vallentine Mitchell, 2010), 214–31.
62 Such as "bringing Jewish money" to Harbin, a task that was entrusted to the Heilongjiang Academy of Social Sciences. In 1999 Prof. Zhang Tiejiang, a Research Fellow at the Heilongjiang Academy of Social Sciences and the Assistant Director of its Jewish Center, wrote an essay titled Suggestions for the Study of Harbin Jews to Quicken Heilongjiang Economic Development.

economic and cultural encounters of North East China with the World in the 20th century."[63] This suggestion is quite applicable to the Shanghai experience as well.

History can be unveiled through a collaborative effort of varied disciplines to ensure that the imagined past is understood to be just that—a creation in one's mind and not a factual record. Glocalized suitcase memories of an imagined past, nostalgia and tailored remembrance create fiction—a (re)construction of history, depending on the motive of the storyteller. "Understanding of memory is an understanding of the role of experience in shaping our lives,"[64] and experience has several faces, especially when the local integrates with the global and creates new identities, new geography of glocalized past and myth.

Harbin is not an exception, and imagined history also exists in Shanghai.

---

63   Karl Schlögel, letter to author, April 2009: "Reading Time in Space. Mapping Cultural Junctions, Outline of my Contribution for the Harbin Summer School."
64   Ranpura, "How We Remember."

Gabrielle Abram*

Ephemeral Memories, Eternal Traumas and Evolving Classifications: Shanghai Jewish Refugees and Debates about Defining a Holocaust Survivor[1]

Wandering[2]

I

Wander Jew, wander, roam,
For you only a shabby tent.
Nowhere is a peaceful home,
Move on, wander in the world.

---

* Gabrielle Abram was born in London. She earned an undergraduate degree in history at Bristol University and a Master of Studies in Global and Imperial History at Oxford University. She is currently studying for a Graduate Diploma in Law, aiming at a career as a commercial solicitor.
1 Dedicated to Trixie Wachsner, who passed away shortly after our interview, to all Shanghai refugees and their relatives who graciously contributed their time and memories to this study, and to those who were not present to tell their stories, but whose voices are heard through their families and the writings and interviews they have left behind.
2 Quoted in Irene Eber, *Voices from Shanghai: Jewish Exiles in Wartime China* (Chicago: University of Chicago Press, 2008), 85–86.

II
Condemned to ramble
Even in the hoary past.
Remember the Egyptian gamble,
You lost and fled in the Red Sea.

III
And later when the sword of Rome
Destroyed your state,
You set forth once more to roam,
From land to land.

IV
Never more will you find rest,
Ever onward you must move.
Always only as a guest,
No use trying to remain.

V
Wander Jews, roam afar,
These the words that greet you.
Under moon and under star,
Go on roaming, go away.

VI
How much farther need they range,
Over oceans and through states,
To endure what's odd and strange,
Why submit to hardship thus?

VII
Open your eyes at last,
New world that's civilized.
Release us from suffering vast,
Bring us the calm we need.

Hermann Goldfarb (1942)

Hermann Goldfarb, born in 1919, was nineteen in January, 1939, when he left his home in Berlin for Shanghai, fleeing in the aftermath of *Kristallnacht*, November 9, 1938. These events had shown Hermann, a Jewish cabinet-maker supporting a widowed mother and younger brother, the necessity of escape from Nazi-occupied Europe. In the same year that he left for Shanghai, his brother took the *Kindertransport* to France and his mother gained a permit to work in England.[3] His family became scattered and unreachable. In 1942, he presented his poem "Wandering" at a variety evening in Shanghai.[4] Hermann's performance would have reminded his audience of fellow refugees that they fit with a historic pattern of intermittent Jewish homelessness. They had wandered to the other side of the world, but hoped it would not be their last journey. The final verse of Hermann's poem wished for a "new world" to release him from his suffering. He was granted partial release when he entered the United States in October 1949.

When the reality of firsthand suffering was over, the postwar decades saw Holocaust trauma categorized by Holocaust cognoscenti and survivors alike under a "hierarchy of suffering." The Shanghai Jewish refugees are some of the last Holocaust victims to have their suffering formally acknowledged and their identities declared to be those of Holocaust survivors, both by their peers and in their own self-reflections.

At first glance, the subject of this work appears to be quite humble. However, it is about more than the straightforward experiences of the wartime Jewish refugees of Shanghai. It concerns the legitimacy of post-Holocaust memory, of trauma and of becoming part of a "Holocaust survivor" demographic that is both uniquely constructed and rigidly defined. This study examines how debates surrounding the definition of Holocaust survivor have evolved since the initial postwar years and traces how a survivor identity has developed alongside this definition for the community of European Jews who lived in Shanghai as refugees between 1933 and 1949. These issues are of particular relevance today, because they follow the recent "global turn" in historical studies of World War II and the Holocaust. Historians have, with increasingly frequency, turned to

---

[3] Hermann Goldfarb, video interview at Visual History Archive, USC Shoah Foundation, #46853, Rochester, NY, November 13, 1998; Alexandra Garbarini, ed., *Jewish Responses To Persecution*: vol. II: *1938–1940* (Lanham, MD: AltaMira Press, 2011), 49–52. Many of the interviews used as sources in this essay were conducted by the Survivors of the Shoah Visual History Foundation. In 2006, this archive was relocated to the University of Southern California and renamed the USC Shoah Foundation.

[4] Eber, *Voices from Shanghai*, 86.

studying the Third Reich within an international context and World War II as an event with global scope, connecting East and West in one war, rather than depicting them as fighting separate battles.[5] Thus, one might consider this to be a study of the global Holocaust and its survivors in the East.

The relevant historiography is divided between cultural studies of the everyday life of Jewish refugees in Shanghai up to 1945 and wider works about the aftermath of the Holocaust, its memorialization and developments in survivor identity and definitions. The latter group is further split among the themes of memory, trauma and patterns of change in Holocaust history, including the classification of Holocaust suffering. The issue of memory has become a preoccupation within Holocaust history and is an essential part of this case study. Key works are Dominick LaCapra's writings on trauma and the role of psychoanalysis in historical understanding.[6] Early memory is a central focus in studies by Rubin Suleiman, Robert Krell and Sharon Kangisser Cohen, who shed light on child survivors and how they fit into debates surrounding the definition of a Holocaust survivor.[7] These are of particular significance to this study, as the majority of former refugees alive to tell their stories today were children and adolescents during their years in Shanghai. Works produced recently have sought to address the traumas associated with the "myth of silence" promulgated by historians up to the mid-90s.[8]

Beth B. Cohen's notion that survivors took time to acculturate to their new homes and plan for the future, while at the same time maintaining a desire to look back on their past traumas as part of a collective, is central to this study. Where Shanghai survivors reminisced on their mutual past as a collective, few outside of their community acknowledged their story as significant in the hierarchy of Holocaust experience. The shaping of a

---

5   Richard J. Evans, *The Third Reich In History And Memory* (London: Oxford University Press, 2015), VI–IX.
6   See Dominick LaCapra, *Writing History, Writing Trauma* (Baltimore: Johns Hopkins University Press, 2001); Dominick LaCapra, *History and Memory after Auschwitz* (Ithaca, NY: Cornell University Press, 1998), 180–210.
7   See S. Rubin Suleiman, "The 1.5 Generation: Thinking About Child Survivors and the Holocaust," *American Imago* 59, no. 3 (2002): 277–95; Robert Krell, ed., *Child Holocaust Survivors: Memories and Reflections* (Victoria, British Columbia: Trafford Publishing, 2007); Sharon Kangisser Cohen, *Child Survivors of the Holocaust in Israel: Finding Their Voice* (Brighton, UK: Sussex Academic Press, 2005).
8   See Beth B. Cohen, *Case Closed: Holocaust Survivors in Postwar America* (New Brunswick, NJ: Rutgers University Press, 2007); David Cesarani and Eric J. Sundquist, eds., *After the Holocaust: Challenging the Myth of Silence* (London: Routledge, 2012).

Holocaust survivor definition by US institutions offers insight into the reasons for the underrepresentation of the Shanghai episode. The recent inclusion of Shanghai refugees into the fold of "Holocaust survivors" is explained by expansions in definitions. Myra Giberovitch's 2014 study examines Holocaust survivor identity and changing perceptions of survivors, helping to explain how a Holocaust survivor "identity crisis" affected the speed with which those who suffered the Holocaust adopted the survivor label.[9] Dahlia Ofer, Françoise Ouzan, and Judy Baumel-Schwartz turned a new page in Holocaust studies in 2012 by drawing attention away from research focused on survivors' impact on the societies to which they immigrated, instead investigating their personal lives in the aftermath of the war.[10] This essay builds on this new approach by looking at a specific group, previously uncategorized within Holocaust history. Thus, this study will merge new approaches to the Holocaust with a new approach to the wartime Jewish refugee community of China.

In order to offer distinct insights into the wartime Jewish refugee community of Shanghai and their place in debates surrounding the definition of a Holocaust survivor, a variety of primary source materials will be drawn upon. Following Raul Hilberg's advice, documentary sources such as diaries, memoirs and newspaper articles have been used alongside oral history testimonies, in order to counter the omnipresent issue of reliability that surrounds discussions about survivor memory.[11] Indeed, such issues are somewhat immaterial in this work, given that the intention here is not to reconstruct events of the past, but instead to explore how memory has been changed and experiences repositioned in line with the adoption of the "Holocaust survivor" label, and how such a repositioning fits within existing definitions surrounding the classification of survivors. The voices of the former Shanghai refugees will be heard through their testimonies archived at the USC Shoah Foundation and the United States Holocaust Memorial Museum, and in interviews conducted by this author through a range of media. The aim of the interviews collected for this work has been to represent a cross section of refugees who escaped from Austria following the

---

9   See Myra Giberovitch, *Recovering From Genocidal Trauma: An Information and Practice Guide for Working with Holocaust Survivors* (Toronto: University of Toronto Press, 2014).
10 Dalia Ofer, Françoise S. Ouzan, and Judy Tydor Baumel-Schwartz, eds., *Holocaust Survivors: Resettlement, Memories, Identities* (New York: Berghahn Books, 2012), 2.
11 LaCapra, *Writing History, Writing Trauma*, 86.

Anschluss, from Germany after *Kristallnacht,* and from Poland after the Nazi invasion. It also aims to represent both the orthodox and secular strands of European Jews who found a safe haven in Shanghai. This is particularly important, as distinctions between the two communities had a significant effect on the building of Holocaust identity in refugees' post-Shanghai lives. The limitation of a study of the Holocaust conducted today is that only the youngest of survivors could be spoken with in person, and the age range of the individuals who were able to give unique testimonies for this work ranges from those born in Shanghai to twelve at the time of arrival. The stories of older generations of refugees are told by their relatives and through the documents and writings donated by their families.

This essay explores how the Shanghai Jews fit with existing classifications of Holocaust survivors, how such definitions have evolved, and how a new classification, that of the "Shanghai survivor," is in its early stages of development. It opens by considering developments in private memory at the beginning of the former refugees' postwar years. It addresses similarities with the "child survivor" generation concerning age and experience, and how such issues have created ephemeral memory. It will then identify how Shanghai refugees have re-remembered events and reclassified them in order to create more "legitimate" wartime memories that can be repositioned within a Holocaust chronology.

I then consider how former refugees took time to acclimate to their new homes in the United States and how, having unlocked and repositioned traumatic memory, they dealt with these issues, while at the same time advancing in careers and building families. The particular focus of this section will be on the issue of "survivor silence" and three specific models of thought within it, exploring how the classification of "silence" has been applied to Holocaust survivors in general and how the Shanghai refugees fit within such categories. Pivotal to this section is how they perceive the "hierarchy of suffering" and the position on its scale where they identify themselves. It will conclude by considering the importance of recognition and "community identity" in breaking the silence and allowing for the creation of a new kind of Holocaust survivor identity.

The final section addresses recent patterns in the way Holocaust survivors have been defined and the involvement of the second generation in the development of survivor identity in former Shanghai refugees. It will consider how return visits to Shanghai with younger family members, whom Marianne Hirsch calls the "generation of post-memory," have aided in this mission. It will also explore the extent to which wider recognition by those outside of their families is important in the development of a new category of Holocaust survivors. I conclude by considering how a people who arrived in the United States as "outsiders" to the Holocaust are gradually taking on the "survivor" definition, and how this is affecting Holocaust historiography more generally, with the birth of a new kind of survivor identity. The United States will be the focal point as the destination that the majority of Shanghai refugees immigrated to after liberation.[12] It is not my objective to say whether or not the Shanghai Jews deserve the survivor label, nor is it to define accurately what a Holocaust survivor is. Rather, I will be exploring the former refugees' journey towards considering themselves legitimate recipients of this label and how this compares to other groups of Holocaust survivors with similar and different experiences who have been classified as conforming to distinct labels. The fact that numerous definitions exist is significant only in so far as each definition affects the Holocaust consciousness of my focal community.

Ephemeral Memories: Child Survivors and the Outsider Generation

"We are the middle. We are the in-between generation, the one and a half generation, the forgotten ones."[13] For Maurice Halbwachs, collective memories are the DNA that link generations in their communal identities.[14] To be considered a part of a generation and be given identity as a member, an event needs to have been collectively experienced with shared memory of that experience. While generations at different phases of the life cycle may have different memories of the same event, it is problematic for a single generation, brought together as a collective on the basis of sharing a collective memory, to have members with conflicting memories.[15] This is the issue presented by child survivors of the Holocaust. They do not exist within the adult "first generation" of survivors, nor within the second generation of children of survivors. They are the one and a half generation, those who

---

12 Steve Hochstadt, *Exodus To Shanghai: Stories of Escape from the Third Reich* (New York: Palgrave Macmillan, 2012), 201.
13 H. Dasberg, "Children of The Holocaust Now and Then," in *Child Holocaust Survivors*, 58.
14 See Maurice Halbwachs, *On Collective Memory*, trans. Lewis A. Coser (Chicago: University of Chicago Press, 1992).
15 A. B. Spitzer, "The Historical Problem of Generations," *American Historical Review* 78, no. 5 (1973): 1363.

have witnessed the war, but cannot use their ephemeral and fragmentary memories to bear witness in the same way as their older contemporaries. Lacking a generational consciousness of their own and the memories to join with an established group are strong reasons why the self-identification of child survivors as Holocaust survivors in the postwar world was more delayed than those of their mature survivor peers.[16] Late adoption of the survivor label is a consistent pattern among children who lived through the Holocaust, both in camps and in hiding.

A parallel between child survivors and former Shanghai refugees, both young and old, can be drawn. Like child survivors, Shanghai refugees did not fit with one specific Holocaust generation. The majority who have been interviewed or have written memoirs were under twenty on arrival in Shanghai and a number considerably younger than this.[17] In addition, like this 1.5 generation they shared few memories in common with the older survivors of camps and ghettos. Those experiences they did have in common were often lived through at a young age and their recall of these was, at best, ephemeral and fragmentary. Shanghai refugees did not become self-conscious members of a survivor generation until they were able to see their experiences and memories as part of the Holocaust.[18] Issues of age and locational experience have created repressed, fragmented and lost memory; in order for these memories to become worthy to be considered recollections of Holocaust experiences, they had to be re-remembered and reclassified. Child survivors and former Shanghai refugees did this at different rates, based on their own unique experiences, both during and after the Holocaust. The search for memory became a necessary first step in the creation of a "survivor experience" that formed the basis for creating a new generational classification.

For child survivors who were repressing memory, the United States provided a safe environment to open up (in time). For hidden children and the Shanghai survivors, it provided an environment for education. Arriving in the United States between 1945 and 1949, both hidden children and former Shanghai refugees learned, for the first time, alongside their new countrymen, of the atrocities that had been carried out by the Nazis

---

16 Suleiman, "The 1.5 Generation," 287.
17 Hochstadt, *Exodus To Shanghai*, 8.
18 Karl Mannheim, "The Problem of Generations," in *Karl Mannheim: Essays on the Sociology of Knowledge*, ed. P. Kecskemeti (London: Routledge and Kegan Paul,1952), 309.

in Europe against their coreligionists and the family members they had left behind.[19] So began a period of passive Holocaust education for the refugees that was crucial in allowing them a new context in which to place their memories. Recollections of life before Shanghai began to evolve from personal instances of discrimination and maltreatment into Nazi inspired and conducted persecution, as part of a wider plan to exterminate European Jewry.[20] As Yehuda Bauer contends, the only way to deal with the trauma of events was to weave the Holocaust into their own historic events.[21] The Shanghai Jews began this process after 1949.

Memory is not neutral and, unlike history, it does not have to follow a distinct chronology. For Holocaust survivors, memory can be severely disordered. It cannot be used to certify facts nor is it useful as a lone source in reconstructing events.[22] There is fluidity to memory, and Shanghai refugees experienced changes to their memory in three stages: on leaving their hometowns, on arriving in Shanghai and on immigrating to the United States. The testimonies of those who witnessed the Holocaust demonstrate that there is a certain agency to memory. Where some are eager to take on an "amnesia," others believe "it is better to remember too much than to forget."[23] Many concentration camp survivors, young and old, desired to disremember that which they had experienced. For many hidden children, as well as Shanghai Jews, this was the reverse: they desired to remember that which they had not experienced.[24] Lacking memories of key episodes of persecution made later traumas feel illegitimate, as they could not be placed on a timeline with earlier events.[25] For former refugees, such incidents as the November pogrom and the *Anschluss* became these defining experiences, as they were the last memories of Nazi persecution that they shared with other German-speaking survivors. Memories that might once

---

19   Gary Matzdorff, video interview at Visual History Archive, USC Shoah Foundation, #18665, Ventura, CA, August 13, 1996.
20   Gertrude Kracauer, *Memories and Images of my Shanghai Years*, manuscript (New York, 1991), 78.
21   Yehuda Bauer, *Rethinking The Holocaust* (New Haven: Yale University Press, 2001), XII.
22   Lawrence L. Langer, *Admitting the Holocaust: Collected Essays* (Oxford: Oxford University Press, 1995), 13.
23   Irene Eber, *Wartime Shanghai and the Jewish Refugees from Central Europe: Survival, Co-Existence, and Identity in a Multi-Ethnic City* (Berlin: De Gruyter, 2012), 4.
24   Aaron Haas, *The Aftermath: Living with the Holocaust* (Cambridge, UK: Cambridge University Press, 1996), 95.
25   Harry Katz, telephone interview by author, February 6, 2014; Audrey Marcus, Skype interview by author, January 23, 2014.

have been faint were replayed as pivotal experiences of self-identification. It is important to note, however, that such memories of key events that allowed the Shanghai Jews to feel "legitimate" as survivors were not fabrications, but were often logically repositioned remembrances.

Harry Katz was just six years old when he experienced *Kristallnacht* in Berlin. He described a memory of "large black boots at the top of the stairs" during the night of November 9, 1938, and his mother's fearful reaction to them. While he himself did not remember the exact context within which this memory was created, nor have any idea who was wearing the boots, he was keen, upon arriving in America, to have his mother confirm that it was a memory from that time, in order to legitimize his identity as someone who had experienced the Holocaust. He admitted that at such a young age he might have adopted memories that did not relate to his own personal experience, but came from hearing an older relative's narrative. Harry's experiences at age six would all have been processed through the prism of his own youth. His most distinct memory from the time, beyond the boots, was that the disruption had caused his sixth birthday party to be cancelled.[26]

Both Evelyn Pike Rubin and Elie Grasse had faint memories of their time in Germany and Austria respectively, but both have reexamined their experiences to place them within a Holocaust chronology. Elie recalls being chased through the streets of Vienna at age nine by classmates who were screaming "Dirty Jew."[27] At age seven, Evelyn Pike Rubin remembers that signs were put up reading "*Juden sind hier unerwünscht*" ("Jews are not welcome here"), but not understanding why on one day she was allowed into the park and the next day she was not. As a child, it took time to associate these memories with their discriminatory contexts. Following Susan Rubin Suleiman's premise, those children who were removed from their native countries to find safety in a foreign land were delayed in developing a survivor identity.[28] Early memories did not conform with those experienced in Shanghai, and thus had to be separated from them and clarified, to have them form part of a distinct timeline of persecution.

For those who were particularly young on arrival in Shanghai, such as Harry, the unique experience in China overpowered memories of life in Germany. Indeed, even early memories of Shanghai were fragmented.

---

26 Harry Katz, interview by author.
27 Elie Grasse, Skype interview by author, March 26, 2014.
28 Suleiman, "The 1.5 Generation," 286.

After spending almost a decade in China, the majority of his living years, the Shanghai experience became the "ordinary," with few recollections of a time before.[29] However, what marks Harry out from both his younger peers and those who escaped Germany and Austria before *Kristallnacht* is that he had some claim to memory from this defining episode. Those who were unable to piece together any memories of persecution in Europe had more difficulty coming to terms with a Holocaust identity. Horst Eisfelder was thirteen when he left Berlin, departing for Shanghai on October 30, 1938, crucially missing the events of the November pogrom by just ten days. He commented that he was "ambivalent about considering myself a Holocaust survivor. Having escaped from Germany before the notorious 9th November 1938, I have not experienced the extremes of Nazi behavior."[30] With a similar background and aged just five on his escape, Claus Hirsch shared this ambivalence.[31] Werner Glass arrived in Shanghai in 1933 aged six and made a clear distinction in his testimony between survivors and children of survivors. He explained that he believed the "defining factor" was that, unlike his parents, he made no "deliberate decision that would influence my fate."[32]

Taking on the survivor definition was yet more difficult for those with no claim to any memory of a time in Europe. Individuals who were born in China to Holocaust-escapee parents are referred to collectively as "Shanghai babies" by their peers. While they did not experience persecution in their parents' hometowns, they did suffer the traumas associated with life in Shanghai, particularly after 1943 when the Japanese enforced ghettoization. Like hidden children, they have disturbing memories from this time that are more difficult to fit with the common Holocaust survivor timeline. Indeed, it took time for young refugees and "Shanghai babies" to appreciate the horrors of their time in China, given that they had known nothing else until their arrival in the United States or elsewhere after liberation.

Hearing of the heartbreaking fates that relatives and friends had suffered at the hands of the Nazis in Europe was another form of Holocaust

---

29 Rolf Preuss, *Growing up in Shanghai*, manuscript (Seattle, 1990).
30 Horst Peter Eisfelder, *Chinese Exile: My Years in Shanghai and Nanking* (Melbourne: Ayotaynu Foundation, 2003).
31 Claus Hirsch, video interview at Visual History Archive, USC Shoah Foundation, #20002, New York, NY, September 19, 1996.
32 Werner Glass, interview by Gratz College Hebrew Education Society, Philadelphia, PA, April 7, 1992, accessed May 8, 2015, https://collections.ushmm.org/search/catalog/irn508724.

education that aided in the establishment of survivor identity. The American Red Cross informed Harry Katz that his older brother, who he thought had immigrated to Palestine, had actually been transported from Berlin to Buchenwald before he could make his escape.[33] Lotte Marcus learned of her relatives' terminal fate in 1948, two years after arriving in the United States. For the majority, it took until the 1990s for information to be collected concerning their lost families. Such a delay, undoubtedly, postponed their survivor identity formation. Gerda Haas did not know that her parents had been picked up by the SS in Berlin in 1943 until the 1990s, and Alfred Adler had to wait until 1993 to hear that his parents had been murdered in Auschwitz.[34] Gary Matzdorff explained in an interview that, not long after his escape to Shanghai, his grandparents were transported to Breslau (now Wrocław), later to be conveyed to Theresienstadt, where they both perished.[35] His wife Nancy informed me that her husband did not hear from the American Red Cross about his grandparents' demise until 1994.[36]

No matter the differences of experiences in Shanghai, loss was something they shared with every other Holocaust survivor. Lawrence Langer has identified a pattern in survivor behavior that he called the "disintegrated self."[37] In postwar life, survivors coexisted with those who did not survive, whose deaths became an essential part of their own self-identification. Fred Marcus became a Jewish educator not long after his arrival in the United States.[38] He felt that the shared experiences of loss allowed him to identify with the other Holocaust survivors with different experiences whom he met through his work.[39]

Once aware of their families' fate in Europe, it was the Shanghai refugees with some memory of post-*Anschluss* Austria or *Kristallnacht* who chose to speak first. Just as these individuals have been quicker to identify themselves as worthy of the "survivor" classification, they have been quicker

---

33 Harry Katz, interview by author.
34 Gerda Haas, video interview at Visual History Archive, USC Shoah Foundation, #19837, Tacoma, WA, October 6, 1996; Alfred Adler, video interview at Visual History Archive, USC Shoah Foundation, #9024, Tamarac, FL, November 21, 1995.
35 Gary Matzdorff, video interview at Visual History Archive.
36 N. Matzdorff to author, email "Shanghai correspondence," November 20, 2013.
37 Lawrence Langer, "Holocaust and Jewish Memory in the Paintings of Samuel Bak" (lecture at Strassler Family Center for Holocaust and Genocide Studies, Clark University, Worcester, MA, September 25, 2002).
38 Audrey Friedman Marcus and Rena Krasno, *Survival in Shanghai: The Journals of Fred Marcus, 1939–49* (Berkeley, CA: Pacific View Press, 2008), 244.
39 Audrey Marcus, interview by author.

to acknowledge the importance of telling their stories. Memoirs began to be published in the 1990s and Ernest Heppner and Sigmund Tobias were some of the first to produce texts, having strong memories of *Kristallnacht* and other incidents of pre-Shanghai persecution.[40] Others who were younger were left with memories so fragmentary that they felt unable to give testimony. Rolf Preuss has still not published his diaries and private memoirs, as he believes that they do not form a continuous and coherent narrative.[41]

The formation of a collective "child survivor" generation marked a significant change in how Holocaust survivors were defined. This change came about in 1981 with the founding of the World Federation of Jewish Child Survivors of the Holocaust and Descendants.[42] This was followed by the gradual emergence of other child survivor organizations around the world. At a conference for child survivors in New York in 1991, Elie Weisel commented that "the enemy changed your identity but in most cases, failed to change your memory."[43] The idea of using this memory to give testimony about the events of the Holocaust and to deny the Nazi ambition to eliminate the Jews, children first, finally came to the fore. Child survivors began to take on a more active role in the retelling and reliving of their experiences. Having acquired the collective identity of child survivors, they gained the confidence and the mission to make their stories known.[44] The creation of such a generation sped up the survival self-identification for former Shanghailanders. Hearing others with unique experience of escape and similarly fragmented memories tell their stories allowed the Shanghai refugees greater legitimacy in telling their own. Indeed, Jerry Moses commented that being able to count himself "among the eleven percent of Jewish children that, by some miracle, survived" was significant in allowing him to reappraise past events.[45]

If child survivors were able to consider themselves as a survivor generation in the mid-1980s, it took until the late 1990s and early 2000s

---

40 See Sigmund Tobias, *Strange Heaven: A Jewish Childhood in Wartime Shanghai* (Champaign, IL: University of Illinois Press, 1999); Ernest G. Heppner, *Shanghai Refuge: A Memoir of the World War II Jewish Ghetto* (Lincoln, NB: University of Nebraska Press, 1995).
41 Preuss, *Growing up in Shanghai*.
42 Cohen, *Child Survivors of the Holocaust in Israel*, 15–16.
43 Elie Wiesel, "Hidden Memories," in *Child Holocaust Survivors*, 44.
44 S. Moskovitz, "Making Sense of Survival: A Journey with Child Survivors," in *Child Holocaust Survivors*, 16–21.
45 Jerry Moses to author, email "Shanghai Jewish Refugees," April 13, 2014.

for the Shanghai refugees to reclassify their own communal identity. Re-remembering past events was the crucial first step in allowing the Shanghai Jews to recognize their experiences as falling within a Holocaust chronology. However, other obstacles also had to be overcome. Having accessed traumatic memory, the second stage was learning to live with such distressing recollections. The voices collected in this thesis represent individual experiences. Each person dealt with their relationship to the past in a different way during their early postwar lives. Each had a different relationship with "survivor silence" and the "survivor guilt" associated with a hierarchy of Holocaust suffering. Becoming part of a community and recognizing each other as survivors have been crucial to their identity formation. Just as child survivors found an audience for their testimony at events run by and for their community, many of the Shanghai refugees have required forums in which to share memories and identities. Private memory, now reclassified, had to become public memory through sharing and recognition.

Langer has asserted that survivors have marked their lives across two separate chronologies.[46] So far, I have focused on the first chronology, how Shanghai refugees lived according to the narrative of their Holocaust experiences. Next I will consider the second chronology, how they lived within the conventional calendar, going about everyday life through a veil of the irreversible trauma that they had experienced and uncovered, and how this affected their perceptions and the mental and physical health of themselves and their families.[47] This will help to place the Shanghai refugee community into existing classifications of survivor silence and survivor guilt.

Eternal Traumas: Silent Survivors and the Shanghai Generation

Since the mid-1990s, "silence" has become a common and contradictory feature within Holocaust historiography that considers the lives of Holocaust survivors in the postwar world, specifically in the United States and in Israel. "Survivor silence" in its earliest incarnation was held responsible for the lack of historical research undertaken in the 1950s up until the trial of Adolf Eichmann in 1961.[48] It was argued that, after the war, survivors participated in a "silence" through which they sought to forget their

---

46 Langer, *Admitting the Holocaust*, 13–20.
47 Cohen, *Case Closed*, 116.
48 Cesarani, "Introduction," in *After the Holocaust*, 1.

trauma and overwrite old memories with early positive experiences in their postwar lives. The Eichmann trial was considered the turning point, when they felt able to begin speaking, having now acclimated to their postwar homes and been empowered by hearing the voices of survivors called as witnesses by Gideon Hausner's prosecution. Thus, historians were finally granted sources for their research.

The "conspiracy of silence," a model of thought outlined in 1982 by Yael Danieli, has recently been more widely supported.[49] Danieli reasoned that a self-established and magnified "hierarchy of suffering" was preventing many survivors with unconventional stories of escape from speaking out, as they either did not consider themselves to have experienced the Holocaust or thought their experiences were incomparable to those further up the hierarchy. In addition, she argued that older survivors stayed silent, so as not to pass their own traumas on to their children. Having been denied the agency to protect their loved ones during the Holocaust, they took the opportunity to do so now. More recently, historians such as Beth Cohen, David Cesarani and Eric Sundquist criticized the 1990s definition of "survivor silence" as a historical construction that has been applied too universally.[50] They approved of Danieli's theories, but advanced upon them by creating the concept of the "myth of silence." Holocaust survivors had a strong desire to recount and remember, but a receptive audience did not exist, beyond their own communities. Indeed, proponents of this school of thought argue that survivors were not encouraged to share their testimonies, and those who were willing to listen were quick to condemn survivor recollections as untrue.[51] Each of these models of "silence" can be applied to the postwar lives of the Shanghai Jews.

On leaving Shanghai from 1946 to 1949, former refugees who immigrated to the United States escaped the shocking conditions of the Designated Area in Hongkou, where they had spent over two years.[52] Some refugees had been living longer than that in *Heime*, "thirty-four people to

---

[49] Y. Danieli, "Families of survivors of the Nazi Holocaust: Some short- and long-term effects," in *Stress and Anxiety*, vol. 8, ed. Charles D. Speilberger, Irwin G. Sarason and N. A. Milgram (New York: Hemisphere Publishing, 1982), 405–421; Cohen, *Child Survivors of the Holocaust in Israel*, 83.
[50] Cesarani, "Introduction," 2; Cohen, *Case Closed*, 115.
[51] Cohen, *Case Closed*, 155–58.
[52] J. E. Greene, "Diary Entries 1946–7," ME1495, Leo Baeck Institute, New York; Anon, "More Jewish Refugees Reach Shanghai from Germany and Austria," *China Press*, October 19, 1938, 3.

a room, women, men and children altogether . . . [with] bathroom facilities [that were] indescribably bad."[53] Laura Margolis, head of the American Jewish Joint Distribution Committee (JDC) in Shanghai, described privacy in the *Heime* as "an unknown event . . . there was a horde of human beings all put into large dormitories with double-decker beds for convenience . . . it was unbelievable that human beings could live as these people were living."[54] It is understandable why, having experienced this squalor, many former refugees threw themselves into new careers in the United States, hoping to avoid having to live in such conditions ever again. Indeed, Fred Marcus was keen to make a living in order to afford spacious accommodation, remembering that the overcrowding in Hongkou meant "people became contentious. Arguments among families and between neighbors were frequent. The divorce rate soared, and there were reports of suicides."[55] Former Shanghai refugees were not alone in describing the traumas that were brought about as a result of ghettoization. One American soldier wrote back to his family having observed that "a . . . kid . . . lives in a room 5 yards long and 4 yards wide. He lives with his father, mother, brother, another family of 4 people and a third family of three, all in one little stinking room."[56]

The suffering associated with such past experiences affected different generations of former refugees in different ways and each experienced a different form of survivor silence. The older generation had felt a greater uprooting from their Western lifestyles when they arrived in Shanghai than their children and grandchildren, thus they held on to their trauma for longer. Henry Moser acknowledged that his mother "had a harder time," while Chaya Small commented that in "the beginning . . . my parents wouldn't speak."[57] Lotte Marcus believed unquestionably that the older community of former refugees were much more resistant to sharing their experiences than their younger peers and much more concerned with a

---

53   A. F. Witting, "Letter to friends, July 1939," in *Voices from Shanghai*, ed. Irene Eber, 34.
54   Speech by Laura Margolis, Annual Members Meeting, National Refugee Service, January 15, 1944, accessed November 5, 2015, http://archives.jdc.org/educators/topic-guides/refuge-in-shanghai.html.
55   Marcus and Krasno, *Survival in Shanghai*, 25.
56   Letter by American soldier in Shanghai to his family, October 31, 1944, accessed May 27, 2015, http://archives.jdc.org/educators/topic-guides/refuge-in-shanghai.html.
57   Henry Moser, video interview at Visual History Archive, USC Shoah Foundation, #11179, Westminster, CA, January 24, 1996; Chaya Small, Skype interview by author, November 18–19, 2013.

"survivor guilt." She divulged that her mother never got her life back again; she suffered from a "deep depression" in Shanghai that did not loosen its grip in the United States. Indeed, as a psychologist, Lotte tried to speak to her mother, but commented that she could not access her "locked up memories."[58]

Lotte herself, alongside her younger former neighbors, was more concerned with the future than the past.[59] They were silent because of their concentration on new careers and new relationships. Indeed, Lotte, like many Holocaust survivors, was eager to find a husband and start a family as soon as possible.[60] Elie Grasse, offered an interview in the 1970s, turned it down as she was busy raising a family.[61] Aaron Haas has argued that those who were silent in the initial postwar period, in order to concentrate on bettering their quality of life, were keen to speak out once they had retired and their children had left home.[62] Children leaving home were a reminder to survivors of the other people and other aspects of prewar life they had missed, while, at the same time, it allowed them more free time to reflect on their memories and their identity. While the memoirs of Shanghai survivors reflect a desire to share their experiences in the 1970s and 1980s, these were delayed until the 1990s for reasons that had not prevented many camp and ghetto survivors from speaking out, namely, the self-perceived and aggrandized hierarchy of suffering.[63]

In interviews, former refugees described the horrors they had suffered in Shanghai, but were quick to express their gratitude for being so "lucky" as to avoid the atrocities in Nazi-occupied Europe. Gerry Lindenstrauss and his brother Kurt lived with their parents in one bedroom of a seven-bedroom house. They described how "dead babies in gutters were a common sight," and both pointed out that they had escaped, not experienced, the Holocaust.[64] Similarly, Jerry Breur referred to life in Shanghai after 1943 as

---

58 Lotte Marcus, Skype interview by author, April 19, 2014.
59 Lotte Marcus, interview by author; Elie Grasse, interview by author; Heppner, *Shanghai Refuge*, 164–71; Evelyn Pike Rubin, *Ghetto Shanghai* (New York: Shengold, 1993), 16.
60 Haas, *The Aftermath*, 103.
61 Elie Grasse, interview by author.
62 Haas, *The Aftermath*, 107.
63 Kracauer, *Memories and Images of my Shanghai Years*; Theodor Friedrichs, *Berlin Shanghai New York: My Family's Flight from Hitler* (Nashville, TN: Cold Tree Press, 2007), 283.
64 Gerald Lindenstraus, video interview at Visual History Archive, USC Shoah Foundation, #18216, New York, NY, August 5, 1996.

"the years of starvation," but suggested his suffering was incomparable with that of camp inmates.[65] Lotte Marcus commented, rather bluntly, that "we apologized because we weren't gassed."[66]

Those who had lived for some time in better conditions outside Hongkou and with some happy memories of their time in Shanghai have also been slower to speak, considering their experiences less legitimate. Trixie Wachsner arrived in Shanghai from Austria in 1938, but lived in the comparable luxury of the French Concession until 1943, when she and her family were confined to the Designated Area. She was also lucky to be able to trade her home in the French Concession with one owned by a Japanese family in Hongkou that was one of the newest houses in the Designated Area. She explained that she was one of the very few lucky enough to have separate living and bathroom facilities. Trixie had met her husband Frank within the confines of the Designated Area and was less confident to speak out as a survivor whilst including these happy memories in her testimony. Indeed, in 2013 she commented that she was still unsure about her identity, referring to herself as a Holocaust survivor only "in a way."[67] Those who suffered through more devastation in Shanghai have been slightly quicker than their peers (many of whom are still silent) to begin telling their stories. Elie Grasse had no doubt that she was a survivor of the Holocaust, having lived in Hongkou from her arrival from Vienna in 1939 until her departure to the United States in 1946.[68] Similarly, Lotte has been more eager to speak, having asserted that she belongs to a Holocaust survivor generation as she suffered the loss of her father and other tragedies during her time in Shanghai.[69] Indeed, at age nineteen on her arrival in the United States, she was quicker to speak than her parents. A survey of the published memoirs suggests that a clear majority were written by those who were young children in Shanghai or by children of Shanghailanders.[70]

Older former refugees often sought to shield their children from their traumatic memories by refusing to speak. Judy Becher acknowledged that

---

65 G. Breuer, *Mon Sejour depuis May 1940*, MW1459, Leo Baeck Institute, New York.
66 Lotte Marcus, interview by author.
67 Trixie Wachsner, Skype interview by author, March 4, 2014.
68 Elie Grasse, interview by author.
69 Lotte Marcus, interview by author; Evelyn Rubin, Skype interview by author, March 7, 2014.
70 For example, Tobias, *Strange Heaven*; D. Strobin and I. Wacs, *An Uncommon Journey: From Vienna to Shanghai to America, A Brother and Sister Escape to Freedom During World War II* (Fort Lee, NJ: Barricade Books, 2011).

her parents spoke infrequently with her about their Shanghai experiences. When they did speak with one another about their experiences, they did so in Shanghai dialect, in order to make such memories inaccessible to their children.[71] Chaya Small commented that she was particularly overprotective with her children in the initial postwar years and would "freak out" if she did not know where they were at all times.[72] This is a common theme among the Shanghai Jews. They had been lucky enough to be shielded from the horrors of the Holocaust in Europe by their parents and now, in the United States, they sought to protect their own children both from the dangers of everyday life and from the suffering associated with their time in Shanghai. However, choosing not to speak meant that silence perpetuated silence. As so few spoke out about their experiences, many took the opinion that because others had not spoken of Shanghai, it was not worth speaking about. Indeed, the longer the silence, the more legitimate it was perceived to be and the more benign the experience was considered. Thus, Evelyn Pike Rubin felt a responsibility to end her silence in the late 1980s and 1990s.[73] Despite this, it was not until 2000 that the first national institution, the United States Holocaust Memorial Museum, recognized their experiences and suffering.[74]

While the post-Eichmann years have been categorized as the "era of the witness" for Holocaust survivors, former refugees remained silent throughout the 1960s due to a combination of self-identified hierarchical inferiority and because they were not being recognized by the institutions that had only just begun their more fervent Holocaust research.[75] Early collections of testimony ignored the full and "multi-colored" population of Holocaust survivors and have continued to leave the full spectrum unexplored. Although Steven Spielberg's Foundation did collect testimonies from the Shanghai Jews in the 1990s, some complained that these interviews were targeted at camp survivors, and it was difficult to contain their testimonies within such a predisposed structure of questioning. Evelyn

---

71 Judy Becher, Skype interview by author, January 24, 2014.
72 Chaya Small, interview by author.
73 Evelyn Rubin, interview by author.
74 *Flight and Rescue*, exhibition catalogue, United States Holocaust Memorial Museum (Washington, D.C.: 2001), 3–17.
75 E. J. Sundquist, "Silence Reconsidered," in *After the Holocaust*, 202; Peter Novick, *The Holocaust in American Life* (New York: Houghton Mifflin, 1999), 7.

Pike Rubin commented that her Shoah Foundation interviewer did "not ask the right questions."[76]

Finding a suitable audience for their testimony was a significant contributing factor in allowing former refugees the confidence to consider themselves to have legitimately suffered through the Holocaust and therefore be classified as survivors. Unlike camp survivors, former refugees did not form a cohesive community upon arrival in America. Whilst each camp was liberated at one moment, Shanghai Jews reached the United States at different times and settled in different areas.[77] Indeed, children were sometimes able to leave Shanghai before their parents or grandparents, because the children had been born in Germany, but the older generations had immigrated earlier from Eastern Europe.[78] The rediscovery of a community identity was essential for the breaking of silence and survivor categorization.[79] Those groups that were able to stay together in Shanghai and later in the United States were some of the first to consider their survivor identities. Within such communities the "myth of silence," in regard to the sharing of experiences specifically within close knit communities, is particularly convincing. Having a group of like-minded peers with the same set of beliefs and having experienced the same traumas meant there was less reason to avoid speaking with one another; there was no hierarchy of suffering.

Mir Yeshiva students remained such a cohesive group. They had traveled together from Poland and Lithuania through Kobe, Japan, and arrived in Shanghai in 1941.[80] Having a primarily religious focus, they lived separately from the German and Austrian Jews in Hongkou and had little communication with the secular community. Chaya Small observed that the Yeshiva was the "support system" that the German and Austrian Jews did not have. Indeed, she argued that there was a distinct split in Shanghai between those who focused on their faith and religious education and those who clung on to their European cultural identity, building restaurants, serving German cuisine and performing opera. Members of the Yeshiva community have thus defined their survival within a religious context and, in line with many of the

---

76 Evelyn Rubin, interview by author.
77 Marcia R. Ristaino, *Port of Last Resort: The Diaspora Communities of Shanghai* (Stanford, CA: Stanford University Press, 2001), 2–7.
78 Trixie Wachsner's parents were not able to acquire an affidavit to the United States until the 1960s and moved to Canada in the interim.
79 Henry Moser, video interview at Visual History Archive.
80 Nathan Lipschitz video interview at Visual History Archive, USC Shoah Foundation, #11174, Brooklyn, NY, January 24, 1996.

Orthodox Jews who survived the Holocaust in camps and ghettos, consider their fate to have been a "blessing from God . . . I consider myself chosen."[81] Like Chaya, Eric Chaim was quick to compare his fate with Old Testament Jewish suffering. He described his flight to the United States as a journey to the Promised Land.[82] Indeed, the Mir Yeshiva recognized the end of their suffering in Hongkou as a further step by the Jewish people towards the coming of the messiah. In 1946, as their ship pulled away from the dock and towards the United States they sung the "Ani Ma'amin" (אֲנִי מַאֲמִין): "I believe with total faith . . . the *Moshiach* [messiah] will come."[83]

For those secular Jews who did not have the faith to consider themselves "chosen" nor a religious community to house them in the United States, reunions and conferences beginning in the late 1970s took on a key role, just as they had done for child survivors. Reunions were organized from within the community and began in 1977.[84] Early reunions were attended by few former refugees, and it was not until the 1980s and early 1990s that such events came to be attended in greater numbers.[85] The delay from arrival in the United States to the organization of reunions in the late 1970s was crucial in preventing the formation of new survivor identities. By 1977, the older generation of former refugees was no longer present and events were largely attended by young Shanghai refugees and their children. It is important to note the distinct difference in self-classification between those who have attended reunions and those who have not. Older generations did not get the chance to share their experience with their peers and, as such, held on to their survivor guilt. Those who did attend reunions were quicker to let go. Indeed, those who attended the Illinois gathering in August 2013 felt suitably comfortable to accept a medal honoring their time in Shanghai.[86] In comparison to reunions, academic conferences have

---

81 Chaya Small, interview by author.
82 Erwin Chaim, video interview at Visual History Archive, USC Shoah Foundation, #21788, Denver, CO, Oct 25, 1996.
83 Chaya Small, interview by author.
84 Trixie Wachsner, interview by author. Smaller groups of former Shanghai refugees got together in New York in the 1950s. Larger reunions were held in 1980, 1985, and 1988.
85 About 1,000 former refugees and their relatives attended an event in Oakland, California, in August 1980, a significant increase from the handful that attended the event in New York in 1977.
86 See the passport for the Chicago event: Danny Spungen, *Shanghai Memory: An Educational Experience at the World's Fair of Money*, August 15, 2013, accessed May 27, 2015, http://www.whynotcollectibles.com/uploaded_pictures/Dinner%20Event%20Passport_Amended-3_small.pdf.

been slower to organize, with few individuals and institutions outside of the refugee community taking an interest in perpetuating the Jewish refugees' episode in Shanghai until the 1990s.[87] Indeed, now in the 2010s the community has finally aroused more academic attention and is the focus of recent symposia and exhibitions. In 2011, the Chinese took an interest in the refugees they had sheltered, albeit involuntarily, some 70+ years previously, and founded the Shanghai Jewish Refugees Museum which is now attracting visitors from around the world.

Recognition is perhaps the most crucial stage in the creation of a new definition for the term "Holocaust survivor" and is the stage that former Shanghai refugees have yet to achieve. While many of those who were children in Hongkou have been eager to judge themselves to be survivors, we will never know the thoughts of older refugees on the matter. Earlier studies of the community did not judge them as Holocaust relevant and therefore never asked these decisive questions. Furthermore, the creation of a new classification within the "Holocaust survivor" definition is not something that this community can bring about on its own. It will take an adaption from within academic institutions by academics, and also needs a new generation that can tell the stories for this diminishing community. The final section will consider the progress that has been made thus far towards a widening of the Holocaust survivor definition and also the importance of the "second generation" to the establishment of the new "Shanghai survivor" classification.

Evolving Classifications: Shanghai Survivors and the Second Generation

"Open for us a gate at a time when the gates are being closed. It is never too late to open the gates."[88] Haim Dasberg, quoting from the Yom Kippur prayer book at a conference of child survivors in 1992, encouraged those who had not spoken yet to release their memories by opening the gates. He told his audience that it was their turn to speak and for the world to listen. These gates opened in 1990 for child survivors of the ghettos, camps and those who were in hiding, but they have yet to open wide enough to allow

---

87 The first conference to focus on Jews in China was held at Harvard University in 1992, "Jewish Diasporas in China." In 1994, Pan Guang organized the "International Seminar on Jews in Shanghai" in Shanghai.
88 Dasberg, *Child Holocaust Survivors*, 60.

the Shanghai Jews to pass through. Contentious disputes about the definition of "survivor" began in the early aftermath of the war. They have yet to be answered with one authoritative definition.[89] Despite this, there has been a pattern of widening classifications since 2004.[90] As former Shanghai refugees struggle to create a consistent sense of their identity and belonging within their communities, a broader definition could aid in the acceptance of their narratives, as they speak out. Here I will review the advancements that have been made toward recognition and the creation of a new breed of Holocaust survivors, which includes the "Shanghai survivor." Within such broadening definitions has been the desire to include others, such as the "second generation," those who are children of Holocaust survivors. This chapter will also consider how children of refugees can play a fundamental part in this journey toward inclusion within the Holocaust lexicon and how they have done so already. Marianne Hirsch's work on the second generation, the "generation of postmemory," explores how memory is passed on to the offspring of Holocaust survivors and how this generational transfer helps to legitimize survivor identity. Her methodology will be considered in so far as it applies to the Shanghai Jews.

Eminent Holocaust historian Yehuda Bauer noted that a gradation of human suffering was not possible when comparing the Holocaust with other lesser genocides. He argued in 2002 that "extreme forms of human suffering are not comparable."[91] When interviewed in 2004, he applied a rigid definition to Holocaust survivors, describing them as "people who lived in ghettos and concentration camps or compulsory labor frameworks, who hid or who joined the partisan ranks. I don't mean to denigrate the suffering of people who suffered from race laws and anti-Semitic decree, or those who fled with nothing in their possession, but these are not Holocaust survivors."[92] He considers the Shanghai Jews not to have ventured into such extreme suffering. Yad Vashem, the Israeli Holocaust museum, on the other hand, having chosen not to create a definition at its founding, has recently published a much more liberal definition than Bauer's. On its website, it

---

89 A. Barkat, "Who Counts As A Holocaust Survivor?" *Haaretz*, April 18, 2004, accessed May 27, 2015, http://www.haaretz.com/print-edition/news/who-counts-as-a-holocaust-survivor-1.119868.
90 Hanna Yablonka, "Holocaust Survivors in Israel: Time for an Initial Taking of Stock," in *Holocaust Survivors*, 185.
91 Bauer, *Rethinking The Holocaust*, 13.
92 Barkat, "Who Counts As A Holocaust Survivor?"

defines Shoah survivors as "Jews who lived for any amount of time under Nazi domination, direct or indirect, and survived."[93] Such a new definition marks an expansion over time, rather than a sudden change. Such alterations in definitions were due to political and social changes, as well as those in public consciousness since the testimonies of Holocaust survivors were publicly accepted in the aftermath of Eichmann.[94] Changes occurred in different locations for different reasons. Developments that came about in the United States were in tune with what Peter Novick called a "Holocaust fixation" that began in the 1990s. Consciousness of the Holocaust increased among the American population, particularly among American Jewry due to a number of factors. The first was that the American Jewish community was growing more secular and required common histories to unite their communities, rather than a common faith.[95] Another reason was that a rise in the number of Holocaust deniers made proving legitimacy more important. Richard Evans concedes that American Jews were on the offensive against deniers in the 1990s and works such as Deborah Lipstadt's *Denying the Holocaust: The Growing Assault on Truth and Memory* (1994) were published with increasing frequency.[96] American public memory of the Shoah had been growing since the first newspaper reports concerning the genocide were published in 1943. Jewish and American memory had become entwined by the 1990s when the Holocaust was used to form a juxtaposition with American civic values. Many of the Holocaust monuments constructed in the United States, such as Nathan Rapoport's *Liberation* located in Liberty State Park, could just as well be shrines to immigration and liberty.[97]

With wider appreciation for the Holocaust came wider appreciation for its survivors and more inclusive definitions. Another important reason for an expansion in classification has been the tragically inevitable disappearance of Holocaust survivors over time. It has now become necessary to turn to other witnesses, formerly not deemed to be survivors, for firsthand

---

93 Yad Vashem, "How Do You Define A Shoah Survivor?," accessed May 30, 2015, http://www.yadvashem.org/yv/en/resources/names/faq.asp.
94 Yablonka, "Holocaust Survivors in Israel," 185.
95 Novick, *The Holocaust in American Life*, 10, 202, 268.
96 Richard J. Evans, *Telling Lies About Hitler: The Holocaust, History and The David Irving Trial* (London: Verso, 2002) 31; Deborah Lipstadt, *Denying The Holocaust: The Growing Assault on Truth and Memory* (New York: Free Press, 1994).
97 James E. Young, *The Texture of Memory: Holocaust Memorials and Meaning* (New Haven: Yale University Press, 1993), 287–322.

accounts of the atrocities perpetrated by the Nazis.[98] Indeed, survivors have been recognized chronologically in line with their age. While child survivors were called upon for their testimony in the late 1980s and 1990s, from the mid-2000s children of Holocaust survivors, or "the generation of postmemory," have been sought out to recall their parents' suffering.[99] Former refugees have been increasingly approached for their own testimonies in recent years as well. While they have yet to see recognition on a national scale, in their own local communities they have been invited to speak at community centers and local schools, becoming educators in a Holocaust experience that was completely unknown in the 1980s.[100] Zoë Vania Waxman and Tony Kushner have observed that a greater commitment to multiculturalism and antiracism in education has fueled an increase in interest in and demand for Holocaust edification.[101] As camp and ghetto survivors are no longer able to give such presentations, the pool of presenters has widened to include the Shanghai Jews.

In her 2012 article, Hanna Yablonka based her definition of Holocaust survivors on three measures, each representing a transition in the classification since it first came about in the 1940s and 1950s. She called a person a survivor if they considered themselves to be a survivor, if the community in which they lived in their initial postwar years regarded them to be a survivor, and if they held a strong historic consciousness having witnessed devastation or having been affected by it "directly, individually or by families."[102] Yablonka's definition represents the most modern development in the evolving classification of Holocaust survivors. Former Shanghai refugees are just beginning to achieve her first measure and, with the widening of definitions, should achieve the second. The third, achieved by the refugees some time ago, is particularly interesting when applied to their "second generation" of children and grandchildren and it is to this subject that I finally turn.

The second generation of family members, with a living connection to the Holocaust, were suitably close to their relatives' suffering to become

---

98 Novick, *The Holocaust in American Life*, 272.
99 See Marianne Hirsch, "The Generation of Postmemory," *Poetics Today* 29, no. 1 (2008): 103–128.
100 Chaya Small, interview by author.
101 Zoë Vania Waxman, *Writing The Holocaust: Identity, Testimony, Representation* (Oxford: Oxford University Press, 2006), 102.
102 Yablonka, "Holocaust Survivors in Israel," 185.

"guardians" of their family memory.[103] As former refugees have aged, they have become more communicative. Children and grandchildren (with an innocent lack of sensitivity to their grandparents' suffering), have come to ask more about the Shanghai experience, and recollections have thereby been transmitted across generations. As a group growing up in the United States when Holocaust remembrance was at its peak, children and grandchildren of the Shanghai Jews have, crucially, been able to ask the right questions. They have become interpreters, acting between their family members and the wider community of Holocaust literati. While Shanghai Jews attempted to filter their trauma for the ears of their children, the second generation has been eager to educate themselves about their parents' experiences. Judy Becher recalled that her parents would only tell her and her brother the funny aspects of their Shanghai experiences. It was only later that she became aware of the suffering they had experienced, when socializing with other children of refugees.[104] For those who are no longer present to tell their stories, the responsibility has fallen on the shoulders of their relatives. There is a common pattern within this community of second generation Shanghai refugees appreciating the stories of the wartime refugees and keeping them alive. Audrey Marcus was struck by the deprivation that her husband had experienced in Shanghai as she read his diaries after he had passed away.[105] It was she who decided that they should be made available to a greater audience and she who published them, alongside some of her husband Fred's later memoir writings, in 2002 shortly after his passing. Similarly, others of the second generation have been eager to donate the documents and photos of their parents to museums around the world. Children of Shanghailanders have donated many of the permits, visas and other papers collected by their parents to local museums and enquiring historians. David Sokal, as the son and grandson of Shanghai refugees, has been eager to "re-activate" and share his family's experiences. He described his father, Robert Sokal, a professor of ecology and evolution educated in Shanghai, as always keen to share his experiences with his family. David assisted his father with the compilation of his memoirs in 2008, but commented that those memories he chose to publish were "selective."[106] In some ways therefore, David is able to be more open than his father. As Hirsch

---

103 Hirsch, "The Generation of Postmemory," 104.
104 Judy Becher, interview by author.
105 Audrey Marcus, interview by author.
106 David Sokal to author, email "Dissertation," July 13, 2014.

observes, "the language of family [is] . . . a form of expression that is both more direct and more ruthless than social and public speech."[107]

The second generation has also played a key role in "validating" their relatives' experiences.[108] Numerous children of refugees have actively encouraged their parents to make return trips to China.[109] In 1998, after her father passed away, Judy Becher took her mother back to Shanghai to "see it through her eyes," and encouraged her to remember as her memories were fading. They located the apartment her mother had stayed in for ten years in Hongkou, still containing the same furniture, and Judy described her mother as feeling an incredible sense of legitimacy as a survivor on seeing her old home once more and the squalor in which she had lived.[110] Shanghai has become a symbolic destination for former Shanghai refugees and their children. Like the ghettos of Europe, Hongkou has become a representative site, a memorial and a tourist attraction. Tim Cole has suggested that return visits by survivors to their Holocaust landscape of Auschwitz has become a hugely significant act. The same can be said of Hongkou and the former refugees.[111] Like Auschwitz, it has become a site of both the mind and the body. Memories of their time in Shanghai, on revisiting, become heightened and often, muscular memory returns. Indeed, Trixie Wachsner commented that she could find her way around without a map, thirty years after she left.[112] Judy Becher noted that her mother's shaky Shanghai dialect was restored to her with greater fluency during their trip to the former ghetto.[113] The second generation, pushing to learn more of their parents' and relatives' time in Shanghai, allowed their relatives greater legitimacy in classifying themselves as survivors. By taking their parents back to Shanghai physically on memorial pilgrimages, they were able to contextualize their family members' suffering within the Holocaust and remind them of the traumas of their experience after the initial postwar years had diminished these memories within a hierarchy of suffering. The donation of documents and memories to museums, foundations, and historians has

---

107 Hirsch, "The Generation of Postmemory," 112.
108 Judy Becher, interview by author.
109 Audrey Marcus, interview by author.
110 Judy Becher, interview by author.
111 Tim Cole, "Crematoria, Barracks, Gateway: Survivors' Return Visits to the Memory Landscapes of Auschwitz," *History & Memory* 25, no. 2 (2013): 123.
112 Trixie Wachsner, interview by author.
113 Judy Becher, interview by author.

granted memorial sites in the United States and a position in the Holocaust library to the former refugees.

The inclusion of a "Shanghai survivor" subgroup alongside such others as "child survivor" and "camp survivor" seems more likely as definitions continue to widen and the second generation continues to fight their parents' cause. Such an inclusion is important to the former refugees, as it allows them a sense of belonging and a community identity that has not existed since their exodus from Shanghai. If they were able to find an empathetic audience for their testimony, outside of their own community, this would also facilitate the articulation of their narratives: "What survivors say, how they say it, whether they say it at all, will depend, in part, on their perceptions of those listeners, as well as on the ways the listeners have made their own hopes, fears and expectations known."[114] As Myra Giberovitch concedes, understanding who survivors believe themselves to be, using their own individual definitions in the light of their own unique experiences, will both improve relationships with them and enhance our understanding of their testimony.[115] It is also important to recognize the similarities of experience, both during and after the war, between Shanghai survivors and their peers already classified as Holocaust survivors. These refugees also experienced the trauma of losing their loved ones in Europe, but not learning the fate of their relatives until much later. Many of them lost their childhoods in the distress of escape. Those who were adults felt a deep uprooting from a lifestyle they had grown up into. While they did not suffer in the camps of Europe, they did witness some of the extremes of Nazi behavior before 1939. Had they stayed in their hometowns, they would very likely not be alive to tell their history today.

One survivor community that has been explored widely is that of the *Kindertransport*, a rescue mission of some 10,000 Jewish children from Nazi-occupied territories in 1938–1939 to the United Kingdom.[116] Nearly twice as many Jews were saved in Shanghai, but they have not gained half the recognition. However, the view taken of the former has demonstrated that one can be considered a Holocaust survivor without wearing a tattoo. This shows that the hierarchy of suffering only partly accounts for the

---

114 Henry Greenspan, *On Listening to Holocaust Survivors: Recounting and Life History* (Westport, CN: Praeger, 1998), 30.
115 Giberovitch, *Recovering From Genocidal Trauma*, 45–46.
116 Vera K. Fast, *Children's Exodus: A History of the Kindertransport* (New York: I. B. Tauris, 2010).

non-existence of Shanghai in the Holocaust anthology, perhaps ignorance of it is a significant factor. Another is undoubtedly the failure of the community to subscribe wholeheartedly to this narrative. As Yablonka has pointed out, self-identification is a precondition to survivor classification. However, this is changing and in interviews with the author the overwhelming majority wish to be so defined.

The Shanghai Jews, taken here as a case study to reflect upon how survivor identity was and continues to be established in postwar America, show how different events and issues can impact the development of identity and self-definition. Such lessons are crucial to understanding why the Shanghai Jews may want to be defined as survivors, but also are important to the more general future of Holocaust studies. They show how a wider range of individuals, previously categorized as escapees, can fit patterns that have been established in order to classify the lives of those already determined to be Holocaust survivors. Thus, they demonstrate that the widening of survivor definitions is less an exercise of inclusion and more one of recognition. If a "Shanghai survivor" classification were to be established on a national and international level, it could mark the beginning of a new kind of Holocaust survivor, survivors without a tattoo, and a new beginning for Holocaust education. Just as the establishment of child survivor identity aided the former refugee community in building and justifying their self-identification as survivors, so the Shanghai survivor label itself may do the same for some other previously neglected group. The final words are Trixie's: "We did not perish in Europe but lived in China ... we were a strange community in a strange land and were strangers once more in the United States ... I've had the opportunity for freedom. ... I can speak at reunions and in [museums] and I am grateful to tell my story."[117]

---

117 Trixie Wachsner, interview by author.

Bibliography

Books by Authors

Ben-Canaan, Dan. *The Jewish People and Their Place in History—The Jews of China and Harbin*. Harbin: Harbin Municipal Government, 2009.

———. *The Kaspe File—A Case Study of Harbin as an Intersection of Cultural and Ethnical Communities in Conflict, 1932–1945*. Harbin: Heilongjiang People's Publishing House, 2009.

Goldstein, Jonathan, ed. *China and Israel, 1948–1998: A Fifty Year Retrospective*. Westport, CT: Preager Publishers, 1999.

———. *The Jews of China*, 2 vols. Armonk, NY: M. E. Sharpe, 1999 and 2000.

Goldstein, Jonathan. *Jewish Identities in East and Southeast Asia: Singapore, Manila, Taipei, Harbin, Shanghai, Rangoon, and Surabaya*. Berlin: De Gruyter Oldenbourg, 2015.

Ho, Feng Shan. 外交生涯四十年 [Forty Years of My Diplomatic Life] (Hong Kong, Chinese University Press, 1990), 75-78.

Hochstadt, Steve. *Shanghai-Geschichten: Die jüdische Flucht nach China*. Teetz, Germany: Hentrich und Hentrich, 2007.

———. *Exodus to Shanghai: Stories of Escape from the Third Reich*. New York: Palgrave Macmillan, 2012.

Meyer, Maisie Joy. *From the Rivers of Babylon to the Whangpoo: A Century of Sephardi Jewish Life in Shanghai*. Lanham, MD: University Press of America, 2003.

———. *Shanghai's Baghdadi Jews: A Collection of Biographical Reflections*. Hong Kong: Blackman Books, 2015.

Rubin, Evelyn Pike. *Ghetto Shanghai*. New York: Shengold, 1993.

Willens, Liliane. *Stateless in Shanghai*. London: China Economic Review Publishing (HK) Limited for Earnshaw Books, 2010.

Xin, Xu., ed. *Encyclopaedia Judaica*. Shanghai: The Shanghai People's Publishing House, 1993.

Xin, Xu. *The Jews of Kaifeng, China: History, Culture, and Religion*. Jersey City, NJ: KTAV Publishing House, Inc., 2003.

———. *Aliens in a Strange Land: Jews and Modern China*. Taipei: National Taiwan University Press, 2017.

Other Memoirs

Eisfelder, Horst Peter. *Chinese Exile: My Years in Shanghai and Nanking*. Melbourne: Ayotaynu Foundation, 2003.
Friedrichs, Theodor. *Berlin Shanghai New York: My Family's Flight From Hitler*. Nashville, TN: Cold Tree Press, 2007.
Heppner, Ernest G., *Shanghai Refuge: A Memoir of the World War II Jewish Ghetto*. Lincoln, NE: University of Nebraska Press, 1993.
Iwry, Samuel. *To Wear the Dust of War: From Bialystok to Shanghai to the Promised Land, an Oral History*. New York: Palgrave Macmillan, 2004.
Krasno, Rena. *Strangers Always: A Jewish Family in Wartime Shanghai*. Berkeley, CA: Pacific View Press, 1992.
Marcus, Audrey Friedman, and Rena Krasno. *Survival in Shanghai: The Journals of Fred Marcus, 1939–49*. Berkeley, CA: Pacific View Press, 2008.
Mühlberger, Sonja. *Geboren in Shanghai als Kind von Emigranten, Leben und Überleben im Ghetto von Hongkew. 1939–1947*. Volume 58 of *Jüdische Miniaturen*. Berlin: Hentrich und Hentrich, 2006.
Tobias, Sigmund. *Strange Haven: A Jewish Childhood in Wartime Shanghai*. Champaign, IL: University of Illinois Press, 2009.
Strobin, D., and I. Wacs. *An Uncommon Journey: From Vienna to Shanghai to America, A Brother and Sister Escape to Freedom During World War II*. Fort Lee, NJ: Barricade Books, 2011.

Media Sources

Cheng, X.-h., and N. Sawada. *The Last Refuge: The Story of Jewish Refugees in Shanghai* [Documentary]. Teaneck, NJ: Ergo Media, Inc., 2004.
Grossman, J., and P. Rosdy. *Port of Last Resort: Zuflucht in Shanghai* [Documentary]. Munich: Winter & Winter, 1998.
Janklowicz-Mann, D., and A. Mann. *Shanghai Ghetto* [Documentary]. N.p.: New Video Group, 2002.
Ottinger, U. *Exil Shanghai* [Documentary]. Berlin: Ulrike Ottinger Filmproduktion, 1997.
Perelsztejn, D. *Escape to the Rising Sun* [Documentary]. Waltham, MA: National Center for Jewish Film, 1990.
Shopsowitz, K. *A Place to Save Your Life: The Shanghai Jews* [Documentary]. New York: Filmakers Library, 1994.
Shalom Show. *Footage of Chicago Survivors Reunion*, [Youtube Clip] (August 2013). Accessed May 18, 2015, http://www.youtube.com/watch?v=6R2WMN7bkoM&feature=c4-overview&list=UUf3K-o1nYPhUOuV0clZ7RKw.
Shanghai Live. *Gary Matzdorff's Return Visit to Shanghai*, [Youtube Clip] (May, 2013). Accessed May 18, 2015, http://www.youtube.com/watch?v=Y13GTGy6DZI.

Secondary Works

Altman, A., and I. Eber. "Flight to Shanghai, 1938–1940: The Larger Setting." *Yad Vashem Studies* 28 (2000): 65–82.

Armbrüster, Georg, Michael Kohlstruck, and Sonja Mühlberger, eds., *Exil Shanghai 1938–1947: Jüdisches Leben in der Emigration*. Teetz, Germany: Hentrich und Hentrich, 2000.

Bei, Gao. *Shanghai Sanctuary: Chinese and Japanese Policy toward European Jewish Refugees during World War II*. New York: Oxford University Press, 2013.

Booker, Edna Lee, and John Stauffer Potter. *Flight from China*. New York: Macmillan Co., 1945.

Buxbaum, Elisabeth. *Transit Shanghai: Ein Leben im Exil*. Vienna: Edition Steinbauer, 2008.

Coble, Parks M., Jr. *The Shanghai Capitalists and the National Government, 1927–1937*. Cambridge: Harvard University Press, 1980.

———. *Facing Japan, Chinese Politics and Japanese Imperialism, 1931–1937*. Cambridge: Harvard University Press, 1991.

Cornwall, Claudia. *Letter from Vienna: A Daughter Uncovers Her Family's Jewish Past*. Vancouver: Douglas & McIntyre Ltd., 1995.

Eber, Irene. *Chinese and Jews, Encounters Between Cultures*. London: Vallentine Mitchell, 2008.

———, ed. Jewish Refugees in Shanghai 1933–1947: A Selection of Documents. Göttingen, Germany: Vandenhoeck & Ruprecht, 2018.

———. *Voices from Shanghai: Jewish Exiles in Wartime China*. Chicago: University of Chicago Press, 2008.

———. *Wartime Shanghai and the Jewish Refugees from Central Europe: Survival, Co-Existence, and Identity in a Multi-Ethnic City*. Berlin: De Gruyter, 2012.

Friend, Beverly. "A Big Weekend with Former Shanghai Refugees." *Points East* 28 (November 2013): 1–12.

Goodman, David G., and Masanori Miyazawa. *Jews in the Japanese Mind: The History and Uses of a Cultural Stereotype*. New York, Free Press, 1994.

Gruenberger, Felix. "The Jewish Refugees in Shanghai." *Jewish Social Studies* 12 (October 1950): 329–48.

Henriot, Christian, and Wen-hsin Yeh, eds. *In the Shadow of the Rising Sun, Shanghai under Japanese Occupation*. Cambridge, UK: Cambridge University Press, 2000.

Henriot, Christian. "Shanghai and the Experience of War, The Fate of Refugees." *European Journal of East Asian Studies* 5 (September 2006): 215–245.

Jakubowicz, Andrew. "Stopped in flight: Shanghai and the Polish Jewish refugees of 1941." *Holocaust Studies: A Journal of Culture and History* 23 (2017): 1–18.

Kranzler, David. *Japanese, Nazis and Jews: The Jewish Refugee Community of Shanghai 1938–1945*. New York: Yeshiva University Press, 1976.

Levine, Hillel. *In Search of Sugihara: The Elusive Japanese Diplomat who Risked His Life to Rescue 10,000 Jews from the Holocaust*. New York: Free Press, 1996.

Malek, Roman, ed. *Jews in China, from Kaifeng... to Shanghai*. Sankt Augustin, Germany: Monumenta Serica, 2000.

Messmer, Matthias. *Jewish Wayfarers in Modern China: Tragedy and Splendor*. Plymouth, Lexington Books, 2012.

Reichman, Alice I. "Community in Exile: German Jewish Identity Development in Wartime Shanghai," *1938-1945*. BA thesis, Claremont McKenna College, 2011.

Ristaino, Marcia Reynders. *Port of Last Resort: The Diaspora Communities of Shanghai*. Stanford, CA: Stanford University Press, 2001.

Ross, James. *Escape to Shanghai: A Jewish Community in China*. New York: Free Press, 1994.

Schwarcz, Vera. *In the Crook of the Rock: Jewish Refuge in a World Gone Mad—The Chaya Leah Walkin Story*. Brighton, MA: Academic Studies Press, 2018.

Sergeant, Harriet. *Shanghai: Collision Point of Cultures, 1918-1939*. New York, Crown Publishers, 1991.

Shillony, Ben-Ami. *The Jews and the Japanese: The Successful Outsiders*. Tokyo: C.E. Tuttle, 1991.

Tokayer, Marvin, and Mary Swartz. *The Fugu Plan, the Untold Story of the Japanese and the Jews during World War II*. London: Paddington Press, 1979.

Flight and Rescue. United States Holocaust Memorial Museum exhibition catalogue, Washington, D.C., 2001.

Wakeman, Frederic, Jr., and Wen-hsin Yeh, eds. *Shanghai Sojourners*. Berkeley, CA: Institute of East Asian Studies, 1992.

Xun, Zhou. *Chinese Perceptions of the "Jews" and Judaism: A History of the Youtai*. New York: Routledge, 2000.

Index

Abraham family, 37, 44, 46–47, 54–56, 60–61, 134
   D. E. J., 36, 56
   Ezekiel, 33, 42, 55
   Isaac, 48–49, 54
   Julie, 33, 60
   Reuben, 37, 69
Abram, Gabrielle, 25, 203–231
Aden, 151
Adler, Leo, 49
Afghanistan, 30
Agran, Paul, 196
Aguinaldo, Emilio, 111
Ahlers, John, 46
American Jewish Joint Distribution Committee, 11, 17, 19–20, 23n75, 24, 91, 93, 102n4, 120, 121n5, 134–135, 138, 153, 218
Anschluss, 12, 19, 116–119, 122, 124–125, 143, 145–146, 149, 162, 167, 208, 211, 214
antisemitism, 5, 74–75, 107, 127, 145, 150–151, 156, 159–160, 162, 167, 187, 191, 225
   Nazi, 94, 106, 117, 131
   Russian, 5, 33, 89, 185, 187, 190, 198
Arabs, 119, 135, 151, 167
Argentina, 69
Ascher, Abraham, 112–113
Atkinson, Anne, 5, 73–84
Auschwitz, 148, 214, 229
Australia, 5, 7, 16, 25, 63, 67, 69–70, 79–80, 82–84, 146
Austria, 7, 12, 19–20, 23, 25, 92, 107, 109, 116–119, 121–125, 134, 143, 146, 160, 162, 165, 167, 175, 207, 212–214, 220

Bachrach, Emil, 101
Baghdad, 29–30, 34–35, 37, 63, 186
Bahamas, 67
bar mitzvah, 34, 54
Basra, 29–30
Batavia, 30, 151
Battle of Britain, 39

Bauer, Yehuda, 211, 225
Baumel-Schwartz, Judy, 207
Becher, Judy, 220–221, 228, 229
Beijing, 80, 105, 193n34, 201n60
Bekhor, Helen Reuben, 55, 61
Belgium, 92, 147, 184
Ben-Canaan, Dan, 25, 179–202
Bengal, 36
Benjamin, Benjamin David, 31–32
Benz, Wolfgang, 9
Berdichev, 74–75, 78
Berglas, Jacob, 164
Berlin, 67, 92, 104, 110, 125, 144, 148, 153, 154n26, 205, 212–214
Betar, 190
Beth Aharon Synagogue, 34, 47, 58, 69
Birman, Meir, 103–105, 107–108
Black Hundred, 198
Bolsheviks, 85–87, 195, 198
Bombay, 4, 30, 134
Boston, 90
Brazil, 44, 137
Breslau, *also* Wrocław, 6, 112, 125, 137, 214
Buchenwald, 7, 119, 124, 137, 139, 147–148, 214
Buddha, 184
Buddhism, 34, 41, 65
Buenos Aires, 3
Bund, 103, 108
Burak family, 5–6, 73–84
Burma, 30, 172

Cairo, 30
Calcutta, 4, 30
Cambridge, 90
Canada, 25, 63–64, 67–70, 88, 92, 94, 123, 146, 180n3, 186–187, 193n34, 222n78
Canton, 70
Cathay Hotel, 35, 66–67
Center of Jewish Studies Shanghai, 4, 156
Cesarani, David, 217
Chapei Camp, 56, 61
Channel Islands, 69
Chanukah, 140

Chiang Kai-shek, 61, 63, 88, 93–94
Chicago, 196
China League for the Protection of Civil
    Rights, 159
China Press, 12, 13n32
China, *passim*
    Communist 61, 63–70, 83, 88, 94–95,
        124, 161, 173, 195
    Nationalist, 51, 61, 63–64, 66, 68, 88, 94,
        118n2, 121–122, 125, 164, 166,
        168–169, 172, 175–176
Chinese Civil War, 63, 90, 94, 96
Chinese Eastern Railway, 75, 85–86
Chinese Nationalist Party, *see* Kuomintang
Chongqing, 122, 161–162, 169, 171, 176
Christianity, 8, 87, 143
    Catholic, 80, 186–189
    Orthodox, 185, 187, 191n29, 199
Cleveland, 67
Clurman, Charles, 195
    Ethel, 184, 190–191, 194
Cohen, Beth B., 206, 217
Cohen, Israel, 101, 104, 108–109
    Moselle, 33, 47
Collège Municipal Français, 89
colonialism, 35, 38, 102, 131, 173, 183
Communism, 5, 66, 77, 81, 173
Communist Party of China, 37, 64, 81, 161
"Conte Biancamano", 12–14, 127
"Conte Rosso", 13
"Conte Verde", 7, 13–14, 61
Coolidge, Calvin, 95
Cuba, 122, 137, 181
Culman, Ernest, 151
Curacao, 15
Czechoslovakia, 7, 19–20, 23, 25, 133, 147

Dachau, 119, 124
Dangoor, Ezra Reuben, 63
    Maurice, 30, 43, 58–59, 64
Danieli, Yael, 217
Darwin, 83
Dasberg, Haim, 224
Designated Area, 93, 130, 131, 140–141, 144,
    150, 217
Didner, Dr. Samuel, 22
Dobrolovskaya, Vera, 185–187
Dominican Republic, 113

Eber, Irene, 5, 133
Egypt, 30
Eichmann, Adolf, 117, 216–217, 221, 226
Eisfelder, Horst, 213
Elias, Flower, 32

Reginald Marcus, 43, 71
Embankment Building, 45
Ephraim, Frank, 101n4, 106
Epstein, Israel, 161
    Lazar, 108–109
Evans, Richard, 226
Evian Conference, 109, 117
Ezra, Edward, 32, 35, 41
    N. E. B., 32, 39, 159

fascism, 89, 159, 161–162, 165, 167, 173, 191,
    198
Feingold, Henry L., 111
Final Solution, 117
Fine, Alvin, 60
Foerder, Martin, 114–115
France, 30, 34, 39, 53, 56, 79–81, 87–90, 92,
    94–95, 109, 137, 147, 162, 167, 173,
    183–184, 205
Frankfurt, 8, 67
Fremantle, 82
Frieder brothers, 102n4, 110–111, 114
Frieder, Philip, 106–107, 109
Friedlander, Saul, 117

Galatzky, Alexander, 192
Gao Bei, 5, 156
Garrick, Leah Jacob, 34, 35, 42, 43, 57
Gelbe Post, 7, 164
Genoa, 12
German Consulate in Shanghai, 11, 14–16, 61,
    133n6, 159n3
Germany, 4, 9, 12, 15–16, 19–20, 22–24, 30,
    34, 39, 53, 56, 59–60, 90–94, 105–107,
    109, 112–113, 115–117, 119, 123–125,
    129, 137, 139, 141–142, 145–149, 151,
    156, 159–160, 162, 165, 167, 173, 175,
    183–184, 206, 208, 212–213, 222
Gestapo, 13n32, 92, 123, 147
Ghoya, Kanoh, 140, 150
Giberovitch, Myra, 207, 230
Gilbert, Martin, 124
"Gneisenau", 99–100, 105, 107–108, 111,
    113–114
Goldfarb, Hermann, 203–205
Goldstein, Jonathan, 6, 99–115
Grasse, Elie, 212, 219–220
Great Depression, 73, 80
Greening, Ilse, 148
Grey, Doris, 148
Grossman, Vasilii, 160

Haifa, 67, 70, 186
"Hakozaki Maru", 137–138

Hamburg, 67
Hannover, 148
Harbin, 5, 25, 75–77, 78n8, 80, 84–87, 89–90, 93, 103–105, 107–108, 180–202
Hardoon family, 30, 32, 34–35, 40–41, 57, 69, 188–189
　Catherine Levy, 30, 69, 71
　Maple, 34, 57, 69
　Silas, 34, 40, 41, 69, 189
Harvard, 154, 196, 224n87
Hausner, Gideon, 217
Hayashi, Senjuro, 54
Hayim family, 38, 44
　Ellis, 39, 164
　George, 38
Heime, 20–21, 130, 152–153, 217–218
Heppner, Ernest, 113, 215
HICEM, 46n47, 104–105, 107–109
hidden children, 210–211
Hilberg, Raul, 207
Hillaly family, 31
Himmler, Heinrich, 15, 117
Hirohito, 50, 59,
Hiroshima, 94, 141, 165
Hirsch, Claus, 213
　Marianne, 208, 225, 228–229
Hitler, Adolf, 39, 91, 94, 99, 101–103, 117–119, 121, 148, 160, 162, 167
Ho, Dr. Feng Shan, 6, 116–126, 133–134, 136, 145, 162
　Manli, 6, 116–126, 162
Hochstadt, Steve, xi, 3–25, 143–157
Hochstädt, Amalia and Josef, 143–145, 149
Holland, 15, 30, 43, 92, 151
Hollywood, 39, 52
Holocaust Memorial Museum, 207, 221
Holocaust, 6, 9–10, 22, 25, 99, 102, 113, 116, 149, 155, 158–161, 165, 203, 205–217, 219–231
　Survivors, 203–231
Hong Kong, 30–31, 37, 62–64, 66–67, 69–70, 94, 101, 160, 186
Honolulu, 63, 69
Horowitz, Rose Jacob, 31, 42–43, 46–49, 51, 57, 59, 68, 71
Hull, Cordell, 146
Hungary, 77, 80n12, 152, 181n5

"Idzumo", 49
India, 12, 37, 40, 64, 129, 144, 184, 199
Indiana, 106
Indianapolis, 113

International Committee for the Organization of European Immigrants in China (IC), *also* Komor Committee, 16, 132, 152
International Refugee Organization (IRO), 69
Isaac family, 31
Israel, 25, 62–63, 69–70, 95, 110–111, 113–114, 116, 154–156, 186–187, 190n28, 216, 225
Israel's Messenger, 39, 164
Italy, 12–13, 19, 53, 56, 61, 70, 122, 135, 137, 144, 151, 153, 160, 173, 184, 187

Jacob family, 30, 36, 41–43, 56–61, 63
　David, 57
　Ellis, 51–53, 58–60, 64, 68, 69, 71
　Isaiah, 33
　Joe, 33–37, 48, 70
　Leah, 63
　Saul, 57
　Silas Isaiah, 30
Jacoby, Sasson, 33, 42, 57, 62
Jakarta, 30, 151
Jakubowicz, Andrew, 16
Japan, 4–12, 14, 15–17, 22–23, 30–31, 35, 39, 41, 43, 49–61, 63, 66, 74, 81–83, 89–95, 100, 103, 106–107, 109–111, 118, 120–122, 129–133, 135, 138–141, 144, 146, 150, 153n21, 156, 158, 161–162, 165, 180n3, 183–184, 187, 190–192, 194–195, 198–199, 213, 220, 222
Jerusalem, 42, 62
Jesuit L'Aurore University, 90
Jewish Agency, 67, 69
Jews, *passim*
　American, 6, 19, 33, 61, 91, 106, 109, 111, 120, 124, 153–154, 166, 226
　Ashkenazi, 5, 16, 33, 48, 58–59, 68, 89, 91, 93, 96, 101, 191n29
　Austrian, 6–7, 12, 19–20, 23, 25, 46–47, 92, 116–136, 143–146, 148–149, 153, 162, 167, 207, 212–214, 220, 222
　Baghdadi, 3–6, 20, 29–72, 93, 133–134, 138, 152, 153, 164, 186
　German, 6–9, 11, 19–20, 23–24, 48, 59–60, 66, 91–92, 99–100, 103, 105–106, 110–111, 113, 115, 117, 121–123, 125, 130, 133, 137, 145–149, 151, 153–154, 160–161, 164–165, 173, 207–208, 211–213, 222
　Lithuanian, 7, 15, 33, 103, 154, 222
　Orthodox, 33–34, 48, 76, 154, 208, 223

Polish, 6–7, 9, 15–16, 19–20, 22–23, 25, 48, 74, 92, 103, 112, 154, 167, 208, 222
Russian, 3, 5–6, 23, 33, 48, 56, 60, 71, 73–96, 138, 152–154, 167, 193
Sephardi, 4–5, 36–37, 41, 48, 56, 58, 63, 87, 89, 91–92
Johannesburg, 3

kaddish, 46–47
Kadoorie family, 35, 39, 41, 44, 47, 61, 67, 152
 Elly, 36, 41, 55
 Horace, 46, 47, 56, 67–68, 134, 152–153
 Lawrence, 47, 61, 63, 67
Kadoorie School, *see* Shanghai Jewish Youth Association School
Kangisser Cohen, Sharon, 206
Katz, Harry, 212–214
Kempeitai, 93, 195, 198
Kerr, Archibald, 45
Kiev, 75, 78, 86
Kindertransport, 143, 205, 230
Kobe, 7, 9, 15, 30, 33, 222
Kohbieter, Gérard, 153
Komor, Paul, 16, 152
Kong Xiang Xi, 164, 169, 176
Korea, 144, 184, 193n34
kosher, 34, 42, 54, 78
Kotlerman, Ber, 110, 113,
Kranzler, David, 5, 7–8, 16, 132
Krasno, Rena, 5, 154
Krips family, 154
Kristallnacht, 6, 14, 18–19, 91, 109, 110, 122–124, 137, 145, 148–149, 162, 205, 208, 211–215
Kuomintang, *also* Chinese Nationalist Party, 88, 90, 94, 161
Kushner, Tony, 227

LaCapra, Dominick, 206
Lahusen, Thomas, 185
Langer, Lawrence L., 214, 216
League of Nations, 170–171, 176
Lebanon, 30
Levy, Clive, 42, 43, 70
Lewis, Judith Herman, 132
Lin Hu, 193–194
Lincoln Avenue Camp, 56
Lipstadt, Deborah, 226
Lithuania, 7, 15, 103, 115n31, 184, 222
Lloyd Triestino, 8n14, 12–13
Loewenberg, Lisbeth, 18, 143n13

Log Angeles, 67, 81
Lunghwa Camp, 54–56, 60–62

MacDonald, Charles H., 107–108
Madagascar, 111
Malaysia, 30
Manchukuo Government, 191, 198
Manchuria, 74–75, 77, 81, 85–86, 89, 91, 93, 103, 183, 192, 195, 197–198
Manila, 7, 69, 99–115
Mao Tse-tung, 88
Marcus, Lotte, 6, 127–136, 214, 218–220
Margolis, Laura, 134–136, 218
Massachusetts, 90
McNutt, Paul V., 102n4, 105–106, 107n12, 109, 114
Meisinger, Col. Joseph, 92
Melbourne, 67
Meyer, Maisie, 4, 29–72
Middle East, 3–4, 25, 180n2
Mindanao Island, 101n3, 108–111, 113,
Mir Yeshiva, 33, 48–49, 222–223
Moalem, Daniel, 33, 35, 47, 50–51, 54, 60–61, 64
Moscow, 81
Mühlberger, Sonja, 8
Munich, 118

Nagasaki, 89, 94, 141, 165
Nanking, *also* Nanjing, 30, 81, 130–131, 161, 165
Naples, 137
Nassau, 67
Natowic, Hermann, 22
Nazis, 6–8, 11–12, 15, 19–20, 22, 34, 39, 44, 52, 56, 71, 90–94, 105–106, 110, 113, 116–117, 119, 122–125, 130–131, 137, 143–144, 146–147, 149–151, 156, 158–162, 165, 183, 195, 205, 208, 210–211, 213, 215, 219, 226–227, 230
Netherlands, 15, 30, 92, 147
New Jersey, 145
New York, 39, 49, 67, 70, 104, 107, 137, 144, 192, 215, 223n85
New Zealand, 16
Nicholas II, 85, 87
Nissim, Matook, 33, 42–44, 48, 49, 55, 61–62
Norddeutscher Lloyd, 13, 100, 105
Normandy, 59
Novick, Peter, 226
Novosibirsk, *also* Novonikolaevsk, 86–87
Nuremberg Laws, 117

October Revolution, 74, 77, 85–86, 138, 183, 195
Ohel Moshe Synagogue, 89
Ohel Rachel Synagogue, 35, 54, 58, 60, 68, 186
Olmert family, 201
Opium Wars, 30, 87
Ortiz, Fernando, 181
Ottoman Empire, 4, 29

Pacific War, 7, 50, 93–94, 141
Pale of Settlement, 74, 87
Palestine, 18
Pan Guang, 10, 155
Pao Chia, 53
Paris, 69, 81, 104, 107–108, 192
Passover, 37, 54, 58
Pearl Harbor, 7, 49, 91, 136
Peitaiho, 80, 89
Persia, 30
Perth, 83
Philippines, 6, 63, 69–70, 99–114, 115n31, 122
pogroms, 75, 84, 86–87, 109, 124, 190, 211, 213
Poland, 6–7, 15, 19, 74, 92, 103, 112, 137, 147, 149n13, 167, 184, 208, 222
Polillo Island, 111
Portugal, 63, 80, 184, 186–187
"Potsdam", 14, 113
Protocols of the Elders of Zion, 198

Qiqihar, 201
Quezon, Manuel L., 102–103, 105–106, 109–114

Radomyshl, 86
Rapoport, Nathan, 226
Red Cross, 55, 59, 70, 83, 214
Red Sea, 151
Reisman, Eric, 151–152
Reuben, Victor, 54
Romania, 95
Roosevelt, Franklin, 81n13, 91, 111
Rosenfeld, Jacob, 7, 124
Rubel, Marcella, 31
Rubin, Evelyn Pike, 6, 124, 137–142, 212, 221–222
Russia, 4–5, 33, 52, 56, 65, 74, 75n4, 76–81, 87, 89–90, 93–95, 103, 140, 167, 183–188, 190, 192, 197–200
Russian Fascist Party, 89, 198
Russian Revolution, 77, 79, 84, 85–87, 183, 197

Russians, White, 5, 33, 56, 58, 66, 76–77, 88–89, 93, 185, 190–191, 195, 198
Russo-Japanese War, 75n4, 195

"S.S. General Gordon", 63, 69–70
Sabbath, 34, 36, 47, 140
Sachsenhausen, 124
Safdie, Ritchie Jacob, 57, 63
"Sakaria", 123
San Francisco, 46, 62, 67–70, 153, 184
Sassoon family, 30–32, 59, 66, 152
    David, 30
    Helen, 30–31
    Reuben, 30
    Victor, 35, 39, 41, 44–46, 49, 62, 66–67, 134
Schacter, Daniel, 196
Schnepp, Otto, 148
Schwarz, Lotte, 147–148
Seattle, 67
Second Sino-Japanese War, 31, 100, 131, 138
Shanghai Ashkenazi Jewish Communal Association, 93
Shanghai Ashkenazic Collaborating Relief Association (SACRA), 16, 21–23
Shanghai, *passim*
    Chapei, 82, 87, 90
    Designated Area, 9, 11, 18n56, 21–23, 59, 93, 130n1, 131, 140–141, 144, 150, 155, 174, 217, 220
    French Concession, 35, 78–80, 87–89, 91, 94, 138, 220
    Hongkou, 14, 17, 18n56, 21, 23, 35, 45, 49, 59, 89–91, 93, 127, 130–131, 133n6, 135, 140, 144, 150, 153–155, 217–218, 220, 222–224, 229
    Hungjao, 65
    International Settlement, 14, 30–32, 35, 37–38, 43, 48–50, 60, 83, 86–87, 89–91, 130-131, 144, 146
    Nantao, 87
Shanghai Jewish Hospital, 91, 130, 134
Shanghai Jewish Refugees Museum, 4, 10–11, 25, 155–156, 224
Shanghai Jewish School, 35, 38, 47, 58, 61, 68, 89, 127, 138–140
Shanghai Jewish Youth Association School, 46, 152–153
Shanghai Judaic Studies Association, 154–155
Shanghai Municipal Council, 8, 14, 37, 132, 133n5, 146

Shanghai Municipal Police (SMP), 11–12, 13n33, 15n45, 16, 18n58, 20n65, 21
Shanghai University of International Business and Economics, 4
Shanghai's Baghdadi Jews, see Meyer, Maisie
Shapiro, M.B., 103–105, 108
Siegel, Manuel, 134
Singapore, 30, 40, 101, 189
Small, Chaya, 218, 221–223, 227
Sokol, Robert, 228
Somekh family, 32
Song Qingling, 159
Sopher, Arthur, 33, 39
  Stephen, 65–66
  Theodore, 33, 39
Soviet Union, 7, 15, 52, 56, 61, 65, 77, 79, 81, 84, 90, 92–94, 160, 167, 173, 192, 195, 197–198
Spain, 34, 110
Spielberg, Steven, 221
Stalin, Joseph, 65, 90
Sternbuch, Recha, 122
Storfer, Adolf, 7, 164
Sudilkov, *also* Sudylkiv, 74
Suez Canal, 12
Sugihara, Chiune, 15
Suleiman, Susan Rubin, 206, 212
Sun Fo, *see* Sun Ke
Sun Ke, 118n2, 124, 162–165, 166–176
Sun Yat-sen, 61, 93, 118n2, 159, 162, 170
Sundquist, Eric, 217
Switzerland, 70, 105, 119, 122, 184
Sydney, 70, 81, 84
Syria, 30, 101n3, 109, 135
Szalet, Leon, 7

Ta Tao Government, 49
Tagore, Rabindranath, 36
Taiwan, 64, 94
Theresienstadt, 214
Tibet, 36
Tientsin, *also* Tianjin, 80, 82, 103–104, 108, 160
Tobias, Sigmund, 215
Toeg family, 31, 56
  Ezekiel, 38
  Isaac, 31
  Rebecca, 38, 49, 57, 70
Tokyo, 69, 92, 95
Tomsk, 77
Topas, Boris, 93
Toronto, 69, 185n16, 187, 193n34

Touro Law Center, ix-xi, 3
Trans-Siberian Railroad, 5, 7, 77, 85–87
Treaty of Nanking, 30
Trujillo, Rafael, 113
Turkey, 30

Ukraine, 5, 74–75, 86, 184–185
United Kingdom, 4, 29n1, 30, 34, 36–41, 43, 45, 49–53, 56–57, 61, 63–64, 67, 69–71, 75, 80, 87, 89–90, 92–94, 101, 104, 112, 119, 122, 124, 134, 137, 139–140, 143, 146, 151, 163, 167, 171, 173, 183–184, 189, 205, 230
United Nations Relief and Rehabilitation Administration (UNRRA), 60, 149
United States Holocaust Memorial Museum, 207, 221
United States, 4–6, 18, 20, 22, 24–25, 33, 38, 47, 49–53, 56–57, 59–64, 67–70, 75, 80, 81n13, 87, 89, 91–96, 99–109, 111–112, 119–120, 121n5, 122–123, 129, 134–138, 140–146, 156, 163, 167–168, 183–184, 193n34, 210, 212, 214, 218–219, 222–223, 226, 231
USC Shoah Foundation, 207

Venice, 150, 153
Versailles Treaty, 137
Vichy, 53, 56, 91
Vienna, 6, 12, 19, 25, 46, 116–121, 123–127, 134, 143–145, 148, 149n13, 153, 162, 212, 220
Vietnam, 172, 174
Vladivostok, 61, 85–86, 185

Wachsner, Trixie, 203n1, 220, 229, 231
Wang Ching-wei, 56, 93
Warsaw, 92, 112, 150
Wasserstein, Bernard, 110
Waxman, Zoë Vania, 227
Weiss, Jacob, 106
Weizmann, Chaim, 114
Wiesel, Elie, 215
Willens family, 5–6, 85–96
  Liliane, 5, 85–96, 154
World Federation of Jewish Child Survivors of the Holocaust and Descendants, 215
World War I, 30, 37, 73, 76, 82, 130, 137
World War II, 3–5, 34, 39, 43, 56n70, 69, 73, 91, 95, 102, 111, 116, 125, 127, 146, 150, 158, 165, 197, 205–206
Wuhan, 162

XGRS, 94
Xiao San, 161
Xu Buzeng, 154
Xu Xin, 6, 155, 158–176

Yablonka, Hanna, 227, 231
Yad Vashem, 113, 123n9, 134, 225
Yangon, *also* Rangoon, 30

Ye Hua, 161
YMCA, 58
Yom Kippur, 224
Yunnan Plan, 124, 156, 159, 161–176

Zionism, 36, 40, 90, 101, 117, 155, 159
Zurich, 67
Zwartendyk, Jan, 15

www.ingramcontent.com/pod-product-compliance
Lightning Source LLC
Chambersburg PA
CBHW061937220426
43662CB00012B/1939